The Gospel of John

THE GOSPEL OF JOHN

Worship for Divine Life Eternal

JOHN PAUL HEIL

▲ CASCADE *Books* • Eugene, Oregon

THE GOSPEL OF JOHN
Worship for Divine Life Eternal

Copyright © 2015 John Paul Heil. All rights reserved. Except for brief quotations in critical publications or reviews, no part of this book may be reproduced in any manner without prior written permission from the publisher. Write: Permissions, Wipf and Stock Publishers, 199 W. 8th Ave., Suite 3, Eugene, OR 97401.

Cascade Books
An Imprint of Wipf and Stock Publishers
199 W. 8th Ave., Suite 3
Eugene, OR 97401

www.wipfandstock.com

ISBN 13: 978-1-4982-3116-9

Cataloging-in-Publication data:

Heil, John Paul

The Gospel of John : worship for divine life eternal / John Paul Heil.

viii + 196 p. ; 23 cm. —Includes bibliographical references and index(es).

ISBN 13: 978-1-4982-3116-9

1. Bible, John—Commentaries. 2. Bible, John—Criticism, interpretation, etc. 3. Worship. I. Title.

BS2615.53 H3 2015

Manufactured in the U.S.A.

Contents

Abbreviations | vii

1. Introduction | 1

2. Hymnic Prologue Introduces Worship
Celebrating the Gift of Divine Life Eternal (John 1:1–18) | 5

3. Disciples and the Worship of Jesus (John 1:19–51) | 16

4. Jesus Reveals True Worship
in the Spirit and Truth (John 2:1—4:54) | 29

5. Jesus Transcends Jewish Festival Worship (John 5:1—10:42) | 49

6. Jesus' Sacrificial Worship for Divine
Life Eternal Glorifies God (John 11:1—12:50) | 76

7. Jesus' Farewell Teaching about the
Worship for Divine Life Eternal (John 13:1—17:26) | 95

8. Jesus' Self-Sacrificial Death Produces
Divine Life-Giving Worship (John 18:1—19:42) | 117

9. The Risen Jesus Establishes the Worship
for Divine Life Eternal (John 20:1—21:25) | 146

10. Conclusion | 167

Bibliography | 173
Scripture Index | 179
Author Index | 194

Abbreviations

AB	Anchor Bible
ABRL	Anchor Bible Reference Library
AnBib	Analecta Biblica
Anton	*Antonianum*
AYBRL	Anchor Yale Bible Reference Library
BDAG	Danker, Frederick W., Walter Bauer, William F. Arndt, and F. Wilbur Gingrich. *Greek-English Lexicon of the New Testament and Other Early Christian Literature*. 3rd ed. Chicago: University of Chicago Press, 2000
BECNT	Baker Exegetical Commentary on the New Testament
Bib	*Biblica*
BNTC	Black's New Testament Commentaries
CBET	Contributions to Biblical Exegesis and Theology
CBQ	*Catholic Biblical Quarterly*
CBQMS	Catholic Biblical Quarterly Monograph Series
CTQ	*Concordia Theological Quarterly*
EDNT	*Exegetical Dictionary of the New Testament*. Edited by Horst Balz and Gerhard Schneider. ET. 3 vols. Grand Rapids: Eerdmans, 1990–1993
ETL	*Ephemerides Theologicae Lovanienses*
EvQ	*Evangelical Quarterly*
Int	*Interpretation*

ITQ	*Irish Theological Quarterly*
JBL	*Journal of Biblical Literature*
JSNT	*Journal for the Study of the New Testament*
JSNTSup	Journal for the Study of the New Testament Supplement Series
LNTS	Library of New Testament Studies
NICNT	New International Commentary on the New Testament
NIDB	*New Interpreter's Dictionary of the Bible.* Edited by Katharine Doob Sakenfeld. 5 vols. Nashville: Abingdon, 2006–2009
NIDNTTE	*New International Dictionary of New Testament Theology and Exegesis.* 2nd ed. Edited by Moisés Silva. 5 vols. Grand Rapids: Zondervan, 2014
NovT	*Novum Testamentum*
NTS	*New Testament Studies*
PRSt	*Perspectives in Religious Studies*
SBLDS	Society of Biblical Literature Dissertation Series
SNTSU	Studien zum Neuen Testament und seiner Umwelt
SP	Sacra Pagina
WBC	Word Biblical Commentary
WUNT	Wissenschaftliche Untersuchungen zum Neuen Testament
ZNW	*Zeitschrift für die neutestamentliche Wissenschaft und die Kunde der älteren Kirche*

I

Introduction

Worship in the Gospel of John

The Gospel of John has been examined from many different perspectives, but a comprehensive treatment of the rich theme of worship in this Gospel has not yet appeared.[1] With this book I will offer a contribution toward a remedy of this deficiency by analyzing the entire Gospel of John from the perspective of its various dimensions of worship. I aim to illustrate that three different but complementary dimensions of worship dominate this Gospel. Indeed, these different types of worship represent the ways one expresses and demonstrates the faith that includes having divine life eternal, which is the stated purpose for writing the signs Jesus did in this Gospel—"that you may believe that Jesus is the Christ, the Son of God, and that, believing, you may have life in his name" (John 20:31).

A first dimension of worship is the confessional worship that takes place through verbal expressions and/or gestures of devotion or reverence. This type of liturgical worship includes individual and communal professions of faith, various kinds of prayer, hymns, doxologies, etc. In the Fourth Gospel Jesus prays several times, repeatedly addressing God as "Father" (11:41; 12:27, 28; 17:1, 5, 11, 21, 24, 25). But Jesus himself is also an object of confessional worship by various individuals before his resurrection, e.g., Nathanael (1:49), the man born blind (9:38), Martha (11:27), and Mary (11:32). The confession addressed to the risen Jesus by Thomas, "My Lord

---

1. As Neyrey (*Give God the Glory*, 167) notes, "To be sure, discussions of worship in the Fourth Gospel are rare, and in most commentaries worship does not even rate a place in the topical index." Some brief treatments of worship in John include Cullmann, *Early Christian Worship*, 37–119; Borchert, *Worship*, 43–57; Lee, *Hallowed*, 61–84; Koester, *Word*, 203–9.

and my God!" (20:28), climaxes this type of confessional worship in John. It reaffirms the basis for the communal act of doxological worship proclaimed in the prologue: "We observed his glory, glory as of the unique one from the Father, full of a gift of truth" (1:14).

A second type of liturgical worship is the sacramental worship that includes not only verbal expressions but ritual actions. The two primary sacraments involved in John are baptism and the Eucharist. Baptism involves the ritual immersion or cleansing in water which gives believers a new birth into the kingdom of divine life eternal (3:3–5) as children of God (1:12). The Eucharist or Lord's Supper involves a ritual meal consisting of bread and wine transformed into the body and blood of Jesus, which is based upon the life-giving blood and the water symbolic of the Spirit that went out from the pierced side of Jesus after his self-sacrificial death (19:34) as the Passover Lamb of God (1:29, 36). It nourishes and maintains the believer's divine life eternal (6:51–58).[2]

A third dimension of worship is the ethical worship constituted by the way a believer behaves and conducts his life. In John this primarily involves believers keeping Jesus' new commandment to love one another in the self-sacrificial (ethical rather than cultic) way that he has loved them (13:34; 15:12). This is part of what it means to be a true worshiper who worships the Father in Spirit and truth (4:23–24). The Spirit of truth is given to believers as a result of Jesus being glorified by God (7:39) through his self-sacrificial death. The Spirit will guide believers in all the truth (16:13; cf. 14:17, 26; 15:26) that includes keeping the commandment to love one another in a self-sacrificial way in order to have divine life eternal (12:50).[3]

Methodological Presuppositions

In the following analysis of John from the perspective of its various dimensions of worship I will employ a narrative-critical, audience-oriented approach. While not denying a diachronic dimension which recognizes that John has developed from earlier traditions and perhaps undergone different editions over time, I will treat John synchronically, including all twenty-one

---

2. "The Johannine references to these two sacraments [baptism and Eucharist], both the more explicit references and those that are symbolic, are scattered in scenes throughout the ministry" (Brown, *Introduction*, 234). See also Cullmann, *Early Christian Worship*, 37–119; Hurtado, *Christian Worship*; Neyrey, *Give God the Glory*, 171–90; Campbell, "Worship," 70–83; Gieschen, "Baptism," 23–45.

3. For a detailed treatment of various dimensions of biblical worship, see Block, *Glory of God*.

chapters we have today, as well as the story of the adulteress (7:53—8:11).[4] The focus will be on the responses that the text evokes from its implied, textual, or ideal audience in the sequential manner in which the Gospel would have been performed orally, most likely in a communal worship context.[5]

Along with most commentators I consider John to be one of the later documents in the NT. Considered to be the Fourth Gospel, John was most likely completed later than the letters of Paul as well as the three Synoptic Gospels of Matthew, Mark, and Luke, whether or not John is directly dependent on any of these Gospels. Although we cannot presume that the audience of John was familiar with any of the other documents of the NT as we have them, the text of John presupposes its audience's knowledge and practice of common forms of Christian worship alluded to elsewhere in the NT, such as baptism, Eucharist, professions of faith, prayers, hymns, etc.[6] Other significant presuppositions include the audience's knowledge of Jewish forms of worship and festivals as well as the OT scriptures. Significant for its theme of worship, the Fourth Gospel presents itself as not only the fulfillment and completion but also the continuation of the Jewish scriptures and thus, like the Jewish scriptures, functions as a source for listening to the word of God in Christian worship services.[7]

Preliminary Overview

The following chapters will treat the theme of worship in John in the sequential order in which the audience would have heard this Gospel performed within a context of communal worship. With its communal pronouncement

---

4. Although for some reason this story was omitted very early on in the manuscript tradition, there is very strong internal evidence for considering it original, as it fits quite well into its narrative context. See Heil, "Jesus and the Adulteress," 182–91; Heil, "Rejoinder," 361–66.

5. This literary, narrative-critical approach is very similar to that articulated by Brown, *Gift*, 11–15.

6. For various forms of worship in the letters of Paul, see Heil, *Rituals of Worship*. "What we see in this Gospel is a strong emphasis on events in Jesus' ministry that foreshadow the sacramental life of the church. The evangelist speaks to a Christian audience that depends upon baptism and the Eucharist for that life. Thus, he does not mention these institutions, but presupposes them through references to living water and rebirth, as well as living bread and the wine of the new dispensation" (Brown, *Gift*, 247). On the various practices of early Christian worship, see McGowan, *Ancient Christian Worship*.

7. "The author has written his story that the readers may come to life as a result of this exposure to the Word of God: a story of Jesus he already understood and passed on as Scripture (20:31)" (Moloney, "John as Scripture," 467). See also Smith, "Gospels Become Scripture," 3–20; Brown, *Gift*, 70–78; Moloney, "Know the Scripture," 97–111.

celebrating Jesus' gift of divine life eternal, the hymnic prologue in 1:1–18 sets a preliminary tone of communal worship for the rest of the narrative. In 1:19–51 the first four days of the narrative present scenes focused on the worship of Jesus. In 2:1–4:54 Jesus reveals that the "place" for true worship is not physical or geographical but rather "in Spirit and truth" (4:23–24). In 5:1—10:42 Jesus perfects and transcends various aspects of Jewish festival worship. In 11:1—12:50 Jesus reveals that sacrificial worship for divine life eternal glorifies God. In 13:1—17:26 Jesus presents his farewell address to his disciples at his last supper with them, revealing further aspects of true worship and concluding with an extensive prayer. In 18:1—19:42 Jesus' self-sacrificial death provides the foundation for a life-giving worship. And finally, in 20:1—21:25 the risen Jesus establishes the worship for divine life eternal.

2

Hymnic Prologue Introduces Worship Celebrating the Gift of Divine Life Eternal (1:1–18)

Translation and Structure of the Prologue (1:1–18)

The Word—The Life—The Light (1:1–5)[1]

¹ In the beginning was the Word, and the Word was with God, and the Word was God. ² This one was in the beginning with God. ³ All things through him came to be, and without him came to be not one thing. What had come to be ⁴ in him was life, and the life was the light for human beings. ⁵ And the light shines on in the darkness, for the darkness has not overcome it.[2]

The Light into the World and the Gift to Become Children of God (1:6–13)

⁶ There came to be a human being, sent from God, his name John. ⁷ This one came for testimony, that he might testify about the light, that all might believe through him. ⁸ That one was not the light, but (he came) that he might testify about the light. ⁹ The true light, which enlightens every human being, was coming into the world. ¹⁰ He was in the world, and the world through him came to be,

---

1. All translations throughout are my own. The aim is for a literal, exegetical translation.

2. The fourfold rhythmic duplication of the expressions "in the beginning" (1:1, 2), "with God" (1:1, 2), "light" (1:4[2x]), and "darkness" (1:5[2x]) establishes the integrity of the first unit (1:1–5). These expressions are unique within the prologue. Lincoln (*John*, 94) points out the step parallelism of repeated terms that lends a poetic character to this hymnic unit. On this unit as a hymn, see Miller, "Logos Hymn," 552–61.

but the world did not know him. ¹¹ To his own he came, yet his own people did not accept him. ¹² But as many as did receive him, he gave them authority to become children of God, those who believe in his name, ¹³ who not from bloods, nor from the will of flesh, nor from the will of a man, but from God were born.[3]

The Word Became Flesh—Jesus Christ, the Gift of Truth (1:14-18)

¹⁴ And the Word became flesh and dwelt among us, and we observed his glory, glory as of the unique one from the Father, full of a gift of truth. ¹⁵ John testifies about him and had cried out, saying, "This one was he of whom I said, 'the one after me coming, before me had come to be, for prior to me he was!'" ¹⁶ For from his fullness we all received, and gift in place of gift. ¹⁷ For while the law through Moses was given, the gift of the truth through Jesus Christ came to be. ¹⁸ No one has ever seen God; the unique one, God, who is in the bosom of the Father, that one made him known.[4]

The Word—The Life—The Light (1:1-5)

Although the opening phrase, "in the beginning [ἐν ἀρχῇ]" (John 1:1a), alludes to the identical opening phrase of the OT (LXX Gen 1:1), the immediate concern is not what God made or created but the preexistent status of the personified "Word" (λόγος) of God before anything took place.[5] Before God began to act, the Word not only was in a position "with," "toward," or "beside" (πρός) God, but the Word shared God's identity (John 1:1). To

---

3. A literary inclusion formed by the only occurrences in the prologue of the term "God" (θεοῦ) in the genitive case at the beginning (1:6) and end (1:12, 13) of the second unit (1:6-13) establishes its integrity.

4. A literary inclusion formed by the only occurrences in the prologue of the terms "unique one" and "Father" at the beginning (1:14) and end (1:18) of the third unit establishes its integrity. In addition, a literary inclusion formed by the only occurrences in the prologue of the term "God" in both the nominative and accusative cases at the beginning (1:1-2) and end (1:18) of the prologue establishes its integrity. Note that the nominative occurrences refer to Jesus as the Word (1:1) and as the "unique one" (1:18), whereas the accusative occurrences refer to God the Father (1:1, 2, 18). For a recent detailed discussion of the structure of the prologue, see Kim, *Sourcebook*, 38–51. On the prologue as a didactic hymn, see Gordley, "Prologue," 781–802.

5. "But whereas in Genesis the reference is to the beginning of creation, in this Gospel it is to the absolute beginning in the sphere of God" (Lincoln, *John*, 94). "The Gospel of John is not particularly interested in creation. Like the other Gospels, its focus is on revelation and redemption, the new creation if you will" (Michaels, *John*, 46).

emphasize the preexistent position of the Word before God began to act, it is repeated with a pointed stress that "*this one* [the Word] was in the beginning with God" (1:2). The Word is thus presented to the audience not only as a worthy object of worship himself, since he was God, but, as "*the* Word," the one who uniquely communicates or reveals the God to be worshiped, since "this one" was with God from the absolute beginning.[6]

That "all things through him," the Word, "came to be" (ἐγένετο), not "were created" or "were made," and that "without him came to be [ἐγένετο] not one thing" (1:3a) confirms the focus not merely on creation but on the broader scope of everything that took place within salvation history. Through the Word that was with God from the beginning (1:1-2), God brought about everything without exception that occurred within God's plan of salvation. This reinforces the uniquely preeminent status of the preexistent Word as a communicator or revealer for the worship of God as the absolute origin through the Word of everything that has taken place in salvation history.[7]

Among all the things that "through him [the Word] came to be [δι' αὐτοῦ ἐγένετο]" (1:3a), was the life that "had come to be in him [γέγονεν ἐν αὐτῷ]" (1:3b-4a).[8] This refers to the preexistent divine life eternal that "was" (ἦν) and that had come into existence in the personified Word and that "was [ἦν] the light for human beings" (1:4b), the preexistent Word that "was" (ἦν) not only with God, but "was" (ἦν) God (1:1-2). The perfect tense of the verb "had come to be" (γέγονεν) indicates that this divine life eternal not only had come into existence in the personified Word, but is still presently available as the light for human beings.[9]

In accord with the fact that the life not only had come to be but still is present, the light that was the life still "shines on" (φαίνει, present tense) "in

6. "Just as in the Jewish Scriptures Wisdom can be placed at God's side without this figure being seen as a threat to monotheism, so from the Fourth Gospel's perspective the Word as in God's presence would not have been thought as transgressing the bounds of Jewish monotheism but as a vivid way of talking about God's self-communication" (Lincoln, *John*, 97).

7. Miller, *Salvation-History*; Ashton, *John*, 145-55.

8. For the reasons to take the relative clause "what had come to be" (ὃ γέγονεν) with 1:4 rather than with 1:3, see Phillips, *Prologue*, 162-64; Ashton, *John*, 152-55. See also Miller, *Salvation-History*; Cohee, "John 1.3-4," 470-77.

9. Ashton (*John*, 155) offers the following interpretive paraphrase of 1:1-4: "From the very beginning God held his thought (the Logos) close to him, and his thought was a facet of his divinity. All human history, every single thing that has ever happened, took place through the mediation of the Logos, but what has come about *in* the Logos (that is, the special event of God's intervention on behalf of his people), this was life, a life that it was God's prerogative to bestow, a life that was also light—illumination and revelation" (emphasis original).

the darkness, for the darkness has not overcome it" (1:5; cf. 12:35).[10] This life is thus presently available to all in the audience, as the light still shines on in the darkness, a realm associated with death, a power which has not overcome, not prevailed over nor extinguished, the light which is the life.[11] This is the divine life eternal that had come to be and still is in the Word who reveals the God to be worshiped as its giver by the human beings for whom the life was the light (1:4).

The Light into the World and the Gift to Become Children of God (1:6–13)

Among the things that "came to be" (ἐγένετο) in salvation history through the Word (1:3), and among the "human beings" (ἀνθρώπων) for whom the life was the light (1:4), "there came to be a human being [ἐγένετο ἄνθρωπος], sent from God, his name John" (1:6). Whereas in the beginning the Word was "with" (πρός) God (1:1, 2), John was sent "from" (παρά) God.[12] In contrast to the Word, emphatically pointed out as "this one" (οὗτος) who "in the beginning was with God" (1:2), as "this one" (οὗτος), John "came for testimony, that he might testify about the light, that all might believe through him" (1:7). John's role is thus to provide divinely authoritative evidence for "all" (πάντες) the human beings for whom the life is the light (1:4) to believe "through him" (δι' αὐτοῦ), implicitly, in order to experience this life/light as among "all things" (πάντα) that came to be "through him" (δι' αὐτοῦ), the Word (1:3). And worshiping is a preeminent way of expressing and demonstrating believing.

It is then pointedly clarified that "that one" (ἐκεῖνος), John, was not himself the light, and it is reiterated and thus emphatically underscored that John came "that he might testify about the light" (1:8; cf. 1:7). The light about which John testified was "the true light" (1:9a), which is the divine life eternal that had come to be in the Word (1:3–4). That this true light "enlightens every human being [ἄνθρωπον]" (1:9b) deliberately asserts that the life was the light for each and every individual among all "human beings

---

10. "I add the preposition 'on' to the verb 'shines' in order to capture the full force of the present tense, and I sometimes even suggest adding or putting in parentheses after 'shines on' the words 'still, even now' to make this present-tense reality as clear as possible" (Bruner, *John*, 18; emphases original).

11. For an example in the biblical tradition of the close association of darkness with death, see Isa 9:1 (also quoted in Matt 4:16), where "in darkness" is paralleled by "in a region and shadow of death." See also Köstenberger, *John*, 32.

12. "The phrase 'sent from God' is reminiscent of the OT description of a prophet whose role was to function as a spokesperson for God" (Köstenberger, *John*, 32).

[ἀνθρώπων]" (1:4b). It still shines on for every individual in the darkness that connotes death (1:5). When John testified about the light, this true light, the Word, was "coming [ἐρχόμενον] into the world" (1:9c) of human beings from its preexistent position with God (1:1-2), in distinction to John, who "came [ἦλθεν]" (1:7) not from a preexistent position with God but as one who came to be and was sent by God (1:6).

Having come into the world (1:9), the Word that previously "was" (ἦν) with God (1:1-2) "was" (ἦν) now "in the world" (1:10a) of human beings. As among all things that "through him came to be [δι' αὐτοῦ ἐγένετο]" (1:3), the world "through him came to be [δι' αὐτοῦ ἐγένετο]" (1:10b). "But the world did not know him" (1:10c), and thus did not recognize the Word in whom divine life eternal had come to be as the light for all human beings in the world (1:3-4). "To his own he came [ἦλθεν], yet his own people did not accept him" (1:11), even though John "came [ἦλθεν] for testimony, that he might testify about the light, that all might believe though him" (1:7).[13] Ironically, his own people "did not accept him" (αὐτὸν οὐ παρέλαβον), the Word, in whom was the life that was the light for all human beings, and thus did not believe.[14] But this alliteratively alludes to and reminds the audience, that, nevertheless, the darkness connoting unbelief and associated with death "did not overcome it" (αὐτὸ οὐ κατέλαβεν), the light (1:5) that was divine life eternal (1:3-4).

"But as many as did receive him" (1:12a), the Word, implicitly could include some who were not of his own people who as a whole did not accept him (1:11).[15] To those who did receive him, the Word "gave them authority to become [γενέσθαι] children of God" (1:12b) in the salvation history in which all things through the Word "came to be [ἐγένετο]" (1:3).[16] To become children of God implies participating in the divine life eternal that "had come to be [γέγονεν]" (1:3) in the Word. Those who did receive the Word are further specified as "those who believe [πιστεύουσιν] in his name" (1:12c), implying that they accepted the testimony of John who came that "all might believe [πιστεύσωσιν] through him" (1:7). Believing in his

13. "Here there are two uses of the phrase 'his own', the first is a neuter plural, signifying his own possession, property or domain, while the second is a masculine plural, signifying his own people" (Lincoln, *John*, 102).

14. "Perhaps the most obvious of John's ironic incongruities is summarized in 1:11" (Duke, *Irony*, 111).

15. "This sets up a kind of rhetorical contrast, even contradiction. Jesus' 'own did not receive him,' *yet* many of them did receive him" (Michaels, *John*, 67; emphasis original).

16. "Their 'authority' to become God's children (1:12) presumably emphasizes divine authorization to become what no human effort could accomplish" (Keener, *John*, 1.403).

"name," that is, his identity and status, refers to believing in the Word who not only was with God in the beginning, but was God (1:1-2), and in whom had come to be the divine life eternal that was the light for all human beings (1:3-4).[17]

After an emphatic threefold denial of a merely physical, human origin—"not from bloods, nor from the will of flesh, nor from the will of a man" (1:13a), it is climactically clarified that those whom the Word gave the authority to "become" (γενέσθαι) children of God have a spiritual, divine origin. They are those who were "born" (ἐγεννήθησαν) from God himself (1:13b).[18] Believing in the name of the Word who not only was with God in the beginning, but was God (1:1-2), in order to become children of God who are born from God and who thus experience and share in the divine life eternal of God implicitly is expressed and demonstrated by worshiping God.[19]

The Word Became Flesh—Jesus Christ, the Gift of Truth (1:14-18)

The Word, who in the beginning was with God and was God (1:1-2), and through whom the world (1:10), indeed all things "came to be [ἐγένετο]" (1:3), himself "became flesh [σὰρξ ἐγένετο]" (1:14a), and thus entered the world of human beings who are born "from the will of flesh [σαρκός]" (1:13). John "came to be" (ἐγένετο) as a human being in salvation history (1:6), and the Word also "became" (ἐγένετο) flesh, a human being, for his role in salvation history. And the Word "dwelt among us" (1:14b), that is, among all of the human beings for whom the Word was the light of divine life eternal (1:4, 9). That the Word "dwelt" (ἐσκήνωσεν), literally, "pitched his tent/tabernacle," among us human beings alludes to the OT "tent" or "tabernacle" (σκηνή) where God was present with his people, the forerunner of the temple where God was to be worshiped (cf. LXX Exod 25:9). This implies that the person of the Word, who is both God (John 1:1) and

---

17. "As in the Jewish Scriptures, 'name' indicates more than just the verbal designation of a person. It signifies all that a person represents" (Lincoln, *John*, 103).

18. "Children of God come about neither through the mixing of bloods, the desire of the flesh nor the will of any human being. The initiative is solely with God" (Phillips, *Prologue*, 193). "The unusual plural 'from bloods' (ἐξ αἱμάτων) is probably to be understood as the mixing of the female and the male 'bloods'" (Moloney, *John*, 45).

19. "John 1:12-13 is very possibly the climactic statement of the entire prologue, and by way of *inclusio* epitomizes the very purpose for which the Gospel was written: for people to 'believe' and have life 'in his name' (cf. 20:31)" (Köstenberger, *John*, 38).

a human being (1:14), as God's presence among human beings, is now the place for the true worship of God.[20]

And "we," a collective representative of the human beings among whom the incarnate Word dwelt, "observed his glory, glory as of the unique one from the Father, full of a gift of truth" (1:14). That "we observed his glory [δόξαν]" furthers the allusion of the Word who "dwelt [ἐσκήνωσεν] among us" to the OT tabernacle/temple as the place for worship. When the divine cloud covered the tabernacle of witness, "the tabernacle [σκηνή] was filled with the glory [δόξης] of the Lord" (LXX Exod 40:34, 35). And when the divine cloud filled the house/temple (3 Kgdms 8:10), "the glory [δόξα] of the Lord filled the house/temple" (8:11).

The glory that "we observed" in the Word become flesh, who dwelt "among us" human beings, is further described. It is "glory as of the unique one from the Father, full of a gift of truth" (John 1:14). That the unique one is "from the Father" (παρὰ πατρός) distinguishes the Word from John, who was sent "from God [παρὰ θεοῦ]" (1:6), but not as Son of the Father, not as "the unique one" or "one of a kind" (μονογενοῦς)—the unique Son who was with God and was God (1:1-2), but became a human being.[21] As the tabernacle was "filled" (ἐπλήσθη) with the glory of the Lord (LXX Exod 40:34, 35), and the glory of the Lord "filled" (ἔπλησεν) the temple (3 Kgdms 8:11), indicating the glorious presence of God as the object of worship, the divine Word whose glory "we observed" was "full" (πλήρης) of a gift of truth. This implies that the Word is not only the place for the worship of God, but reaffirms that he is a worthy object of worship. Indeed, that "we observed his glory" is an act of doxological worship, acknowledging the Word's glory and thus "glorifying" the Word, inviting all in the audience to do the same.[22]

---

20. Among the sources for the OT background of "dwelt among us" is "the Priestly cult associated with the ancient Tabernacle and Temple" (Coloe, *God Dwells*, 26–27). "Whereas once the tabernacle in the desert and later the temple in Jerusalem became the dwelling place of God's glory, in the incarnation of the Word that dwelling place is to be found in the 'flesh' or body of Jesus" (Byrne, *Life Abounding*, 32). See also Hoskins, *Temple*, 116–25.

21. On the meaning of μονογενής as "one of a kind," see Keener, *John*, 1.412–16. "Μονογενής therefore means not 'only begotten,' but 'one-of-a-kind' son" (Köstenberger, *John*, 43).

22. "In the narrative structures of the Fourth Gospel δόξα/δοξάζειν principally means divine identity and recognition of this identity" (Nielsen, "Glory and Glorification," 366). "In vv. 14 and 16 there is a switch to the first person plural, as the narrator places himself and those whom he represents among those who have believed and have become children of God, and as this community of believers makes its confession about the Word" (Lincoln, *John*, 103). "Here, the first person plural verb represents another process of inclusion. The reader is now one of us, for we too have seen his glory in that we have read the Prologue. . . . Eye-witnesses, a believing community, readers are all

The glory for which the Word is worshiped includes his being "full of a gift of truth [χάριτος καὶ ἀληθείας]" (John 1:14).[23] This develops the role of the Word as the "true" (ἀληθινόν) light, who enlightens every human being (1:9), the Word in whom divine life eternal had come to be, the life that was the light for all human beings (1:3-4). The Word is full of a "gift" of the "truth" that includes this divine life eternal, since the Word "gave" (ἔδωκεν) to those who believe in his name the authority to become children of God (1:12), and thus to participate in divine life eternal. The audience may receive the gift of becoming children of God and sharing in divine life eternal as those who believe in and worship the Word by acknowledging his divine glory as the unique one from the Father, the Word who is full of a gift of truth.

The John who came "that he might testify about [μαρτυρήσῃ περί] the light, that all might believe through him" (1:7) now "testifies about [μαρτυρεῖ περί] him" (1:15) for the benefit of the faith and worship of the audience. John "had cried out" (κέκραγεν) in the past and continues to cry out presently (perfect tense) for the audience, saying, "This one was he of whom I said, 'The one after me coming, before me had come to be, for prior to me he was!'" (1:15). The emphatic "this one was" (οὗτος ἦν) about whom John is testifying resonates with the emphatic reference to the Word as "this one was [οὗτος ἦν] in the beginning with God" (1:2). John's statement about "the one after me coming [ἐρχόμενος]" recalls that John came to testify about the true light that "was coming [ἐρχόμενον] into the world" (1:9). That before John he "had come to be" (γέγονεν) recalls that what "had come to be [γέγονεν]" (1:3) in him was life (1:4). And that prior to John he "was" (ἦν) reaffirms for the audience that "in the beginning was [ἦν] the Word, and the Word was [ἦν] with God, and the Word was [ἦν] God" (1:1).

After John testifies for the audience that all might believe and thus worship (1:7, 15), all believers in the audience are drawn into another act of worship in accord with celebratory tone of this hymnic prologue, the confession of faith that "from his fullness we all received, and gift in place of gift" (1:16). The "fullness" (πληρώματος) from which we all received refers to a "gift of truth," which includes the gift to become children of God (1:12), and thus share in divine life eternal—a "gift of truth" of which the Word is "full [πλήρης]" (1:14). From this fullness all of us believers "received" (ἐλάβομεν), as among those who "did receive [ἔλαβον] him," "those who believe in his name" (1:12).

---

included" (Phillips, *Prologue*, 200–201). See also Koester, *Word*, 204.

23. The Greek phrase χάριτος καὶ ἀληθείας, literally "gift/grace and truth," is to be understood as a *hendiadys*, with the καί ("and") functioning epexegetically, so that the meaning is "a gift of truth" or "a gift that is truth." Moloney, *John*, 45.

All of us believers received "gift [χάριν] in place of gift [χάριτος]" (1:16), for while the law, the initial revelation of God's will, through Moses "was given" (ἐδόθη) as a gift from God (divine passive), "*the* gift [ἡ χάρις] of *the* truth [ἡ ἀλήθεια]," the final revelation of God's will in salvation history, through Jesus Christ came to be (1:17).[24] The Word who "became" (ἐγένετο) flesh (1:14) and about whom the audience heard that "all things through him came to be [δι' αὐτοῦ ἐγένετο]" (1:3) in salvation history is identified as Jesus Christ, since the gift of the truth "through Jesus Christ came to be" (διὰ Ἰησοῦ Χριστοῦ ἐγένετο). The law that "was given" through Moses was distinct from the person of Moses. But the gift of the truth not only "came to be" (ἐγένετο) through Jesus Christ, but the gift of divine life eternal included in the gift of the truth "had come to be" (γέγονεν) in him (1:3-4), in his very person.[25] This further indicates for the audience the centrality of the person of Jesus Christ, the personified Word, for the true worship of God.

Although no human being has ever seen God, "the unique one" (μονογενής), himself God, who is "in the bosom of," that is, in the closest intimacy with, God the "Father" (πατρός), "that one made him known" (1:18). This further specifies for the audience "the gift of the truth" that came to be through Jesus Christ (1:17). It reaffirms the doxological worship that, although no one has ever "seen" (ἑώρακεν) God, "we observed" (ἐθεασάμεθα) the Word's glory, the "glory as of the unique one [μονογενοῦς] from the Father [πατρός], full of a gift of truth" (1:14), "the unique one" who is himself God.

Whereas in the beginning the Word "was" (ἦν) with God (1:1-2), now the Word, identified as Jesus Christ, "is" (ὤν) in the bosom of God the Father (1:18).[26] In contrast to the emphatic assertion that "that one" (ἐκεῖνος), John, was not the light (1:8), it is emphatically and climactically asserted

24. "To describe what took place in Jesus Christ, the latter gift, the author again uses an epexegetical καί, or *hendiadys*. The two nouns in the same case, joined by καί, repeat v. 14e, but this time the nouns have the definite article: ἡ χάρις καὶ ἡ ἀλήθεια: 'the gift that is the truth'" (Moloney, *John*, 46).

25. "Both are gifts of God. One cannot 'replace' the other. One prolongs and perfects the never-ending graciousness of God. The gift of the Law is perfected in the gift of the incarnation" (Moloney, *John*, 46).

26. "[T]here is an important distinction between the two affirmations concerning the intimate relationship between the Word and God (v. 1) and Jesus Christ and the Father (v. 18). The author has caught this by means of the expression εἰς τὸν κόλπον. The expression does not indicate an indwelling, or a return to the preexistent status of the Word, as many would claim. The Greek word κόλπον indicates the bosom, breast, or chest, an external part of the body (cf. 13:23). Jesus Christ is turned toward the Father at all times during the story that is about to be told. The present participle ὁ ὤν makes the durative aspect of this oneness clear" (Moloney, *John*, 46-47).

that "that one" (ἐκεῖνος), the unique one, Jesus Christ, the light, made God known (1:18). This assures the audience that in the communal doxological profession of observing the glory of, thus "glorifying" and worshiping, the unique one, *the* Son (1:14), they are seeing completely illuminated and fully made known the God to be worshiped as *the* Father.[27]

Summary on 1:1-18

As one who not only was with God but was God from the absolute beginning (1:1-2), the Word, through whom everything came to be within salvation history (1:3), is not only a worthy object of worship himself, but communicates and reveals to human beings the God to be worshiped. The divine life eternal that had come to be and still is in the Word shines on as the light for all human beings, since the darkness of death has not overcome it (1:4-5). This divine life eternal is thus presently and continually available for all human beings to share.

Although not the true light, a human being named John came into salvation history to testify about the light of divine life eternal, so that all might believe through him (1:6-8). Although the world of human beings came to be through the Word, they did not know the Word, the true light of divine life eternal (1:9-10). Even his own people did not accept him (1:11). But to as many as did receive him, who believe in his name and thus worship him, the divine Word gave the authority to become children of God and thus share in divine life eternal by being born from God (1:12-13).

That the Word "dwelt," literally, "pitched his tent/tabernacle," among us human beings (1:14) alludes to the OT "tent" or "tabernacle" where God was present with his people, the forerunner of the temple where God was to be worshiped. As the tabernacle was "filled" with the glory of the Lord, and the glory of the Lord "filled" the temple, indicating the glorious presence of God as the object of worship, the divine Word whose glory "we observed" was "full" of a gift of truth (1:14). This implies that the Word is not only the

---

27. "For Jesus to 'make God known' implies more than communicating a visual image; the term suggests that Jesus fully interprets God, confirming the sense of the context: Jesus unveils God's character absolutely" (Keener, *John*, 1.424). "[T]he entire Gospel to follow should be read as an account of Jesus 'telling the whole story' of God the Father" (Köstenberger, *John*, 50). "[B]ecause 'No one has seen God, ever,' hearing takes the place of seeing. . . . and this is all the more appropriate in a setting where Jesus Christ has been introduced as 'the Word.' He is now said to have acted as the Word when he 'told about' God. . . . Because he is himself God, and 'right beside the Father,' he (and he alone) has seen God and can therefore 'tell about' God" (Michaels, *John*, 92-93).

place for the worship of God, but reaffirms that he is a worthy object of worship. Indeed, that "we observed his glory" is an act of doxological worship, acknowledging the Word's glory and thus "glorifying" the Word, inviting all in the audience to do the same.

After John testifies for the audience that all might believe and thus worship (1:7, 15), all believers in the audience are drawn into another act of worship in accord with the celebratory tone of this hymnic prologue, the confession that "from his fullness we all received, and gift in place of gift" (1:16). The "fullness" from which we all received refers to a "gift of truth," which includes the gift to become children of God (1:12), and thus share in divine life eternal—a "gift of truth" of which the Word is "full" (1:14). From this fullness all of us believers "received," as among those who "did receive him," "those who believe in his name" (1:12).

The law that "was given" through Moses was distinct from the person of Moses. But the gift of the truth not only "came to be" through Jesus Christ (1:17), but the gift of divine life eternal included in the gift of the truth "had come to be" in him (1:3–4), in his very person. This further indicates for the audience the centrality of the person of Jesus Christ, the personified Word, for the true worship of God. In contrast to the emphatic assertion that "that one," John, was not the light (1:8), it is emphatically and climactically asserted that "that one," the unique one, Jesus Christ, the light, made God, whom no one has ever seen, known (1:18). This assures the audience that in the communal doxological profession of observing the glory of, thus "glorifying" and worshiping, the unique one, *the* Son (1:14), they are seeing completely illuminated and fully made known the God to be worshiped as *the* Father.

With its communal professions of faith expressed by repeated acts of communal worship, the hymnic prologue (1:1–18) has drawn the audience into a celebratory tone of worship in preparation for the narrative to follow. It has positioned the audience for a further development of their worship not only of Jesus Christ, the unique divine Son, but of the divine Father whom Jesus Christ, the divine Word, has made known.

3

Disciples and the Worship of Jesus (1:19–51)

First Day: John's Testimony to Jewish Leaders (1:19–28)

The narrator announces that "this is the testimony of John , when the Jews from Jerusalem sent [ἀπέστειλαν] priests and Levites, that they might ask, 'Who are you?'" (1:19).[1] This reminds the audience that John, in contrast, came as one "sent [ἀπεσταλμένος] from God" (1:6) for "testimony, that he might testify about the light, that all might believe through him" (1:7). John was sent from God to testify about the light that was the divine life eternal that had come to be in the Word (1:3–4), who "became flesh and dwelt among us" (1:14) as the personified place for worship by those who believe. That the Jews from Jerusalem sent priests and Levites, those in charge of worship in the temple in Jerusalem, indicates their concern with how John and his testimony might impact their worship.[2]

John "confessed [ὡμολόγησεν] and did not deny but confessed [ὡμολόγησεν], 'I am not the Christ!'" (1:20), reaffirming that he "was not the light" (1:8). This emphatically negative "confession" that John is not "the Christ" accentuates for the audience that the Jesus who is the "Christ" through whom came to be the gift of the truth (1:17), which includes the gift to become children of God (1:12) and share in divine life eternal, is the one, not John, that they are positively to "confess" in worship.[3] John's increasingly

---

1. "'[T]he Jews' (οἱ Ἰουδαῖοι) serves here and throughout the Gospel as an umbrella term for both priestly and scribal leaders in Israel, especially in Jerusalem" (Michaels, *John*, 95–96).

2. "That they are identified as 'priests and Levites' alerts readers that they will be interested in John's activity as it pertains to ritual purity and the purification rites that he may be initiating" (Brown, *Gift*, 97).

3. In John "confess" refers to the worship that expresses faith. In 9:22 it is stated that the Jews had already agreed that if anyone "confessed" (ὁμολογήσῃ) Jesus as the

abrupt and emphatic replies that he is not even one of the other expected messianic figures—"I am not!" to the question whether he is Elijah and "No!" to the question whether he is the Prophet (1:21)—underscore that Jesus Christ, not John, is the messianic figure that believers in the audience are to confess in their worship.[4]

Having identified himself negatively, John is pressed to identity himself positively (1:22). The John who emphatically declared that "*I* [ἐγώ] am not the Christ!" (1:20), with another emphatic "I," declares that "*I* [ἐγώ] am a voice of one crying out in the desert, 'Make straight the way of the Lord' [Isa 40:3], as Isaiah the prophet said" (John 1:23). Although John is not the Christ who is "the Word" (1:14, 17) nor "the Prophet" (1:21), he is a "voice" who speaks prophetically in the words of "the prophet Isaiah."[5] John came to testify that all might believe in the Word, Jesus Christ, who was "coming" into the world after John (1:9, 15). His prophetic appeal to make straight the "way/coming" of the Lord is thus a metaphorical appeal to believe in, and implicitly to worship, the one coming after him. Through the prophetic voice of John, the prophet Isaiah's reference to the way of the Lord God now refers to the way/coming of Jesus Christ as Lord, the Word and unique divine Son, worthy to be worshiped as God (1:1, 18) along with God the Father whom he came to make known (1:18).

In addition to the priests and Levites some Pharisees also came to John (1:24), likewise with concerns about worship, as they ask him, "Why do you baptize [βαπτίζεις]?," referring to a ritual cleansing for proper worship, if he is not the Christ, nor Elijah, nor the Prophet (1:25).[6] With another emphatic "I" John answered that "*I* baptize with water; in the midst of you stands one whom you have not known" (1:26).[7] That "*I* baptize [ἐγὼ

Christ, he would be put out of the synagogue, a place for Jewish worship. And in 12:42 it is stated that many believed in Jesus, but because of the Pharisees they would not "confess" (ὡμολόγουν) and thus worship, so that they would not be put out of the synagogue. "John's apparent denial is actually a confession of his faith in 'the Christ,' so that 'the Jews' and their delegation are thwarted" (Michaels, *John*, 97).

4. On Jesus as the new Elijah in John's Gospel, see Gunawan, "New Elijah," 29–53. The designation "the Prophet" alludes to the promised "prophet like Moses" whom God would raise up for his people according to Deut 18:15, 18. Jesus is identified as this prophet like Moses in Acts 3:22; 7:37.

5. "Though Jesus is the Word, the Baptist is 'a voice' directing his audience to Jesus" (Köstenberger, *John*, 62). See also Michaels, *John*, 100–1.

6. "Most likely, there was only one delegation of Jewish leaders, some of whom were Pharisees" (Köstenberger, *John*, 63). See also Bruner, *John*, 77.

7. "Behind John's strange remark lies a traditional Jewish notion of the hidden Messiah who comes into the world but remains incognito until it is time for him to be revealed" (Michaels, *John*, 103).

βαπτίζω] with water" resonates with and complements John's previous emphatic declaration that "*I* [ἐγώ] am a voice crying out in the desert" (1:23). His voiced appeal to make straight the way of the Lord (1:23) by believing is complemented by his ritual activity of baptizing as part of his testimony that all might believe through him (1:7). But that in their midst stands one whom they have not known places the Pharisees among his own people who did not accept the Word (1:11), among the world who did not know the Word (1:10) as the light in whom came to be the divine life eternal for all human beings (1:3–4). They thus have not recognized him as worthy to be worshiped.

The Pharisees have not known the Word as the one coming after John (1:27a; cf. 1:15), the Word who "became flesh and dwelt among us" (1:14) as the personified place for the true worship of God. Resonating with his emphatic declaration that "I am not the Christ!" (1:20) is John's characterization of himself as a lowly servant. He emphatically declared the superiority over him of the Christ, the Lord, coming after him—"I am not worthy that I might loosen the strap of his sandal" (1:27).[8] This accentuates that the Christ coming after him and actualizing the "way of the Lord" (1:23), not John, is the Lord to be worshiped. This first day concludes with the notice that "these things happened in Bethany beyond the Jordan, where John was baptizing [βαπτίζων]" (1:28). This reaffirms that John was baptizing with water (1:26) as a ritual cleansing that was part of his testimony that all might believe in (1:7), and thus worship, Jesus Christ as the Word in whom came to be divine life eternal as the light for all human beings (1:3–4).[9]

Second Day: John's Testimony that Jesus Is the Sacrificial Lamb of God (1:29–34)

The next day John saw Jesus "coming" toward him (1:29a), the one after him "coming" (1:27), recalling that the true light, which was the divine life eternal that had come to be in the Word (1:3–4), was "coming" into the world (1:9). John's pronouncement, "Behold, the Lamb of God, who takes away the sin of the world" (1:29b), identifies Jesus as both the sacrificial Passover lamb (Exodus 12) and the Suffering Servant, who like a lamb was

---

8. "The task of untying the thong of the sandal was given to the least and lowest of all in the hierarchy of servants and slaves" (Moloney, *John*, 58).

9. In the Gospel of Mark it is reported that the Pharisees and all Jews do not eat a meal, which they considered to be an act of worship, unless they are "baptized" (βαπτίσωνται), ritually cleansed, beforehand (Mark 7:4). With reference to this practice Jesus applied to them a scriptural quotation (Isa 29:13) which includes the words "in vain do they worship [σέβονταί] me" (Mark 7:7).

led to a sacrificial death for sins (Isa 52:13–53:12).[10] That he takes away the sin of the "world" recalls that he was in the "world," and although the "world" came to be through him, the "world" did not know him (1:10). By his sacrificial death, then, he takes away the sin of not knowing or believing in him in order to become children of God (1:12) and share in divine life eternal. Jesus is not only an object of worship who makes known the God to be worshiped (1:14-18), but, as the Lamb of God who was led to death, he himself performs a sacrificial act of worshiping God.

The Jesus whom John saw "coming" (ἐρχόμενον) toward him and identified as the Lamb of God who takes away the sin of the world (1:29) he further identified: "This one is he for whom I said, 'After me is coming [ἔρχεται] a man who before me had come to be, for prior to me he was!'" (1:30). This accentuates the superiority over John of Jesus as "the one after me coming [ἐρχόμενος]" (1:27). And it reaffirms John's testimony regarding Jesus as the preexistent Word who became flesh (1:14): "This one was he of whom I said, 'The one after me coming [ἐρχόμενος], before me had come to be, for prior to me he was!'" (1:15). It indicates for the audience that the Jesus who, as the Lamb of God, offered himself as a sacrificial act of worship to God, is also the preexistent Word who was with God and was God (1:1-2), and thus himself an object of worship.

When John, with an emphatic "I," explained to the Pharisees that he is not the Christ, because "*I* [ἐγώ] baptize with water," he added, with an emphatic "you," that "in the midst of you stands one whom *you* [ὑμεῖς] do not know" (1:26). But now, again with the emphatic "I," John admits, "And *I myself* [κἀγώ] did not know him, but that he might be manifested to Israel, on account of this *I* [ἐγώ] came baptizing with water" (1:31). This not only explains the role of John's baptizing with water as a ritual act of worship, but

---

10. "The primary background must be that of the (sacrificial) Passover lamb, as many scholars have contended, although combinations with other sources like the Suffering Servant remain feasible. . . . the writer undoubtedly viewed the Passover as a form of sacrifice. (The LXX uses John's term here for sacrificial lambs approximately one hundred times.)" (Keener, *John*, 1.454). The identification of Jesus as the Lamb of God who takes away the sin of world "appears to combine the imagery from Deutero-Isaiah of the servant-witness who bears the sin of many and is led as a lamb to the slaughter with that of the Passover lamb . . . one of the ways in which this Gospel's narrative portrays Jesus is as the sacrificial victim, whose death removes the primary obstacle to the world's reception of the divine gift of life" (Lincoln, *John*, 113). "While the Gospel writer never speaks of 'the blood of the Lamb,' and stops well short of attributing to John the explicit notion of cleansing from sin through Jesus' blood, he nevertheless allows John's testimony to evoke for his readers just such imagery. . . . the Gospel writer presents him here as 'the Lamb,' but a lamb like no other in that he himself initiates the sacrifice . . . Jesus is priest and sacrifice at the same time" (Michaels, *John*, 111). See also Bruner, *John*, 83-84.

further implies that the Christ who is Jesus (1:17), the Lamb of God (1:29), will baptize differently.

John, who came to testify (1:7-8, 15, 19), testified further, saying, "I have observed [τεθέαμαι] the Spirit descending like a dove from heaven and it remained upon him" (1:32). This resonates with and reinforces for the audience the communal doxological confession that "we observed [ἐθεασάμεθα] his glory, glory as of the unique one from the Father, full of a gift of truth" (1:14b).[11] That the divine Spirit "remained" or "abided" (ἔμεινεν) upon him accords with Jesus being the personified place for the presence and worship of God as the divine Word who "dwelt" (ἐσκήνωσεν) among us (1:14a).

John emphatically reiterated that "*I myself* [κἀγώ] did not know him" (1:33a; cf. 1:31a). But John then reported that the one who sent him to baptize with water, namely God (1:6), said to him, "Upon whom you see the Spirit descending and remaining upon him, this one is he who baptizes with the Holy Spirit" (1:33b). This makes explicit the implication that Jesus in continuity with John would also baptize but in a different way. Whereas John baptizes with water as a ritual cleansing in preparation for worship, Jesus is not only the personified dwelling place for worship (1:14), but he baptizes with the Holy Spirit, providing a divine agent for the proper worship of God.

This second day of John's testimony concluded as he emphatically confessed that "*I myself* [κἀγώ] have seen and have testified that this one is the Chosen One of God!" (1:34).[12] That Jesus is "the Chosen One of God" (ὁ ἐκλεκτὸς τοῦ θεου) as the one upon whom "the Spirit" (τὸ πνεῦμα) of God descended and remains (1:33) coincides with his being "the Lamb of God" (ὁ ἀμνὸς τοῦ θεοῦ), the chosen Passover lamb/Suffering Servant, who takes away the sin of the world (1:29). It alludes to God's pronouncement of the Suffering Servant as "my chosen one" (ὁ ἐκλεκτός μου), the one to whom God gave "my Spirit [τὸ πνεῦμά μου]" (LXX Isa 42:1). John's testimonial confession of faith not only reaffirms that Jesus is the Lamb of God chosen by God to sacrifice himself as an act of worship to God, but provides the

---

11. "θεάομαι in John conveys a more pronounced note of *perception* than other 'seeing' verbs" (Köstenberger, *John*, 69n46; emphasis original). John "becomes here the spokesman for all who have 'looked,' whether literally or spiritually, at the Word in human flesh, and seen 'glory as of a father's One and Only' (v. 14)" (Michaels, *John*, 113).

12. For the reasons to choose the variant reading "the Chosen One of God" rather than "the Son of God," see Quek, "Textual-Critical Study of John 1.34," 22-34; Köstenberger, *John*, 71; Bruner, *John*, 97-98. Note also that if "the Son of God" were the original reading, it would detract from the dramatic rhetorical progression in 1:19-51 in which "the Son of God" title is a climactic confession (1:49).

testimony for the audience to worship Jesus as well, indeed, as the divine Lamb of God, the divine Chosen One of God.[13]

Third Day: First Disciples Prepare for the Worship of Jesus (1:35–42)

The next day again John was "standing," away from two of his disciples (1:35). This associates John with Jesus as the one who "stands" among those who do not know him (1:26). But John made the identity of Jesus known. Looking at Jesus walking by, John said, "Behold, the Lamb of God!" (1:36), recalling that Jesus is the Lamb of God who takes away the sin of the world (1:29). His two disciples heard John speaking and followed Jesus (1:37), implying that they are now becoming disciples of Jesus. This is confirmed as Jesus, turning and observing them following, said to them, "What are you seeking?" (1:38a). They addressed him with the Jewish designation "rabbi," whose Greek equivalent is "teacher" (1:38b), indicating Jesus' relevance as a teacher not only for these two Jews who are now becoming his disciples but for the rest of the (mainly Greek speaking) world as well (cf. 1:9–11).

Based on the context, the implied answer to Jesus' question, "What [τί] are you seeking?" (1:38), is that they are seeking the Holy Spirit that "remains" or "abides" (μένον) upon Jesus and with which he baptizes (1:33), as the Lamb of God who takes away the sin of the world (1:29, 36).[14] Their reply to Jesus with their own question, "Where are you abiding/remaining [μένεις]?" (1:38) confirms this. They are asking where Jesus abides/remains, as the one upon whom the Holy Spirit abides/remains, the one who "dwelt among us" as the personified place for worship (1:14). After Jesus' invitation for them to come and "you will see," the two disciples came and "saw" where Jesus, the one who made known the God no one has ever "seen" (1:18), "was abiding/remaining [μένει]" (1:39). They in turn "abided/remained" (ἔμειναν) beside him that day at a specific time—"the hour was about the tenth" (1:39). This places them at a definite time in a close relationship with Jesus, who baptizes with the Holy Spirit for the proper worship of God.

---

13. "The two perfect tenses—'I myself have seen and have testified'—emphasize the continuing present significance of John's witness as a testimony that remains on record for the readers. The ordinary language associated with the stance of an eyewitness is now used instead to speak of the insight of belief that leads to confession" (Lincoln, *John*, 114).

14. The neuter interrogative pronoun "what [τί]" (1:38) points back to the neuter noun "Holy Spirit [πνεύματι ἁγίῳ]" (1:33).

Andrew, the brother of Simon Peter, was one of the two disciples of John who heard John and followed Jesus (1:40).[15] After having been with Jesus, the first thing Andrew did was to find his own brother and say to him, "We have found the Messiah!" (which is translated "Christ") (1:41). The two disciples of John, who abided/remained beside Jesus (1:39) after "seeking" where Jesus abides/remains (1:38) have "found" that Jesus is not only the Messiah for the Jews but the Christ for the whole world. In finding Jesus as the Christ they have found the Lamb of God who takes away the sin of the world (1:29, 36), the one upon whom the Spirit abides/remains, enabling him to baptize with the Holy Spirit (1:33).

Andrew then led his brother Simon to Jesus, who looked at him and said, "You are Simon, the son of John. You will be called Cephas" (which is interpreted "Peter") (1:42). That Jesus "looked at" (ἐμβλέψας) Simon continues the transferal of disciples of John to Jesus that began when John "looked at" (ἐμβλέψας) Jesus and pointed him out as the Lamb of God (1:36) to two of his disciples (1:35), who then followed Jesus (1:37). Jesus' address to Simon as "the son of John" has a double meaning for the audience. Simon is not only the literal son of someone named John, but the metaphorical "son" of the John who baptizes with water (1:26, 31, 33), the only "John" who has been mentioned previously (1:6, 15, 19, 26, 28, 32, 35, 40).[16] In authoritatively renaming Simon as Cephas/Peter, Jesus has indicated that Simon Peter is no longer a disciple of the John who baptizes with water, but now has been named and claimed as a disciple of Jesus, the Messiah/Christ who baptizes with the Holy Spirit (1:33), a divine agent for the proper worship of God.[17]

Fourth Day: A Disciple Worships Jesus (1:43–51)

The next day, the fourth in this sequence, Jesus "found" and invited Philip to "follow" him to Galilee (1:43), as Philip, along with Andrew and Peter, was from Bethsaida in Galilee (1:44). Jesus continued the process begun by Andrew of "finding" individuals to be disciples who "follow" Jesus rather than

---

15. On the role of Peter in the Gospel of John, see Cassidy, *Peter*, 85–107; Blaine, *Peter*.

16. "The only 'John' mentioned so far is the one who has just proclaimed Jesus as 'Lamb of God' (v. 36), and it is at least as likely that Jesus is addressing Simon as an adherent or disciple of John as that he is making reference to Simon's actual father" (Michaels, *John*, 124).

17. "In OT times, God frequently changed people's names to indicate their special calling (e.g., Abraham, Jacob). Giving someone a new name demonstrated authority (2 Kings 23:34; 24:17)" (Köstenberger, *John*, 77).

John (1:37-38, 40, 41). Philip in turn repeated this process, as he "found" Nathanael and said to him, "The one about whom Moses wrote in the law, also the prophets, we have found [εὑρήκαμεν], Jesus, son of Joseph, from Nazareth" (1:45). This recalls that when Andrew "found" his brother Peter, he said to him, "We have found [εὑρήκαμεν] the Messiah/Christ" (1:41). The Jesus Christ through whom the gift of the truth came to be in place of the gift of the law given through Moses (1:16-17) is thus identified as the Jesus of Nazareth, the son of Joseph, about whom Moses and the prophets wrote.

But Nathanael said to Philip, "From Nazareth can there be anything good?" (1:46a), which stands in ironic contrast to Andrew's declaration that the Jesus who is from Nazareth is the Messiah/Christ (1:41).[18] And so Philip said to him, "Come and see" (1:46b). This echoes Jesus' invitation, "Come and you will see," to those who were seeking where he abides/remains (1:39), which resulted in Andrew's declaration that after abiding/remaining with Jesus they found him to be the Messiah/Christ (1:41). It also echoes John's invitation to "behold/see" that Jesus is the Lamb of God who takes away the sin of the world (1:29, 36). What is the messianic "good" that Philip's invitation will lead Nathanael to see in Jesus from Nazareth?

But Jesus "saw" Nathanael "coming" toward him (1:47a), before Nathanael can "come and see" what good there can be from Nazareth (1:46). Jesus then points out Nathanael to the audience as one whose significance is to be seen: "Behold/see, truly an Israelite in whom there is no deceit" (1:47b). Nathanael is an ideal representative of Israel, since unlike Jacob/Israel, who took away his brother's blessing with "deceit [δόλου]" (LXX Gen 27:35), in Nathanael "there is no deceit [δόλος]." He is thus an ideal representative for the manifestation to Israel of Jesus, the Christ and Lamb of God, the reason for which John came baptizing with water (1:31).[19]

After Nathanael then asked Jesus, "Whence do you know me?," Jesus replied, "Before Philip called you, I saw you under the fig tree" (1:48). That Nathanael was "under the fig tree" indicates that he, as truly an Israelite (1:47), was anticipating the fulfillment of the messianic peace and rest, symbolized by being under a vine and fig tree, which a messianic figure (see

---

18. On the irony in 1:46, see Duke, *Irony*, 84-85.

19. "It was Jacob, whose name meant supplanter or deceiver (cf. Gen. 25.26; 27.35-6), who was first given the name Israel after wrestling with God (cf. Gen. 32.28; cf. also 35.10). Nathanael surpasses the original Israel in being without guile or deceit. His response to Jesus can therefore be viewed as paradigmatic for those who would be faithful Israelites and as what is meant to happen when Jesus is revealed to Israel (cf. 1.31)" (Lincoln, *John*, 120). On the character of Nathanael in John, see Bennema, *Encountering Jesus*, 64-68.

Zech 3:8) would bring, as prophetically promised for Israel in the OT: "'On that day,' says the Lord almighty, 'you will call together, each his neighbor, under a vine and under a fig tree" (LXX Zech 3:10). And in the eschatological age (see LXX Mic 4:1), "each will rest under his vine and under his fig tree" (4:4).[20]

As the ideal representative of Israel (1:47), Nathanael then acknowledged Jesus as the messianic figure for whom the people of Israel were hoping. With a confession of faith that serves as an exuberant act of worship, which provides a model for the audience, he proclaimed, "Rabbi, you are the Son of God; you are the King of Israel!" (1:49). The Nathanael who disparagingly asked, "From Nazareth can there be anything good?" (1:46a), now confesses that Jesus from Nazareth is not only "son" of Joseph (1:45) but the messianic "Son" of God.[21] As the ideal Israelite, Nathanael appropriately confessed Jesus as the messianic King of Israel, thus signaling that the reason John came baptizing with water—that Jesus might be manifested to Israel as their Christ (1:31)—has been realized.[22]

In reply to Nathanael's confession of faith Jesus said, "Because I told you that I saw you under the fig tree, do you believe? Greater things than these you will see" (1:50). The expression of Nathanael's faith in an act of worship continues to indicate that the goal of John's testimony is beginning to be realized, as John came that "all might believe through him" (1:7), with the implication that worship gives expression to faith. Although his own people in general did not accept Jesus (1:11), Nathanael was among those who did receive him, "those who believe in his name," enabling them to become children of God (1:12).

Jesus continues to address Nathanael, but with a climactic revelatory pronouncement directed to a plural "you"—"Amen, amen, I say to you

---

20. Koester, "Messianic Exegesis," 23–34.

21. "The Gospel writer and his readers know that Jesus is God's Son in a more profound sense than Nathanael could have understood (see 1:14, 18), yet he allows Nathanael to speak for him and for the entire Christian community. Nathanael's confession anticipates the writer's hope that all who read, 'might believe that Jesus is the Christ, the Son of God, and believing have life in his name' (20:31). To Nathanael, within the story, 'King of Israel' defines what 'Son of God' means, but for the author and his readers 'Son of God' defines what 'King of Israel' means" (Michaels, *John*, 132). On the contrast between Jesus as "son" of Joseph and as "Son" of God, see Nicklas, "Unter dem Feigenbaum," 195, 197.

22. "The second title, 'the King of Israel,' is precisely what we would expect from 'a true Israelite.' Nathanael, as 'Israel,' acknowledges 'Jesus, son of Joseph, from Nazareth' as his King and Lord. The designation of Israel's king as God's son goes all the way back to the biblical Psalms (compare Pss 2:6–7; 89:26–27), and in the present context the two are virtually synonymous ways of affirming Jesus as 'the Christ' or "Messiah' (compare vv. 41, 45)" (Michaels, *John*, 132).

[ὑμῖν]" (1:51a), which includes Nathanael, his fellow disciples, and ultimately the audience of the Gospel: "You will see heaven opened and the angels of God ascending and descending upon the Son of Man" (1:51b).[23] When Jesus invited the two disciples to "come and you will see" (1:39), it resulted in their discovery of Jesus' identity as the Messiah/Christ (1:40). And now he promises that "you will see" his identity as the "Son of Man." Jesus is thus not only "son" of Joseph and the "Son of God," but the "Son of Man," a heavenly figure with divine authority (see LXX Dan 7:13-14), who has come to earth. Others have pointed out that Jesus is the Lamb of God (1:29, 36), the Messiah/Christ (1:41), the Son of God and the King of Israel (1:49), but Jesus refers to himself as the Son of Man.[24]

Jesus' promise that "you will see heaven opened and the angels of God ascending and descending upon the Son of Man" (1:51) alludes to Jacob's dream in which he saw "a stairway erected on the earth whose head reached into heaven and the angels of God were ascending and descending upon it" (LXX Gen 28:12). When Jacob awoke, he declared that "this place is none other than the house of God" (28:17), that is, the place for the presence and worship of God. The vision of "heaven" opened and the angels of God "descending" upon the Son of Man recalls John's testimony that he saw the Spirit "descending" from "heaven" and remaining on Jesus (John 1:32), indicating that he is the one who baptizes with the Holy Spirit (1:33) for the true worship of God.

Thus, Jesus is not only the messianic Son of God and the King of Israel (1:49), but the heavenly Son of Man who has come down from heaven to be the personified place for the presence and worship of God on earth, the divine Word who became flesh and dwelt among us (1:14). Jesus is the divinely chosen (1:34) Lamb of God who takes away the sin, not just of Israel, but of the whole world (1:29). He is the one who baptizes with the Holy Spirit (1:33) so that all who believe might truly worship God in and through him.[25]

---

23. "The double 'Amen' formula occurs 25 times in John's Gospel as a way of solemnly attesting the truth of what is about to be said. . . . In a sense, the double 'Amen' formula here solemnly attests the truth of *all* that Jesus will say from here on" (Michaels, *John*, 134-35; emphasis original).

24. "'Son of man' is not a title someone else gives to Jesus, but one that he claims for himself, just as in the other Gospels" (Michaels, *John*, 138).

25. "As has been noted, the Jacob story has already been invoked in the conversation with Nathanael. Now it is made clear that this true Israelite will see something greater than Jacob saw. He will see not simply a ladder but a person, the Son of Man, as the connection between earth and heaven. For Jacob the place of his dream became Bethel, the house of God, and the gate of heaven (Gen. 28:17, 19). For the evangelist Jesus now embodies God's address on earth, fulfilling all that was previously represented by

Summary on 1:19–51

On a first day (1:19–28) John emphatically confessed that he is not the Christ (1:20). His increasingly abrupt and emphatic replies to the priests and Levites in charge of temple worship that he is not even one of the other expected messianic figures (1:21) underscore that Jesus Christ, not John, is the messianic figure that believers in the audience are to confess in their worship. Through the prophetic voice of John, the prophet Isaiah's reference to the way of the Lord God (1:23) now refers to the way/coming of Jesus Christ as Lord, the Word and unique divine Son, worthy to be worshiped as God (1:1, 18) along with God the Father whom he came to make known (1:18).

The Pharisees have not known the Word as the one coming after John (1:27a; cf. 1:15), the Word who "became flesh and dwelt among us" (1:14) as the personified place for the true worship of God. Resonating with his emphatic declaration that "I am not the Christ!" (1:20) is John's characterization of himself as a lowly servant (1:27). This accentuates that the Christ coming after him and actualizing the "way of the Lord" (1:23), not John, is the Lord to be worshiped. This first day concluded with a reaffirmation that John was baptizing (1:28) with water (1:26) as a ritual cleansing that was part of his testimony that all might believe in (1:7), and thus worship, Jesus Christ as the Word in whom came to be divine life eternal as the light for all human beings (1:3–4).

On a second day (1:29–34) John's pronouncement, "Behold, the Lamb of God, who takes away the sin of the world" (1:29), identifies Jesus as both the sacrificial Passover lamb (Exodus 12) and the Suffering Servant, who like a lamb was led to a sacrificial death for sins (Isa 52:13–53:12). That he takes away the sin of the "world" recalls that he was in the "world," and although the "world" came to be through him, the "world" did not know him (1:10). By his sacrificial death, then, he takes away the sin of not knowing or believing in him in order to become children of God (1:12) and share in divine life eternal. Jesus is not only an object of worship who makes known the God to be worshiped (1:14–18), but, as the Lamb of God who was led to death, he himself performs a sacrificial act of worshiping God.

John reported that the one who sent him to baptize with water, namely God (1:6), said to him, "Upon whom you see the Spirit descending and remaining upon him, this one is he who baptizes with the Holy Spirit" (1:33). This makes explicit the implication that Jesus in continuity with John would also baptize but in a different way. Whereas John baptizes with water as a

---

such locations as Bethel, the tabernacle or the temple (cf. also 1.14; 2.19–21; 4.21–4)" (Lincoln, *John*, 122). See also Perrin, *Jesus the Temple*, 53.

ritual cleansing in preparation for worship, Jesus is not only the personified dwelling place for worship (1:14), but he baptizes with the Holy Spirit, providing a divine agent for the true and proper worship of God.

This second day of John's testimony concluded as he emphatically confessed that "*I myself* have seen and have testified that this one is the Chosen One of God!" (1:34). That Jesus is "the Chosen One of God" as the one upon whom "the Spirit" of God descended and remains (1:33) coincides with his being "the Lamb of God," the chosen Passover lamb/Suffering Servant, who takes away the sin of the world (1:29). It alludes to God's pronouncement of the Suffering Servant as "my chosen one," the one to whom God gave "my Spirit" (LXX Isa 42:1). John's testimonial confession of faith not only reaffirms that Jesus is the Lamb of God chosen by God to sacrifice himself as an act of worship to God, but provides the testimony for the audience to worship Jesus as well, indeed, as the divine Lamb of God and the divine Chosen One of God.

On a third day (1:35-42) the implied answer to Jesus' question to the two following him, "What are you seeking?" (1:38), is that they are seeking the Holy Spirit that "remains" or "abides" upon Jesus and with which he baptizes (1:33), as the Lamb of God who takes away the sin of the world (1:29, 36). Their reply to Jesus with their own question, "Where are you abiding/remaining?" (1:38) confirms this. They are asking where Jesus abides/remains, as the one upon whom the Holy Spirit abides/remains, the one who "dwelt among us" as the personified place for worship (1:14). After Jesus' invitation for them to come and "you will see," the two disciples came and "saw" where Jesus, the one who made known the God no one has ever "seen" (1:18), "was abiding/remaining" (1:39). They in turn "abided/remained" beside him that day (1:39). This places them at a definite time in a close relationship with Jesus, who baptizes with the Holy Spirit for the proper worship of God.

On a fourth day (1:43-51), as the ideal representative of Israel (1:47), Nathanael acknowledged Jesus as the messianic figure for whom the people of Israel were hoping. With a confession of faith that serves as an exuberant act of worship, which provides a model for the audience, he proclaimed, "Rabbi, you are the Son of God; you are the King of Israel!" (1:49). The Nathanael who disparagingly asked, "From Nazareth can there be anything good?" (1:46a), now confesses that Jesus from Nazareth is not only "son" of Joseph (1:45) but the messianic "Son" of God. As the ideal Israelite, Nathanael appropriately confessed Jesus as the messianic King of Israel, thus signaling that the reason John came baptizing with water—that Jesus might be manifested to Israel as their Christ (1:31)—has been realized.

Jesus' promise, addressed not only to Nathanael but to the broader audience, that "you will see heaven opened and the angels of God ascending and descending upon the Son of Man" (1:51) alludes to Jacob's dream in which he saw "a stairway erected on the earth whose head reached into heaven and the angels of God were ascending and descending upon it" (LXX Gen 28:12). When Jacob awoke, he declared that "this place is none other than the house of God" (28:17), that is, the place for the presence and worship of God. The vision of "heaven" opened and the angels of God "descending" upon the Son of Man recalls John's testimony that he saw the Spirit "descending" from "heaven" and remaining on Jesus (John 1:32), indicating that he is the one who baptizes with the Holy Spirit (1:33) for the true worship of God.

Nathanael confessed Jesus to be the messianic Son of God and the King of Israel (1:49). But Jesus referred to himself as the heavenly Son of Man with divine authority (LXX Dan 7:13-14) who has come down from heaven to be the personified place for the presence and worship of God on earth. He is the divine Word who became flesh and dwelt among us (1:14). Jesus is the divinely chosen (1:34) Lamb of God who takes away the sin, not just of Israel, but of the whole world (1:29). He is the one who baptizes with the Holy Spirit (1:33) so that all who believe might truly worship God in and through him.

4

Jesus Reveals True Worship in the Spirit and Truth (2:1—4:54)

Jesus Transforms Water into Wine for a Worship Celebrating Divine Life (2:1-12)

"And so on the third day there came to be a wedding in Cana of Galilee" (2:1a). The mention of a "third day" ties this scene closely to the previous series of four days (1:19–51), suggesting that they are a preparation for what will happen on this climactic third day. In addition to the things that "came to be" (ἐγένετο) during this sequence of days "in Bethany across the Jordan, where John was baptizing" (1:28), a wedding "came to be" (ἐγένετο) in Cana of Galilee, recalling Jesus' desire to go out to Galilee on the final of the first four days (1:43). Additionally, "on the third day" alludes to the manifestation of God for the giving of the law through Moses, which "came to be" (ἐγένετο) after a preparation of days "on the third day" (LXX Exod 19:16; cf. 19:11). This implies that at this wedding there will be a divine manifestation involving how the gift of the truth "came to be" (ἐγένετο) through Jesus Christ, which transcended the gift of the law through Moses (1:17).

That a Jewish "wedding" took place accords with OT references to the covenantal relationship in terms of nuptial imagery for which the Mosaic law was central and in which God is the "bridegroom" and his people the "bride."[1] A wedding connotes feasting, and there were OT expectations that the arrival of the messianic age would involve celebratory feasting that included the abundance of wine (Amos 9:13–14).[2] Wine was drunk not

---

1. See Hos 2:14–16, 21; Isa 54:4–8; 62:4–5; Jer 2:2; Ezek 16:8; 23:4.
2. "The setting of a marriage feast also summons up biblical images of the messianic era and the messianic fullness, marked by wine and abundance of fine foods" (Moloney, *John*, 66).

only to bring gladness and celebrate life (LXX Ps 103:15; Sir 31:28), but it was even equated with life itself (Sir 31:27) and associated with God's destruction of death, implying the arrival of a new, divine and eternal life (Isa 25:6-8).[3]

Present at the wedding were Jesus and his disciples (2:2) as well as the mother of Jesus (2:1b), who, when the wine ran out, pointed out to Jesus that "they have no wine" (2:3). On the symbolic level this characterizes how the nuptial relationship of the old covenant with its Mosaic gift of the law (1:17) has not yet provided the abundant wine needed for the celebration of divine life eternal. Jesus' reply, "What [is this] to me and to you, woman?" (2:4a), implies what they together, with Jesus as a new "bridegroom" and his mother as a new "woman/wife [γύναι]" on a deeper level, have to do about this situation.[4] But Jesus' additional statement that "my hour has not yet come" (2:4b) inserts a note of dramatic tension, as it indicates that the divine manifestation to take place at this wedding is an early anticipation of the divine manifestation to take place at the later time of his "hour."

Resonating with the statement of faithful obedience, "all the things God has spoken we will do [ποιήσομεν]," uttered by all the people as the "bride" of the old covenant (LXX Exod 19:8; 24:3, 7), Jesus' mother as the "woman/bride" (2:4) of the new covenant of this new wedding feast told the servants, "Whatever he might say to you, do [ποιήσατε]" (2:5).[5] A narrative aside notes that there were six stone water jars lying there for the cleansing/purification of the "Jews," each holding "two to three measures" (2:6), that is, twenty to thirty gallons. Jesus told the servants to fill the jars with "water," and they filled them to the very top, indicating abundance (2:7). This recalls John's statement to those sent by the "Jews" from Jerusalem (1:19) that he baptizes/cleanses with "water" (1:26, 31, 33) to purify people for worship, but Jesus brings this Jewish cleansing and purification for worship to perfection as he baptizes with the Holy Spirit (1:33). Indeed Jesus transforms this

---

3. "In the Jewish Scriptures wine in abundance signifies the salvation of the end time... In addition, wine stands for life and joy (cf. Ps. 104.15; Eccl. 10.19; Sir. 31.27-8; 40.20). In inaugurating the new order, Jesus provides life that is to be enjoyed" (Lincoln, *John*, 129).

4. On the covenantal language indicated by this question, see Brown, *Gift*, 118-20. "His mother's remark that 'they have no wine' (v. 3) is not so much a request for Jesus to perform a miracle as a signal to the reader that he is going to do so. Her subsequent word to the servants, 'Do whatever he tells you' (v. 5), will signal further that this is her expectation as well. In short, Jesus and his mother are thinking along the same lines, not at cross purposes" (Michaels, *John*, 144).

5. "She accepts his challenge just as the children of Israel accepted the covenant at Sinai, and with her imperative sets in motion the revelation" (Brown, *Gift*, 120).

abundance of water for the cleansing of the Jews into an abundance of wine for drinking in a new celebratory worship of divine life eternal.

Jesus told the servants to bring some of the water to the headwaiter (2:8), who tasted the water for cleansing that miraculously "had come to be" (γεγενημένον) wine for drinking (2:9a), resonating with the divine life eternal that "had come to be" (γέγονεν) in Jesus, the divine Word (1:3-4). Although the headwaiter did not know "whence" (πόθεν) the wine came, the servants who drew the water knew that it came from Jesus (2:9b), which associates them with the disciples, one of whom, Nathanael, Jesus told "whence" (πόθεν) he knew him (1:48), with "whence" hinting at the divine origin of Jesus.[6] The headwaiter then called "the bridegroom" (2:9c), who on the deeper, ironic level is now Jesus himself.[7]

The headwaiter said to the bridegroom/Jesus, "Every human being serves the good wine first, and when they are drunk the inferior. But you have kept the good wine until now!" (2:10). At a Jewish wedding Jesus transformed the water to cleanse the Jews for worship into an abundance of wine for the celebratory worship of divine life eternal (2:6-9). But he also transformed a practice not just of Jews but of "every human being," as he provided not just abundant but good wine appropriate for the celebratory worship of divine life eternal available to everyone. This recalls that the life that had come to be in Jesus was the true light that enlightens "every human being" (1:9). With an emphatic "you," Nathanael worshiped Jesus by confessing, "You [σύ] are the Son of God. You [σύ] are the King of Israel!" (1:49). And with an emphatic "you," the headwaiter similarly directs the audience to the worship of Jesus by declaring that "you" (σύ), as the new bridegroom, "have kept and are still providing" (τετήρηκας, perfect tense) the good wine of divine life eternal even until now, so that it is available for all.[8]

That "Jesus did this [ταύτην] as the beginning of the signs" (2:11a) begins to fulfill for the audience his promise to the disciple Nathanael that "greater than these things [τούτων] you will see" (1:50). Whereas John came baptizing with water so that Jesus might be "manifested" to Israel (1:31), in Cana of Galilee Jesus "manifested" for every human being in the audience

---

6. "Within the account, it appears that these anonymous servants to whom Jesus' mother said, 'Do whatever he tells you,' take the disciples' place" (Michaels, *John*, 147).

7. "Jesus . . . fulfils the role of the bridegroom and does so in a way that exceeds all its usual expectations" (Lincoln, *John*, 130).

8. "The water required for the Jewish rite of purification, now become an abundance of best wine, points to the onset of the messianic age when the marital relationship between YHWH and Israel is restored and indeed transcended in the person of Jesus" (Byrne, *Life Abounding*, 56). On the irony in 2:10, see Duke, *Irony*, 83-84.

his "glory" (2:11b), extending to all people the manifestation of the "glory" of God that came down upon Mount Sinai before the sons of Israel at the giving of the law (LXX Exod 24:16–17). This reaffirms the basis for the communal act of doxological worship that "we observed his glory, glory as of the unique one from the Father, full of a gift of truth" (1:14). Whereas earlier the individual disciple Nathanael "believed" (1:50), the group of his disciples now "believed in him" (2:11c), indicating that they have been given the authority to become children of God who share in divine life eternal, as they are among those who "believe in his name" (1:12).

After this first sign Jesus, his mother, brothers, and disciples went down to Capernaum (2:12a), indicating that his disciples, who believed in him (2:11), have become part of the familial household of Jesus, a household oriented toward worship.[9] That they "remained" there "a few days" (2:12b) recalls that the first disciples saw where Jesus "remains" and they "remained that day" with Jesus (1:39), the one upon whom the Spirit of God "remains," so that he baptizes with the Holy Spirit (1:32–33). This gathering of a new familial household of Jesus thus forms an initial community for worship, a model for the audience, as they remained with Jesus, the divine Word who "dwelt among us" (1:14) as the personified place for the true worship of God.

The Risen Body of Jesus Is the New Temple for True Worship (2:13–25)

Jesus replaced and perfected the water for the cleansing/purification of the "Jews" (2:6) with an abundance of good wine for the celebratory worship of the divine life eternal he now provides (2:7–10). Subsequently, Jesus, the Passover Lamb of God (1:29, 36), went up to Jerusalem when the Passover of the "Jews" was near (2:13). After he drove the animals and those who sold them for sacrificial worship from the temple (2:14–15), he said, "Take away [ἄρατε] these things from here, do not make the house of my Father a house of trade!" (2:16).[10] As the sacrificial Lamb of God who "takes away" (αἴρων) the sin of the world (1:29) to enable true worship for all people, and as the

---

9. "With the arrival of the bridegroom and the completion of the wedding celebrations, the disciples are incorporated into the household of Jesus, dwelling with his mother and brothers and sisters" (Coloe, *Household of God*, 56). "Jesus' natural brothers and his disciples are seen together as 'family'" (Michaels, *John*, 156).

10. "The paraphernalia of Israel's cult are displaced, poured out, and overturned in anticipation of a new mode of worship. While the exact nature of the new mode of worship is still to be disclosed, in the dialogue that follows the presence of a new 'Temple' is announced" (Coloe, *God Dwells*, 81). See also Kerr, *Temple*, 67–101.

unique one from the "Father" (1:14), who is in the bosom of the "Father" (1:18), Jesus demands the taking away of the things that do not enable true worship. Indeed they are turning the house of God his Father into a house of trade instead of what God wants it to be: "For my house shall be called a house of prayer for all nations" (LXX Isa 56:7).

The Passover feast was to be a perpetual "memorial" (μνημόσυνον) commemorated in worship for all generations (LXX Exod 12:14). The disciples of Jesus, who are part of his familial household who remained with him as the personified place for worship (2:12), "remembered" (ἐμνήσθησαν), suggesting that they did so as a commemoration in worship, that it is written, "Zeal for your house will consume me" (2:17; cf. LXX Ps 68:10).[11] In other words, the scriptural word of God predicted that Jesus' zeal to make the house of his Father a house of true worship will lead to his sacrificial death as the Passover Lamb.[12] It will totally "consume," "devour," or "eat up," Jesus, just as the Passover lambs were to be "eaten" in their entirety (LXX Exod 12:9).[13]

In reply to the Jews' request that Jesus show them a sign, "since you are doing these things" (2:18), he said to them, "Destroy this temple and in three days I will raise it up" (2:19). Jesus' assertion for them to "destroy" this temple develops the scriptural prediction that zeal for the house of God's worship "will consume" him (2:17), implying that "this temple" refers to Jesus himself as the new temple for worship. In contrast to the previous term for "temple" (ἱερόν) to refer to the literal building (2:14-15), Jesus now employs a synonymous term for "temple" (ναός) metaphorically to refer to himself. The sign he indicates to them is the future sign of his resurrection from the dead. But the Jews misunderstand his metaphorical application of "temple" as literal and question his ability to raise it up in a mere three days (2:20). The narrator, however, clarifies that Jesus was speaking about his body (2:21), confirming that, after being "consumed" as the sacrificial Passover Lamb (2:17) and "destroyed" as the personified temple (2:19; 1:14, 51), Jesus will be raised as the new temple for the true worship of God.

---

11. Whereas LXX Ps 68:10 reads "consumed" (κατέφαγεν), John 2:17 has "will consume" (καταφάγεταί).

12. "At a deeper level, the text is a comment upon what is driving the entire mission of Jesus and will ultimately 'consume' him in the most radical sense of encompassing his death: a zeal to reclaim the world as the place where human beings, as 'children of God' (1:12), are at home in their Father's house, recognizing and worshiping the divine presence and power ('glory') in line with Jacob's experience at Bethel (Gen 28:16-18) and Jesus' promise to Nathanael (John 1:51)" (Byrne, *Life Abounding*, 61).

13. References to the "eating" of the Passover lambs occur an emphatic six times in LXX Exod 12:7-11.

After Jesus was raised from the dead, his disciples "remembered" that he had said this (2:22a), just as they "remembered" the Scripture (2:17). Thus they believed the Scripture that predicted his sacrificial death as well as the word which Jesus had spoken, predicting his resurrection from the dead (2:22b). This provides a model for the audience to likewise "remember," not merely as a one-time remembrance but with the implication of an ongoing commemoration in their worship, the death and resurrection of Jesus as the personified new temple for the presence and worship of God.[14] Such worship is based on their faith in both Scripture and the "word" of Jesus, the divine "Word" become flesh (1:1, 14), whose word, like Scripture, is the very word of God as the focus of the true worship of God.

While Jesus was in Jerusalem at the Passover feast, many "believed [ἐπίστευσαν] in his name" when they saw the signs he was doing (2:23). This might suggest that Jesus gave them the authority to become children of God, as among "those who believe [πιστεύουσιν] in his name" (1:12). This is not the case, however, as Jesus "would not entrust [ἐπίστευεν] himself to them because he knew them all" (2:24).[15] Indeed that Jesus himself knew what was in the human being (2:25) suggests that their faith may be inadequate. The disciples, who "believed" when they saw the beginning of his signs (2:11), exemplify the progression to a more adequate faith as they "believed" the Scripture and the word of Jesus (2:22). Thus the faith of all human beings needs to be based not merely on seeing the preliminary signs of Jesus, but on the ultimate sign of the death and resurrection of Jesus as the personified new temple for the true worship of God.

Nicodemus and the Ritual Worship of Being Born of Water and Spirit (3:1–21)

Nicodemus, one of the "human beings" Jesus knew all about (2:25–3:1), came at "night" to Jesus (3:2a), the divine Word in whom was the life that was the light for all human beings (1:4, 9). His address to Jesus, "Rabbi, we know that you are a teacher who has come from God, for no one is able to do these signs which you are doing, unless God is with him" (3:2b), indicates that he is a representative spokesman for those Jews who believed

---

14. "[I]t is a matter not simply of recalling certain words that Jesus had spoken, but of coming to understand their significance in light of subsequent events" (Michaels, *John*, 169).

15. "As the evangelist indicates by way of a wordplay, though these people 'believed' (ἐπίστευσαν) in *him*, Jesus, for his part, did not 'entrust' (ἐπίστευεν) himself to *them*" (Köstenberger, *John*, 116; emphases original).

when they saw the signs Jesus was doing (2:23). Jesus challenged him to a deeper faith, as he replied, "Amen, amen, I say to you, unless someone is born again/from above, he is not able to see the kingdom of God" (3:3).[16] After Nicodemus misunderstood being born again as a physical rebirth (3:4), Jesus clarified, "Amen, amen, I say to you, unless someone is born of water and Spirit, he is not able to enter into the kingdom of God" (3:5). Thus, someone must be "born" again and from above of water and Spirit, in order to see and enter into the kingdom of God.

To be "born" again and from above of water and Spirit to see and enter the kingdom of God (3:5) develops what it means for those who believe in the name of Jesus to be "born" of God (1:13) in order to become children of God (1:12). To see and enter the kingdom of God is to enter into the community of believers who have become children of God with a share in divine life eternal.[17] Those who have been baptized with water only (1:26, 31, 33) must be baptized again and from above with water and Spirit. And this means being baptized with the baptism of Jesus who baptizes with the Holy Spirit, which descended from heaven above (1:32) and remains upon him (1:33). This baptism again and from above by water and Spirit establishes the basis for the audience to practice a ritual worship of sacramental baptism as the way of entering into the community of believers.[18]

The disciples provided a model for the audience's worship of commemorating the death and resurrection of Jesus as those who believed the Scripture that predicted his death and the word of Jesus that predicted his resurrection (2:22). This is developed in Jesus' further address to Nicodemus: "And just as Moses lifted up the serpent in the desert [Num 21:9], so it is necessary that the Son of Man be lifted up/exalted, so that everyone who believes in him might have life eternal" (3:14-15).[19] The Son of Man's

16. "The Greek adverb ἄνωθεν can have the temporal meaning 'again' as well as the spatial meaning 'from above'" (Byrne, *Life Abounding*, 65).

17. "[L]ike the gift of '(eternal) life' with which it is more or less synonymous, the kingdom is not simply a future destiny awaiting believers but a reality that they already 'see' with the eyes of faith and into which they have already 'entered' in the community of believers" (Byrne, *Life Abounding*, 66).

18. "It is reasonable to see 'water' here as referring to the Christian sacrament of baptism, the physical and communal enactment of the more interior disposition of faith" (Byrne, *Life Abounding*, 65). "In a Christian context there may well be a secondary connotation for water as a reference to baptism, and immediately following there will be references to Jesus baptizing in water (cf. 3.22, 26; 4:1-2)" (Lincoln, *John*, 150). "Contrary to an evident tendency in the early Church to separate Baptism by the Spirit from water altogether, it is here emphasized that in the Baptism of the Christian community the two belong together: water and Spirit" (Cullmann, *Early Christian Worship*, 76). See also Morgan-Wynne, *Cross*, 197-98.

19. "To the lifting up of the snake on a pole that all may live corresponds the lifting

being "lifted up" in crucifixion is simultaneously his being "exalted" or "glorified."[20] As the Son of Man, Jesus is thus not only the personified place for the presence and worship of God (1:51) but the object of worship in and through the sacrificial death by which he is exalted. It is by his sacrificial death, then, that Jesus provides the divine life eternal symbolized by the abundant good wine, so that for his disciples who saw the manifestation of this glory and believed in him (2:11), and everyone else who believes in him, he has become an object of worship.

The narrator then declares, "For God so loved the world, that he gave the Son, the unique one, so that everyone who believes in him may not perish but may have life eternal" (3:16). God so loved the world that he "gave," with the connotation of giving up to sacrificial death, "the Son" who is both the Son of God (1:49) and the Son of Man (1:51; 3:13-14), and, as "the unique one," is also God (1:1, 18). That God so loved the "world" in this way resonates with Jesus being the sacrificial Lamb of God who takes away the sin of the whole "world" (1:29). God "gave" (ἔδωκεν) the Son to the world, as the Word who became flesh by God (1:14), but also in his sacrificial death, so that everyone who believes in him may have life eternal.[21] This provides the basis for the assertion that Jesus "gave" (ἔδωκεν) authority for those who believe in his name to become children of God (1:12) with a share in life eternal. Not only Nicodemus, who came to Jesus at night (3:2), but everyone is invited to come to Jesus as the light (3:19-21) in whom is life (1:3-4), so that everyone who believes in, and thus worships, him may have divine life eternal.

---

up of the Son of Man on a cross that all may have eternal life" (Beasley-Murray, *John*, 50). On the double meaning of "lifted up" (referring to crucifixion) and "exalted" (indicating glorification) for ὑψωθῆναι in 3:14, see Mardaga, "Repetitive Use," 111-17.

20. "'Lift up' certainly refers to the crucifixion here as elsewhere in the Gospel, a usage it can bear very naturally in Palestinian Aramaic and in ancient Mediterranean thought" (Keener, *John*, 1.565).

21. "The giving of the only Son clearly embraces both incarnation and vicarious death; it is the entire mission of the Son that is in view" (Beasley-Murray, *John*, 51). "This draws attention to the sacrifice involved for God the Father in sending his Son to save the world" (Köstenberger, *John*, 129). "The gift has in view the whole of the Son's mission and therefore also the giving up of his life through crucifixion" (Lincoln, *John*, 154). "The notion that God 'gave' or 'gave up' his only Son points unmistakably to Jesus' death, confirming the interpretation of 'lifted up' (v. 14) as crucifixion" (Michaels, *John*, 202). See also Moloney, *Love*, 59.

Bridegroom's Baptism and the Abundant Gift of the Spirit for Life Eternal (3:22-36)

The transition from John's baptism with water to Jesus' baptism with water and the Spirit (1:33) is completed, as John indicates that Jesus is the "bridegroom" and John is the "friend of the bridegroom." After the notice that Jesus was spending time with his disciples and that he was baptizing (3:22), a dispute arose between the disciples of John and a "Jew" about "cleansing/purification" (3:25). This recalls the water jars for the "cleansing/purification" of the "Jews" at the wedding in Cana (2:6).[22] To John's disciples, who informed John that Jesus was baptizing, implicitly with the Spirit, and all were going to him (3:26), John replied, "A human being is not able to receive anything unless it is given to him from heaven" (3:27). This recalls John's testimony that he saw the Spirit descending like a dove "from heaven" and remaining upon Jesus (1:32), thus equipping him to baptize with water and the Spirit (1:33), so that one is able to enter into the kingdom of God by being "born" (baptized) from water and the Spirit (3:5).

John went on to declare, "The one who has the bride is the bridegroom; the friend of the bridegroom, who stands and listens for him, rejoices greatly on account of the voice of the bridegroom. This joy of mine then has been made complete" (3:29).[23] The "bride" refers to those who are being baptized into the community of believers by Jesus, the "bridegroom," and by his disciples (3:22), thus making explicit the implication that Jesus was the actual "bridegroom" at the wedding in Cana (2:1-11).[24] John, as the "friend of the bridegroom," rejoices greatly on account of the "voice/call of the bridegroom" (φωνὴν τοῦ νυμφίου). This reminds the audience that the headwaiter at the wedding in Cana "called the bridegroom [φωνεῖ τὸν νυμφίον]" (2:9), before joyfully declaring to him that "you have kept the good wine until now!" (2:10).[25] John's great rejoicing with a joy that has now been made complete by God (divine passive) thus provides a model for the

---

22. That these are the only occurrences in John of the term "cleansing/purification" (καθαρισμός) enhances this connection for the audience.

23. "He [John] is not the voice of the groom (v. 29). He is the voice of one crying in the wilderness (1.23) who witnesses to the coming one, whom he now characterizes with the messianic image of the bridegroom. . . . he 'rejoices greatly (χαρᾷ χαίρει) on account of that voice" (Brown, "John the Baptist," 162).

24. "The widespread biblical image of Israel as the bride or spouse of YHWH (Isa 54:4-8; 62:4-5; Jer 2:2; Ezek 16:8, 23:4; Hos 2:21; etc.) makes it appropriate, as earlier at Cana (2:1-11), to understand the image in an allegorical sense as well: Jesus is the Bridegroom; John is the Bridegroom's friend; Israel—or rather the renewed Israel being constituted by Jesus—is the Bride" (Byrne, *Life Abounding*, 74).

25. That the term "bridegroom" (νυμφίος) occurs in John only in 2:9 and 3:29 facilitates this connection for the audience.

audience's joyful celebratory worship of the divine life eternal symbolized by the abundance of good wine provided by Jesus as the divine "bridegroom."

To Jesus, who baptizes with the Holy Spirit (1:33), God gives the Spirit "without measure [μέτρου]" (3:34), that is, abundantly. This accords with Jesus, as the divine "bridegroom," providing the abundance (six jars each holding two to three "measures [μετρητάς]," 2:6) of good wine symbolic of divine life eternal (2:1-11). Jesus, as the divine Word, "gave" authority for those who believe in his name to become children of God, and thus share in divine life eternal (1:12). This is because God "gives" to Jesus without measure the Spirit, so that one may be born/baptized from water and the Spirit in order to enter into the kingdom of God (3:5), and so share in the divine life eternal enjoyed by the children of God. This is the eternal life available for anyone who believes in Jesus as the Son (3:36) whom the Father loves and to whom he has given everything (3:35), by worshiping him not only as the Son of God (1:49) but as the Son of Man lifted up and exalted in and through his sacrificial death (3:14-15), his own, unique act of worship as the sacrificial Lamb of God (1:29, 36).

The Samaritan Woman and Worship in the Spirit and Truth (4:1-42)

Jesus continues to act as the metaphorical "bridegroom" when he meets a Samaritan woman at the "fountain" or "well" (πηγή) of Jacob (4:6). In the biblical tradition future bridegrooms and their brides often met at a well before eventually being wed.[26] After Jesus asked the woman to give him a drink (4:7), she objected, pointing out the inappropriateness for him as a Jew to ask her as a Samaritan woman for a drink, since Jews do not have dealings with Samaritans (4:9; cf. 2 Kgs 17:24-41; Sir 50:25-26). Jesus replied, "If you knew the gift of God and who is saying to you, 'Give me a drink,' you would have asked him and he would have given you living water" (4:10). The "gift of God" refers to Jesus, as not just any Jew, but the unique Son whom God "gave" to the world (3:16). But it also refers to the Spirit that God "gives" without measure (3:34). The divine gift of "living water" thus symbolizes the Spirit of God.[27] And that Jesus would have "given" (ἔδωκεν)

---

26. "The meeting at a well between a man and a woman who will become his spouse is a typical motif in the ancestral narratives: Abraham's servant and Rebecca (Gen 24:10-33), Jacob and Rachel (Gen 29:1-14), Moses and Zipporah (Exod 2:15-22)" (Coloe, *God Dwells*, 97-98).

27. According to LXX Isa 44:3 God said to the people of Israel, "I will give water in thirst to those who go in a dry land; I will place my Spirit upon your offspring and my blessings upon your children."

her this resonates with the fact that he has "given" (ἔδωκεν) authority for those who believe in his name to become children of God (1:12).

The Samaritan woman then raised the question of the origin of this "living water" (4:11), and queried whether Jesus is greater than Jacob who gave the Samaritans the well (4:12). Jesus replied, "Everyone who drinks from this water will thirst again; but whoever drinks from the water that I myself will give him will never thirst for eternity, rather the water that I will give him will become in him a fountain of water springing up to life eternal" (4:13-14).[28] As the real "bridegroom" of the wedding at Cana, Jesus replaced the water for the ceremonial cleansing and purification of the Jews with an abundance of good wine for celebratory drinking and worshiping Jesus as the implicit giver of divine life eternal for all (2:1-11). And now Jesus, as indeed greater than Jacob and as the implicit "bridegroom" of the Samaritans, replaces the "fountain" (πηγή) of drinking water that Jacob gave (4:6) to sustain physical life (4:12) with the "fountain" (πηγή) of living water/Spirit for the divine life eternal that he himself will give for all to drink.[29]

Attracted by Jesus' invitation for her to ask him for the living water that quenches thirst and springs up to life eternal (4:10, 13-14), the Samaritan woman asked Jesus to give her this water so that she may not thirst nor need to come "here" (ἐνθάδε), to Jacob's well, to draw water (4:15). But Jesus told her to go and call her husband and come "here" (ἐνθάδε), back to him as the source of the living water she now seeks (4:16). Jesus acknowledged the truth of her reply that she has no husband (4:17), since she has had five husbands and the one she has now is not her husband (4:18). The marital history of this Samaritan woman thus embodies and represents the idolatrous history of the Samaritan people, as the five "husbands" allude to the false gods the Samaritans married/worshiped in the past, and the "husband" they have now is not their true God. This implies that Jesus, the divine "bridegroom" (2:9; 3:29), is their true husband/God.[30] The woman

---

28. The same verb used for the water/Spirit "springing up" (ἁλλομένου) to eternal life is used in LXX Judg 14:6, 19; 15:14; 1 Kgdms 10:10 to refer to the gift of the Spirit of God when it "springs up" (ἥλατο) powerfully upon charismatic figures. See also Coloe, *God Dwells*, 94.

29. The notice that Jesus himself was not baptizing at this point (4:2; cf. 3:22, 26; 4:1) prepares for a transition from Jesus using water for baptizing with the Spirit (1:33; 3:5) to his promise to give living water/the Spirit for drinking (4:10-14). The Spirit, as symbolized by water for drinking, however, will not be given until Jesus is glorified (7:37-39).

30. "[T]he language of 'husbands' alludes to Old Testament language of God as 'husband' to Israel and Israel's 'infidelity' (Isa. 54:5; Jer. 3:20; 31:32). In pointing out the woman's five husbands, John suggests that the Samaritans have not retained their true 'husband,' God. The discussion of worship that follows (John 4:20-24) supports

then recognized Jesus to be a prophet, appropriately as prophets traditionally possessed special knowledge and often called people from false to true worship (4:19).[31]

The Samaritan woman spoke as a representative of her people to Jesus as a representative of the Jewish people, when she pointed to the different geographical places of worship for each people (4:20). But Jesus pointed to a worship that transcends the worship at these places (4:21), a worship whose source is from the Jewish people (4:22). As Jesus declared, "But an hour is coming and now is, when the true worshipers will worship the Father in Spirit and truth, for indeed the Father seeks such as these worshiping him. God is Spirit, and those worshiping him must worship in Spirit and truth" (4:23-24). To worship in "Spirit and truth" means to worship in close association with Jesus. He is the one upon whom the "Spirit" descended and remains (1:32). God gives him the "Spirit" without measure (3:34). He baptizes with the "Spirit" (1:33), so that one may be reborn to divine life eternal by being baptized from water and the "Spirit" (3:5), symbolized by the "living water" Jesus offers (4:10).[32] And Jesus is full of a gift of "truth" (1:14), the gift of the "truth" that came to be through him (1:17).[33]

After Jesus identified himself to the woman as the Christ the Samaritans were expecting (4:25-26), she left her water jar and went into the city (4:28). That she left her "water jar" (ὑδρίαν) indicates that Jesus has attracted her away from the water of Jacob's well with his offer to give the living water that springs up to life eternal (4:10, 14). This accords with Jesus' transformation at the wedding in Cana of the water in the "water jars" (ὑδρίαι) for

---

the identification of an allusion. In their infidelity, the Samaritans have strayed from the true worship of God" (Hylen, *Imperfect Believers*, 49-50). "The true husband/lord of Samaria stands before her in the person of Jesus, the bridegroom. The five previous husbands plus her current one give a total of six, which symbolically indicates the inadequacy of Samaritan worship. . . . A symbolic reading of this part of the dialogue explains the shift from a discussion about the woman's marital status to a discussion about true worship" (Coloe, *God Dwells*, 99). See also Coloe, "Woman of Samaria," 191.

31. Byrne, *Life Abounding*, 84n91. See also Cho, *Jesus as Prophet*, 174-87.

32. "The prerequisite for this worship of God as Father seems to be adoption as a child of God, i.e., having a new relationship with God through the regeneration by the Spirit (1.12-13; 3.5)" (Bennema, *Power*, 189).

33. "Worship in Spirit and truth does not mean that all external forms of worship are rejected at the coming of Jesus. Rather, the emphasis here is on being in the person of Jesus in opposition to any geographical limitation of the worship of God" (Thettayil, *Spirit and Truth*, 164). "Since Jesus is the giver of Spirit and the embodiment of the truth, worship in Spirit and in truth is also worship centred in and mediated by Jesus" (Lincoln, *John*, 177-78). "Readers are expected to recognize themselves in these 'true worshipers,' and in so doing see themselves no longer as Jews or Gentiles, but as Christians" (Michaels, *John*, 255).

Jewish cleansings (2:6-7) into the abundant good wine for the celebratory worship of divine life eternal (2:9-10).[34] After the woman queried to her people whether Jesus could be the Christ (4:29), the Samaritan people came to Jesus (4:30). Jesus then indicated to his disciples, who have returned from the city (4:8, 27), that now that the Samaritans are coming to him, he, as the "reaper," is "gathering fruit for life eternal" (4:36), in accord with his offer to the Samaritan woman.

Many of the Samaritans believed in Jesus on account of the word of the woman who testified that Jesus knew everything she had done (4:39). Many more believed on account of the word of Jesus (4:40-41), the personified Word of God (1:1, 14), thus indicating that they have abandoned their false worship and collectively have become the "bride" for the true worship of Jesus, the divine "bridegroom." This is confirmed by their climactic declaration, as they publicly proclaim that they know Jesus to be a worthy object of worship for all in the audience: "This is truly the savior of the world!" (4:42).

The Samaritans thus affirmed that "salvation" is indeed from the "Jews" (4:22) in the person of Jesus as the representative "Jew" (4:9). But Jesus is to be worshiped not only as the Son of God and King of Israel (1:49) but as the savior of the entire "world" (4:42), indeed as the Lamb of God who takes away the sin of the "world" (1:29). In proclaiming that Jesus is a worthy object of worship as the "savior" of the "world," the Samaritans were confirming that God so loved the "world" (3:16) that he sent his Son into the "world" not to condemn the "world," but that the "world" might be "saved" through him (3:17). The Samaritans then have indicated that the worship of the Father in Spirit and truth is intimately linked to the person of Jesus (4:23-24), the bearer of the Spirit (1:32-33) and embodiment of the truth (1:14, 17), the new personified temple for true worship (2:19-21) by all peoples.[35]

---

34. That these are the only occurrences in John of the term "water jar" (ὑδρία) enhances this connection for the audience.

35. "The (formerly correct) Jewish worship in the temple at Jerusalem and the (wrong) Samaritan worship at Mount Gerizim have both alike been overtaken by worship in the new 'temple' that is the person of the Son (2:19-20)" (Byrne, *Life Abounding*, 86). "Jesus has supplanted Jacob in the gift he offers—the living waters of eschatological salvation—and as the founder of a new form of worship in Spirit and in truth" (Coloe, *God Dwells*, 113). "The universal salvation embodied in Jesus, embracing Jew, Samaritan and Gentile, corresponds to the universal scope of the worship mediated by him, no longer restricted to locations" (Lincoln, *John*, 181).

A Household for Worship by Believers in the Life-Giving Word of Jesus (4:43–54)

After spending two days with the Samaritans, which resulted in their declaration that he is a worthy object of worship (4:42), Jesus returned to Galilee (4:40, 43). Although the Samaritan woman recognized him as a "prophet" (4:19), who revealed to her the worship in Spirit and truth (4:23–24), Jesus himself testified to the proverb that a "prophet" does not have honor in his own fatherland (4:44). This recalls that the Jews in Jerusalem, the central city of "his own" fatherland, did not honor him as a prophet when he called them away from their false worship in the Jerusalem temple to the true worship in the new temple of his body (2:13–21). And it confirms that "to his own he came, yet his own people did not accept him" (1:11). The Galileans, however, welcomed him, since they had seen all the things he had done in Jerusalem at the Passover "feast" (4:45). This associates them with the many who believed in his name when they saw the signs he was doing in Jerusalem during the "feast" of the Passover (2:23), and opens them to a deeper faith that goes beyond a faith based only on seeing signs.[36]

Jesus then came again to Cana of Galilee, where he had transformed the water for Jewish cleansings into wine (4:46a), having provided an abundance of good wine for a celebratory worship of the divine life eternal he will provide (2:1–11). The audience can thus expect a development of this theme of worship for divine life eternal in the scene to follow, which begins when a royal official whose son was sick in Capernaum (4:46b) came to Jesus in Cana (4:47a). The royal official then performed an act of petitionary worship, as he, with implicit faith in the divine power of Jesus, "asked" him to come down and heal his son, who was about to die (4:47b). Jesus then addressed him as a representative of those whose faith is based on seeing signs, "Unless you see [ἴδητε; plural] signs and wonders, you will never believe [πιστεύσητε; plural]" (4:48), acknowledging the need for the seeing of signs to bring people to an initial level of faith.

The royal official then intensified his prayerful request to Jesus with the urgent plea, "Lord, come down before my little child dies" (4:49).[37]

---

36. "But isn't Jesus of Galilean origin—as the gospel makes clear (cf. 1:45; 2:1; 7:41, 52; 19:19)? If he is 'welcomed' by the Galileans (v. 45), how can the proverb apply? An explanation would seem to be that, while Jesus' family origins may indeed be Galilean, the narrative of the gospel has already located much of his ministry in Judea and Jerusalem, the center of his people's life" (Byrne, *Life Abounding*, 91). See also Cho, *Jesus as Prophet*, 144–53.

37. "The writer signals the urgency with a shift from indirect to direct discourse, with the royal official now referring to his 'son' (v. 47) affectionately as 'my little child,' and addressing Jesus as 'Lord' (κύριε). . . . 'Lord, come down' . . . has the sound of a

Rather than coming down, however, Jesus directed the royal official to go and promised, "Your son will live" (4:50a). The royal official "believed the word which Jesus said" to him and went (4:50b). This associates him with Jesus' disciples who "believed the word which Jesus said" (2:22), when he promised to raise up his destroyed body to become a new temple for true worship (2:19-21). Like the disciples, the royal official has progressed from a faith based on seeing signs to a faith based on the life-giving word of Jesus, the personified divine Word (1:1, 14).[38] This word of Jesus' promise at Cana is open to a double meaning—the son will live now physically and he will live eternally. This accords with the promise implied in what Jesus did at Cana previously in making the water wine, a sign pointing to his ability to provide divine life eternal (2:1-11). And it resonates with his promise to give the "living water" that springs up to life eternal (4:10, 14).[39]

After the slaves of the royal official informed him that his boy "is living" (4:51), the father verified that his son became better (4:52) at the same time that Jesus promised, "Your son will live" (4:53a). "He himself believed as well as his whole household" (4:53b). The notice that "this is the second sign Jesus did" (4:54) in Cana (4:46) links this familial household of believers in Capernaum (4:46) to Jesus' familial household (mother, brothers, disciples) that went down to Capernaum (2:12), after Jesus' first sign in Cana when he manifested his glory and his disciples believed in him (2:11).[40] This royal official's "household" (οἰκία) of believers in the life-giving word of Jesus provides a further model for the communal, "household" worship by the audience of believers. It resonates with Jesus' zeal for his Father's "house/household" (οἴκου) of worship (2:17), which led to the promise of his dead body being raised to divine life eternal to serve as the new temple/household (2:19-22) for true worshipers, believers in the life-giving word of Jesus, those who worship in Spirit and truth (4:23-24).[41]

---

genuine prayer" (Michaels, *John*, 279).

38. "The official exercises faith in that word without first having had to see the sign" (Lincoln, *John*, 188).

39. "Jesus' power to save physical life becomes here a metaphor for his gift of eternal life" (Michaels, *John*, 279). See also Byrne, *Life Abounding*, 93.

40. "If revelation of Jesus' glory was the message of the first sign (2:11), the gift of life is the message of its sequel, and as the Gospel story unfolds the reader will learn that revelation and eternal life amount to much the same thing (see 17:3)" (Michaels, *John*, 285).

41. On the significance of a household of believers in "the reliability of Jesus' word as a word of life," see Coloe, *Household of God*, 89.

Summary on 2:1—4:54

At the wedding in Cana (2:1–11) the headwaiter said to the bridegroom/Jesus, "Every human being serves the good wine first, and when they are drunk the inferior. But you have kept the good wine until now!" (2:10). At this Jewish wedding Jesus transformed the Jewish water of cleansing for worship into an abundance of wine for the celebratory worship of divine life eternal (2:6–9). But he also transformed a practice not just of Jews but of "every human being," as he provided not just abundant but good wine appropriate for the celebratory worship of divine life eternal available to everyone. This recalls that the life that had come to be in Jesus was the true light that enlightens "every human being" (1:9). With an emphatic "you," Nathanael worshiped Jesus by confessing, "*You* are the Son of God. *You* are the King of Israel!" (1:49). And with an emphatic "you," the headwaiter similarly directs the audience to the worship of Jesus by declaring that "*you*," as the new bridegroom, "have kept and are still providing" the good wine of divine life eternal even until now, so that it is available for all.

That "Jesus did *this* as the beginning of the signs" (2:11a) begins to fulfill for the audience his promise to the disciple Nathanael that "greater than *these things* you will see" (1:50). Whereas John came baptizing with water so that Jesus might be "manifested" to Israel (1:31), in Cana of Galilee Jesus "manifested" for every human being in the audience his "glory" (2:11b), extending to all people the manifestation of the "glory" of God that came down upon Mount Sinai before the sons of Israel at the giving of the law (LXX Exod 24:16–17). This reaffirms the basis for the communal act of doxological worship that "we observed his glory, glory as of the unique one from the Father, full of a gift of truth" (1:14). Whereas earlier Nathanael "believed" (1:50), the group of his disciples now "believed in him" (2:11c), indicating that they have been given the authority to become children of God who share in divine life eternal, as they are among those who "believe in his name" (1:12).

After this first sign Jesus, his mother, brothers, and disciples went down to Capernaum (2:12a), indicating that his disciples, who believed in him (2:11), have become part of the familial household of Jesus, a household oriented toward worship. That they "remained" there "a few days" (2:12b) recalls that the first disciples saw where Jesus "remains" and they "remained that day" with Jesus (1:39), the one upon whom the Spirit of God "remains," so that he baptizes with the Holy Spirit (1:32–33). This gathering of a new familial household of Jesus thus forms an initial community for worship, a model for the audience, as they remained with Jesus, the divine Word who "dwelt among us" (1:14) as the personified place for the true worship of God.

The disciples believed the Scripture that predicted the sacrificial death of Jesus, as the Lamb of God (1:29, 36), as well as the word which Jesus had spoken, predicting his resurrection from the dead (2:22). This provides a model for the audience to likewise "remember," not merely as a one-time remembrance but with the implication of an ongoing commemoration in their worship, the death and resurrection of Jesus as the new temple for the presence and worship of God (2:13-21). Such worship is based on their faith in both Scripture and the "word" of Jesus, the divine "Word" become flesh (1:1, 14), whose word, like Scripture, is the very word of God as the focus of the true worship of God. The disciples, who "believed" when they saw the beginning of his signs (2:11), exemplify the progression to a more adequate faith as they "believed" the Scripture and the word of Jesus (2:22). Thus the faith of all human beings needs to be based not merely on seeing the preliminary signs Jesus did (2:23) but on the ultimate sign of the death and resurrection of Jesus as the new temple for the true worship of God.

To be "born" again and from above of water and Spirit to see and enter the kingdom of God (3:5) develops what it means for those who believe in the name of Jesus to be "born" of God (1:13) in order to become children of God (1:12). To see and enter the kingdom of God is to enter into the community of believers who have become children of God with a share in divine life eternal. Those who have been baptized with water only (1:26, 31, 33) must be baptized again and from above with water and Spirit. And this means being baptized with the baptism of Jesus who baptizes with the Holy Spirit, which descended from heaven above (1:32) and remains upon him (1:33). This baptism again and from above by water and Spirit establishes the basis for the audience to practice a ritual worship of sacramental baptism as the way of entering into the community of believers.

The disciples provided a model for the audience's worship of commemorating the death and resurrection of Jesus as those who believed the Scripture that predicted his death and the word of Jesus that predicted his resurrection (2:22). This is developed in Jesus' further address to Nicodemus: "And just as Moses lifted up the serpent in the desert [Num 21:9], so it is necessary that the Son of Man be lifted up/exalted, so that everyone who believes in him might have life eternal" (3:14-15). The Son of Man's being "lifted up" in crucifixion is simultaneously his being "exalted" or "glorified." As the Son of Man, Jesus is thus not only the personified place for the presence and worship of God (1:51) but the object of worship in and through the sacrificial death by which he is exalted. It is by his sacrificial death, then, that Jesus provides the divine life eternal symbolized by the abundant good wine, so that for his disciples who saw the manifestation of this glory and believed in him (2:11), and everyone else who believes in him, he has become an object of worship.

The narrator declared, "For God so loved the world, that he gave the Son, the unique one, so that everyone who believes in him may not perish but may have life eternal" (3:16). God so loved the world that he "gave," with the connotation of giving up to sacrificial death, "the Son" who is both the Son of God (1:49) and the Son of Man (1:51; 3:13-14), and, as "the unique one," is also God (1:1, 18). That God so loved the "world" in this way resonates with Jesus being the sacrificial Lamb of God who takes away the sin of the whole "world" (1:29). God "gave" the Son to the world, as the Word who became flesh by God (1:14), but also in his sacrificial death, so that everyone who believes in him may have life eternal. This provides the basis for the assertion that Jesus "gave" authority for those who believe in his name to become children of God (1:12) with a share in life eternal. Not only Nicodemus, who came to Jesus at night (3:2), but everyone is invited to come to Jesus as the light (3:19-21) in whom is life (1:3-4), so that everyone who believes in, and thus worships, him may have divine life eternal.

To Jesus, who baptizes with the Holy Spirit (1:33), God gives the Spirit "without measure" (3:34), that is, abundantly. This accords with Jesus, as the divine "bridegroom," providing the abundance (six jars each holding two to three "measures," 2:6) of good wine symbolic of divine life eternal (2:1-11). Jesus, as the divine Word, "gave" authority for those who believe in his name to become children of God, and thus share in divine life eternal (1:12). This is because God "gives" to Jesus without measure the Spirit, so that one may be born/baptized from water and the Spirit in order to enter into the kingdom of God (3:5), and so share in the divine life eternal enjoyed by the children of God. This is the eternal life available for anyone who believes in Jesus as the Son (3:36) whom the Father loves and to whom he has given everything (3:35), by worshiping him not only as the Son of God (1:49) but as the Son of Man lifted up and exalted in and through his sacrificial death, his own, unique act of worship as the sacrificial Lamb of God (1:29, 36).

Attracted by Jesus' invitation for her to ask him for the living water that quenches thirst and springs up to life eternal (4:10, 13-14), the Samaritan woman asked Jesus to give her this water so that she may not thirst nor need to come "here," to Jacob's well, to draw water (4:15). But Jesus told her to go and call her husband and come "here," back to him as the source of the living water she now seeks (4:16). Jesus acknowledged the truth of her reply that she has no husband (4:17), since she has had five husbands and the one she has now is not her husband (4:18). The marital history of this Samaritan woman thus embodies and represents the idolatrous history of the Samaritan people, as the five "husbands" allude to the false gods the Samaritans married/worshiped in the past, and the "husband" they have now is not their true God. This implies that Jesus, the divine "bridegroom" (2:9; 3:29), is their true husband/God. The woman then recognized Jesus to be a prophet, appropriately as prophets traditionally possessed special knowledge and often called people from false to true worship (4:19).

The Samaritan woman spoke as a representative of her people to Jesus as a representative of the Jewish people, when she pointed to the different geographical places of worship for each people (4:20). But Jesus pointed to a worship that transcends the worship at these places (4:21), a worship whose source is from the Jewish people (4:22). As Jesus declared, "But an hour is coming and now is, when the true worshipers will worship the Father in Spirit and truth, for indeed the Father seeks such as these worshiping him. God is Spirit, and those worshiping him must worship in Spirit and truth" (4:23-24). To worship in "Spirit and truth" means to worship in close association with Jesus. He is the one upon whom the "Spirit" descended and remains (1:32). God gives him the "Spirit" without measure (3:34). He baptizes with the "Spirit" (1:33), so that one may be reborn to divine life eternal by being baptized from water and the "Spirit" (3:5), symbolized by the "living water" Jesus offers (4:10). And Jesus is full of a gift of "truth" (1:14), the gift of the "truth" that came to be through him (1:17).

Jesus is to be worshiped not only as the Son of God and King of Israel (1:49) but as the savior of the entire world (4:42), indeed as the Lamb of God who takes away the sin of the world (1:29). In declaring that Jesus is a worthy object of worship as the "savior" of the "world," the Samaritans confirmed that God so loved the "world" (3:16) that he sent his Son into the "world" not to condemn the "world," but that the "world" might be "saved" through him (3:17). The Samaritans then have indicated that worship of the Father in Spirit and truth is intimately linked to the person of Jesus (4:23-24), the bearer of the Spirit (1:32-33) and embodiment of the truth (1:14, 17), the new temple for true worship (2:19-21) by all peoples.

The royal official intensified his prayerful request to Jesus, an act of petitionary worship, with the urgent plea, "Lord, come down before my little child dies" (4:49). Rather than coming down, however, Jesus directed the royal official to go and promised, "Your son will live" (4:50a). The royal official "believed the word which Jesus said" to him and went (4:50b). This associates him with Jesus' disciples who "believed the word which Jesus said" (2:22), when he promised to raise up his destroyed body to become a new temple for true worship (2:19-21). Like the disciples, the royal official has progressed from a faith based on seeing signs to a faith based on the life-giving word of Jesus, the personified divine Word (1:1, 14). This word of Jesus' promise at Cana is open to a double meaning—the son will live now physically and he will live eternally. This accords with the promise implied in what Jesus did at Cana previously in making the water wine, a sign pointing to his ability to provide divine life eternal (2:1–11). And it resonates with his promise to give the "living water" that springs up to life eternal (4:10, 14).

After the slaves of the royal official informed him that his boy "is living" (4:51), the father verified that his son became better (4:52) at the same time that Jesus promised, "Your son will live" (4:53a). "He himself believed as well as his whole household" (4:53b). The notice that "this is the second sign Jesus did" (4:54) in Cana (4:46) links this familial household of believers in Capernaum (4:46) to Jesus' familial household (mother, brothers, disciples) that went down to Capernaum (2:12), after Jesus' first sign in Cana when he manifested his glory and his disciples believed in him (2:11). This royal official's "household" of believers in the life-giving word of Jesus provides a further model for the communal, "household" worship by the audience of believers. It resonates with Jesus' zeal for his Father's "house/household" of worship (2:17), which led to his dead body being raised to divine life eternal to serve as the new temple/household (2:19–22) for true worshipers, believers in the life-giving word of Jesus, who worship in Spirit and truth (4:23–24).

5

Jesus Transcends Jewish Festival Worship (5:1—10:42)

The Life-Giving Jesus Heals a Man at a Feast of the Jews on the Sabbath (5:1–47)

"After these things there was a feast of the Jews and Jesus went up to Jerusalem" (5:1). This recalls that "the Passover of the Jews was near" when previously "Jesus went up to Jerusalem" (2:13).[1] It thus prepares the audience for a development of the theme of Jesus as the new temple for the true worship of God through his life-giving death and resurrection (2:14–23). Jesus had previously transcended the water for Jewish cleansing meant to enable worship by providing an abundance of good wine for the celebratory worship of divine life eternal (2:1–11). And now he transcends the water that failed to heal a man sick for thirty-eight years (5:2–9), so that he could worship in the Jerusalem temple, by healing him to worship in Jesus as the new temple.[2] Jesus' healing of the sick child with his life-giving word pointed to his ability to provide divine life eternal (4:46–53). His command for the sick man to "rise" (5:8) does the same, as it resonates with his promise that "I will raise up" (2:19) his own dead body to be the new temple (2:21) for true worship by believers who share in divine life eternal (1:12–13; 3:15–16, 36; 4:14, 36).

The healing of the sick man in Jerusalem took place not only in the context of a feast of the Jews (5:1) but on the Sabbath (5:9). Jesus thus transcended Sabbath worship, which prohibited any type of work (Exod 20:8–11), with his divinely authoritative command for the healed man to

---

1. On the Jewish feasts in John, see Yee, *Jewish Feasts*.
2. "According to Jewish law, he is probably prohibited to worship in the temple" (Bennema, *Encountering Jesus*, 101).

49

do the work of taking up his mat and walking (5:8-13). Jesus previously "found" in the Jerusalem "temple" those selling the animals for sacrificial worship (2:14), before he drove them out of the "temple" (2:15) and revealed himself as the new temple for true worship (2:16-21). Similarly, he "found" the healed man in the Jerusalem "temple" and warned him to sin no longer so that nothing worse may happen to him (5:14), implicitly by participating in the worship of the Jerusalem temple rather than believing in Jesus as the new temple. He would thereby risk the loss of the divine life eternal that Jesus gives to believers, which would be worse than his sickness for thirty-eight years.[3]

The man, who initially could not identify Jesus to the Jews as the one who healed him (5:10-13), "went away," implicitly from worship in the Jerusalem temple, and then "announced" to the Jews that Jesus was the one who had healed him (5:15). As the Samaritan woman "went away" (4:28) to lead her people to believe in Jesus as an object of worship (4:42), the one who "will announce" to them everything (4:25), including the place for true worship (4:20-24), so the man offers the Jews the opportunity to believe in Jesus. Instead they began persecuting Jesus for doing these things on the Sabbath (5:16).[4] Jesus then told them that his Father and he are working "until now [ἕως ἄρτι]" (5:17), recalling that Jesus has kept and is still providing the good wine symbolic of divine life eternal "until now [ἕως ἄρτι]" (2:10).[5] "For this reason then the Jews were seeking all the more to kill him, because not only was he breaking the Sabbath, but he was also calling God his own Father, making himself equal to God" (5:18). Ironically, although Jesus did not make himself equal to God, from the beginning, as the Word and the unique one, he was God (1:1, 18).

Jesus' promise to Nathanael, "Greater things than these you will see" (1:50), invited him to a more profound faith in Jesus as the divine Son of Man (1:51) who offers divine life eternal to those who believe in him (3:13-15). Jesus' declaration to the Jews that the Father will show him as the

3. "Jesus admonishes the man to discontinue in sin/unbelief and adopt an attitude of belief.... The 'something worse' than thirty-eight years of illness would be not knowing who Jesus really is, not receiving the divine life that he gives" (Bennema, *Encountering Jesus*, 105).

4. "The man 'announces' to the authorities that Jesus is the One who had healed him. Elsewhere in the gospel the Greek verb *anangellein* [to announce] has a positive sense (cf. 4:25; 16:13-15). The man no longer refers to Jesus as one who had caused him to violate the Sabbath (cf. v. 11) but solely as the person who had brought him healing. Like the Samaritan woman (4:28-29), he may be beginning to 'live out' his deeper conversion by identifying Jesus to others as one who brings healing and enhancement of life" (Byrne, *Life Abounding*, 97-98).

5. On the issue of God working on the Sabbath, see Burer, *Divine Sabbath Work*.

Son "greater works than these, so that you may be amazed" (5:20) similarly invited them to believe that he is the Son, not who makes himself equal to God (5:18), but who shares with the Father the work of giving life even on the Sabbath. As the Father "raises" the dead and gives life, so also the Son gives life to whomever he wishes (5:21). This confirms that Jesus' command for the sick man to "rise" (5:8) indicated his divine power not only to heal him, but to give him divine life eternal.

Jesus then told the Jews that the Father has given all judgment to the Son (5:22), so that all may "honor" the Son just as they "honor" the Father. The one not "honoring" the Son does not "honor" the Father who sent him (5:23). Honoring connotes worship, as indicated by how "honor" parallels "worship" in LXX Isa 29:13: "And the Lord said, 'This people comes near to me; with their lips they *honor* me, but their heart is far away from me; in vain they *worship* me.'" Jesus' exercise of the divine power to heal and give life on the Sabbath indicates that he, as the Son, is worthy to be "honored" and thus worshiped together with God the Father who sent him. To "honor" and thus worship both the Father and the Son presupposes hearing Jesus' word and believing the one who sent him. Whoever performs this honor and worship based on hearing the word of the Son and believing the Father who sent him passes from death into divine life eternal (5:24).[6]

Jesus pointed out to the Jews that he does not receive "glory from human beings" (5:41), recalling that his "glory" as the unique one is "from the Father," which glory inspires a communal act of doxological worship, the confession that "we observed his glory" (1:14). Jesus knows that the Jews do not have the love for God within them (5:42), a necessary basis for the true worship of God, because they would receive one who comes in his own name, but they do not receive Jesus who came in the name of his Father (5:43). He questions how the Jews can "believe" if they receive "glory from one another," but do not seek "the glory that comes from the only God" (5:44). "Seeking" the glory of Jesus, full of a gift of truth (1:14), would make them true worshipers in Spirit and truth, such as the Father "seeks" (4:23). Seeking the glory that comes from the only God could lead them and the audience to the faith necessary for true worship, as indicated when Jesus manifested his "glory" in providing the abundant good wine for

---

6. "'The Jews' who comprise his audience (vv. 16, 18) obviously think they are honoring God by guarding God's uniqueness and trying to kill Jesus for 'making himself equal to God' (v. 18). Yet they are not honoring 'the Father,' for 'the Father' implies a Son, and if they do not recognize 'the Son' they cannot recognize or worship God as 'Father'" (Michaels, *John*, 314). "The honour which belongs to the Father and the Son includes the faith recognition of the believing community and its worship" (Lee, *Hallowed*, 72).

the celebratory worship of divine life eternal, so that his disciples "believed" in him (2:11).[7]

If the Jews believed Moses, they would believe Jesus, for Moses wrote about Jesus (5:46). But if they do not believe the written words of Moses, how will they believe in Jesus' spoken "words [ῥήμασιν]" (5:47), which are the "words" (ῥήματα) of the God who sent him (3:34)? Believing Moses who "wrote" about Jesus could lead them and the audience to the faith necessary for true worship, as indicated when Nathanael, after being told that Jesus was the one Moses "wrote" about (1:45), expressed his faith (1:50) in an act of true worship, confessing Jesus as the Son of God and the King of Israel (1:49). And so, rather than breaking the Sabbath (5:18) with his life-giving words to the sick man (5:8–9), Jesus has transcended the Sabbath worship by revealing himself as the divine Son worthy of worship together with God the Father (5:23), as those who give to believers divine life eternal (5:24).

The New Passover Worship of Jesus as the Bread of Divine Life Eternal (6:1–71)

All of the events of John 6 are placed in a Passover context with the notice that "the Passover, the feast of the Jews was near" (6:4). This recalls and resonates with the similar notice that "the Passover of the Jews was near," when Jesus went up to Jerusalem (2:13). The scriptural prediction of his sacrificial death in terms of his zeal for the true worship of God that will replace worship in the Jerusalem temple (2:14–16) and that will "consume," "eat up," or "devour" him (2:17) accorded with his identity as the sacrificial Passover Lamb of God (1:29, 36). He pointed to his sacrificial death and subsequent resurrection (2:19) as the "sign" that would indicate that he is the new personified temple for true worship (2:18). Many believed in him when they saw the "signs" he was doing "on the feast of the Passover" (2:23). The Passover context plus the fact that a large crowd was following Jesus because they saw the "signs" he was performing on the sick (6:2) prepare the audience for further signs that will develop the theme of believing in Jesus as the sacrificial Passover Lamb of God central to the true worship of God.[8]

---

7. "Jesus' reference to glory 'from the Only God' recalls the Gospel writer's early mention of 'his glory—glory as of a father's One and Only' (1:14), in both instances implying that Jesus' 'glory' as the Son comes from 'the Only God' or from 'the Father,' and from no one else" (Michaels, *John*, 335).

8. "The Passover is a particularly appropriate setting for the exposition of the exodus events that will follow in Jesus' discourse and for the eucharistic motifs that emerge at its end, since the eucharist was instituted at a meal which, if not itself a Passover meal, was associated from the earliest times with the Passover" (Lincoln, *John*, 211).

Within the context of the Passover feast Jesus, after performing an act of worship in "giving thanks" to God (6:11), fed a crowd of about five thousand (6:10) with an overabundance of bread and fish (6:5-13). This was reminiscent of the miraculous feeding through Moses of the Israelites during their wandering in the wilderness following their exodus from Egypt and preceding their entrance into the promised land (Exod 16:4-36), events commemorated by the Passover feast.[9] When they saw the "sign" Jesus did, they declared, "This is truly the Prophet, the one coming into the world!" (6:14). But the true identity of Jesus surpasses that of the Prophet like Moses (Deut 18:15, 18). He is the true light, "coming into the world" (1:9; 3:19), to be worshiped as the "savior of the world" (4:42), the Passover Lamb of God who takes away the sin of the "world" (1:29), so that everyone in the "world" who believes in him might have divine life eternal (3:16). Ironically, they attempt to make Jesus an earthly "king" (6:15), but he has already been worshiped as the divine "King" of Israel, the Son of God (1:49).

After Jesus withdrew again to the mountain alone (6:15), his disciples went down to the sea (6:16) to cross it by boat to Capernaum (6:17). Jesus then miraculously saved them from a stormy, deadly sea, making it crossable by walking upon it, thus trampling it down and subduing it (6:18-21).[10] This was reminiscent of God saving the Israelites by miraculously making the Red Sea crossable for them in their exodus from Egypt (Exod 14:13-31), another one of the events commemorated by the Passover feast. By walking on the chaotic, deadly sea, Jesus revealed to his disciples his unique divine power to save them from the power of death, a sign indicating his power to give divine life eternal (3:15-16, 36; 4:14, 36; 5:24).

The crowd did not know how Jesus crossed the sea, since the disciples took the only boat available (6:22). But other boats came from Tiberius near the place where they had eaten the bread after the Lord "gave thanks" (6:23), reaffirming that the miraculous meal resulted after Jesus "gave thanks" to God as an act of worship (6:11). After they crossed the sea in the boats and found Jesus in Capernaum (6:24-25), he accused them of seeking him not because they "saw," in the sense of understood, "signs," but because they ate their fill of the loaves (6:26).[11] He then challenged them to understand the

---

9. "Passover not only marks the exit from Egypt, but also marks the entry into the land of promise. As such, it provides a ritual frame for the larger story of redemption which includes both exit out of slavery and entry into the freedom of the land" (Gorman, "Passover," 1014).

10. Heil, *Walking on the Sea*, 75-82, 144-70.

11. "Unlike his first disciples (2:11), they did not see his glory revealed in the signs. Unlike those at the first Passover (2:23), they did not 'believe,' or even pretend to believe, because of his signs" (Michaels, *John*, 363).

sign of the miraculous meal, when he told them not to work for the food that "perishes," in contrast to the food of the miraculous meal, which could "perish" (6:12), but for the food that remains to life eternal, which the Son of Man will give them (6:27). This recalls and resonates with the declaration that Jesus, as the Son of Man, must be "lifted up" (3:14) in crucifixion for his sacrificial death as the Passover Lamb of God (1:29, 36), so that everyone who believes in him may have divine life eternal (3:15).

The crowd then asked for a "sign" from Jesus (6:30; cf. 2:18), pointing out that their ancestors ate the manna in the desert, as it is written, "Bread from heaven he gave them to eat" (6:31; see Exod 16:4, 15; Neh 9:15; LXX Ps 77:24), an event commemorated by the Passover feast. Jesus told them that it was not Moses who gave them the bread from heaven, but his Father is giving them the true bread from heaven (6:32), not the "food" that perishes (cf. 6:12), but the "food" that remains to life eternal (6:27). This recalls that Jesus has metaphorical "food" to eat of which his disciples do not know (4:32). His "food" is to do the will of the one who sent him and to complete his work (4:34). Doing the will of God and completing the work of God by his sacrificial death as the Passover Lamb of God (1:29, 36) enables Jesus, as the Son of Man, to give the "food" that remains to life eternal, the true bread from heaven that the Father gives.

After Jesus revealed that he himself is this bread of life eternal, he declared that whoever comes to him will never hunger and whoever believes in him will never thirst (6:35). This recalls and resonates with his declaration to the Samaritan woman that whoever drinks the living water, symbolic of the Spirit, that he will give will never thirst, but the water he will give him will become in him a fountain of water springing up to divine life eternal (4:14). The necessity to believe in Jesus in order to never hunger or thirst (6:36, 40) prepares for a transition to the necessity to eat the food Jesus gives in the sacramental ritual of eucharistic worship in order to never hunger or thirst again, but to have divine life eternal.[12]

That the Jews "murmured" about Jesus because he identified himself as the bread that came down from heaven (6:41, 43) was reminiscent of the "murmuring" by the Israelites during the Exodus event (LXX Exod 17:3; Num 11:1; 14:27, 29; 17:6, 20) commemorated by the Passover feast.[13] Je-

---

12. "The necessity of eating and drinking in a eucharistic sense appears toward the end of a long discourse where faith has been stressed as the required human response, with the motif of 'eating' first introduced (in v. 48) as a metaphor for faith and only subsequently (v. 53) passing over to a clearly literal understanding" (Byrne, *Life Abounding*, 123).

13. "'Grumbling' at God and his messengers was characteristic of the Jews in their wilderness wanderings" (Beasley-Murray, *John*, 93).

sus pointed out that although the ancestors of the Jews ate manna in the desert during the Exodus event, they died (6:49; cf. 6:31). But he is the bread coming down from heaven, so that anyone may eat from it and not die (6:50). Jesus then revealed that the bread that he himself will give is his "flesh" for the life of the "world" (6:51). As the divine Word, Jesus not only became "flesh" (1:14), but, as the Passover Lamb of God who takes away the sin of the "world" (1:29), he will give his "flesh" in an act of sacrificial worship for the divine life eternal of the "world."[14] His sacrificial death as the new Passover Lamb of God enables Jesus to give his flesh in the form of the bread to be eaten in the sacramental meal of eucharistic worship.[15]

Jesus then declared that you must eat the flesh of the Son of Man and drink his blood to have divine life eternal within you (6:53). Just as the overabundance of bread Jesus provided (6:1-13) was a sign pointing to his ability to give his flesh in the bread of the eucharistic meal, so the overabundance of good wine he provided (2:1-10) was a sign pointing to his ability to give his blood in the wine of the eucharistic meal. Whoever not only "eats" the eucharistic bread that is the flesh of Jesus (6:51), but continually "feeds on" his flesh and continually "drinks" his blood in eucharistic worship has divine life eternal (6:54).[16] Whereas the ancestors of the Jews ate but died during the Exodus event commemorated by the Passover feast, Jesus is the bread that came down from heaven, so that whoever feeds on this bread will live forever (6:58). Thus, the bread/flesh and blood/wine Jesus provides in the meal of eucharistic worship for divine life eternal through his sacrificial death as the Passover Lamb transcends the miraculous but non life-giving food of the Exodus event commemorated in the meal of the Passover feast of the Jews.[17]

14. "'My flesh' comes to mean virtually 'my death,' especially with 'flesh' so closely linked to the verb 'I will give' and the preposition 'for'" (Michaels, *John*, 392).

15. "The 'bread' is defined as 'flesh' rather than the 'body,' almost certainly by reason of the Evangelist's insistence that the Word became *flesh* (1:14). But the conjunction of the terms 'give,' 'flesh,' and 'on behalf of' in v 51c strongly suggests a sacrificial death for the sake of others . . . he who is the Living Bread is to die as the Lamb of God for the sin of the world (1:29)" (Beasley-Murray, *John*, 93–94; emphasis original). "Many elements in v. 51c reflect eucharistic traditions found elsewhere in the NT and in the early Church" (Moloney, *John*, 220).

16. John uses the verb τρώγω, "feed on," exclusively as a present participle connoting an ongoing or continual eating (6:54, 56, 57, 58; 13:18). For other tenses the verb ἐσθίω, "eat," is employed. See also Gignac, "Verbal Variety," 195; Byrne, *Life Abounding*, 123n38.

17. "[T]he mention of 'blood' confirms the notion that by his 'flesh' (v. 51) Jesus meant his death, and a violent death at that. . . . the 'eating' of flesh presupposes killing, and 'drinking' blood presupposes the shedding of blood. The notion of eating and drinking the flesh and blood of Jesus inevitably calls to mind the Christian Eucharist,

To unbelieving disciples (6:64) Jesus declared that the "Spirit" is the one who "gives life" (6:63). This complements his previous statement that just as the Father raises the dead and "gives life," so also the Son "gives life" to whomever he wishes (5:21). Jesus then added, with an emphatic first person pronoun, that the "words [ῥήματα] that I myself [ἐγώ] have spoken" are "Spirit" and are "life" (6:63). This recalls that Jesus speaks the "words" (ῥήματα) of God, the God who gives the "Spirit" without measure (3:34). Believing in the words Jesus has spoken in this bread of life discourse, the words that are "Spirit" and are "life," enables one to eat the flesh of the Son of Man and drink his blood in eucharistic worship to have "life" within him (6:53). Whoever feeds on his flesh and drinks his blood has "life" eternal (6:54). Believing in Jesus' words that are "Spirit" and "life," and eating his flesh and drinking his blood that are "true" food and "true" drink (6:55), enables one to be a "true" worshiper who worships in "Spirit" and truth (4:23–24), the truth that came to be in Jesus (1:17), in whom had come to be divine "life" eternal (1:3–4).

When Jesus asked the twelve remaining disciples if they wanted to go away like those who do not believe (6:67), Simon Peter, as spokesman for the believing disciples, answered him, "Lord, to whom shall we go? You have the words [ῥήματα] of life eternal" (6:68). And then, with emphatic personal pronouns, he pronounced a confession of faith, a climactic act of worship: "And we ourselves [ἡμεῖς] have come to believe and have come to know that you [σύ] are the Holy One of God!" (6:69).[18] Peter's answer was in direct correspondence to Jesus' pronouncement that "the words [ῥήματα] that I myself have spoken are Spirit and are life" (6:63). Peter's confession that "you [σύ] are the Holy One of God" appropriately responded to Jesus' revelation that "I myself [ἐγώ] am" the one they saw performing the uniquely divine and life-giving action of walking on the sea (6:20). To Nathanael's climatic confession of worship, "You [σύ] are the Son of God; you [σύ] are the King of Israel!" (1:49), Peter's confession adds yet another divine designation by which the audience may worship Jesus.

Peter's confession of Jesus as "the Holy One of God" (6:69) recalls that Jesus, as the one upon whom the Spirit descended and remains, baptizes with the "Holy" Spirit (1:33) of God. But as the Holy One "of God," Jesus is also the Son (6:40) sent by the Father to be the sacrificial Passover Lamb "of

---

and the various forms of the words of institution found in the synoptic Gospels and Paul" (Michaels, *John*, 395).

18. "Simon Peter articulates for them their faith in Jesus, and this is where we finally encounter the emphatic pronouns that we expect: 'and *we* believe and *we* know that *you* are the Holy One of God' (v. 69, italics added)" (Michaels, *John*, 415).

God" (1:29, 36).[19] The ominous notice that Jesus knew that Judas was going to betray him, literally, "give him over" (παραδιδόναι) to a sacrificial death (6:71; cf. 6:64) reminds the audience of this. This accords with the declaration that God so loved the world that he "gave" (ἔδωκεν) the Son, the unique one (3:16), with the connotation that he gave him over to a sacrificial death as the Passover Lamb of God. The Passover feast of the Jews, which included the eating of a sacrificial Passover lamb, commemorated an eating of bread/manna that did not give life eternal. But the new Passover worship of Jesus as "the Holy One of God," the Lamb of God, whose sacrificial flesh/bread and blood/wine are to be eaten and drunk by believers in their eucharistic worship, gives them divine life eternal.

The Jewish Feast of Tabernacles and the True Worship of Jesus (7:1—10:21)

The Living Water Jesus Gives Transcends the Water Libation of Tabernacles (7:1-52)

The Passover feast of the Jews was "near," when Jesus went up to Jerusalem (2:13) and revealed that his sacrificial death as the Passover Lamb of God and subsequent resurrection would transcend worship in the Jerusalem temple by establishing him as a new temple for the true worship of God (2:14-22). Similarly, the Passover, the feast of the Jews, was "near" (6:4), when Jesus transcended the Jewish Passover by indicating a new Passover worship that includes the sacramental eating and drinking of his flesh and blood as the sacrificial Passover Lamb of God in the eucharistic meal that gives believers divine life eternal (6:1-71). That the festival of Tabernacles, the feast of the Jews, was "near" (7:2) thus prepares the audience to expect Jesus to transcend the worship at this Jewish feast as well.[20]

---

19. "'The Holy One of God' is virtually synonymous with 'the Son of God,' acknowledging and confirming what Jesus himself had said again and again, that the Father 'sent' him (vv. 29, 57; also 3:17; 4:34; 5:23, 24, 30, 36, 37, 38; 6:38, 39, 44)" (Michaels, *John*, 416).

20. The Jewish feast of Tabernacles "included the lighting of giant menorahs in the temple courtyard, all-night dancing to flutes by torchlight, dawn processions ending with libations of water and wine at the bronze altar, prayers for rain and resurrection of the dead ... the Fourth Gospel mentions a celebration of the Feast of Tabernacles itself (John 7:2), with Jesus referring to himself as the living water, perhaps a reference to the high priest performing the dawn water libation" (Jenney, "Tabernacles," 1270-71). "During the feast of Tabernacles, the symbols of the feast (water and light) and the personages of Israel traditionally associated with Tabernacles (Moses and Abraham) highlight the identity of Jesus" (Coloe, *God Dwells*, 116). "The material in 7.1—8.59 has

Jesus' initial reluctance to go up to the feast of Tabernacles (7:8), because the Jews were seeking to "kill" him (5:18; 7:1), accords with the ominous notice that Judas was going to "give him over" to death (6:64, 71), thus making him the sacrificial Lamb of God (1:29, 36). His statement that "I am not going up [ἀναβαίνω]" to this feast, because his time has not yet been fulfilled (cf. 2:4), indicates that this is not the Jewish feast at which he, as the Son of Man, will be "going up" or "ascending" (ἀναβαίνοντα) through his death and resurrection to where he was before (6:62)—with God (1:1–2, 18). But when his unbelieving brothers (7:5) had gone up to this feast, then he himself also went up, not "openly" (φανερῶς) but "in secret" (7:10). This is in contrast to their urging that Jesus not do anything "in secret," but rather "manifest" (φανέρωσον) himself openly to the world (7:4).[21]

When the feast of Tabernacles was already half over, Jesus went up into the "temple" and was teaching (7:14). This recalls that in the "temple" Jesus told the man he healed on the Sabbath to no longer sin (5:14), implicitly by worshiping in the Jerusalem temple, since in that "temple" (2:14) Jesus revealed that his body, which he will raise from the dead after it is destroyed (2:19), is the new temple for the true worship of God (2:15–22). That Jesus, the new temple, was "teaching" in the Jerusalem temple, a place of Jewish public worship, complements his "teaching" in the Capernaum synagogue (6:59) as a place of Jewish public worship (cf. 18:20).[22] He was teaching in that synagogue about himself as the bread of divine life eternal, which would transcend the meal of the Jewish Passover. That he was teaching in the Jerusalem temple thus prepares the audience for a teaching about how he will transcend Jewish Tabernacle worship.

As his teaching is from the God who sent him (7:16–17), and as one who is "truthful," he seeks the "glory" of the one who sent him (7:18). He seeks not only to give glory as an act of worship by doing the will of the God who sent him (4:34; 5:30; 6:38; 7:17), but also to receive the glory from God that makes him a worthy object of divine worship. In the Jerusalem temple Jesus had previously accused the Jews of not seeking the "glory" that comes

---

the Festival of Tabernacles as its setting and draws directly on its imagery, while that in 9.1–10.21 continues with this festival as the implicit backdrop until the setting changes in 10.22 to the Festival of Dedication (Hanukkah)" (Lincoln, *John*, 241).

21. "Tabernacles may be an appropriate time for a would-be messiah to 'go up' to Jerusalem and reveal himself to the world. For the Messiah that Jesus is, the right time (*kairos*) and appropriate feast for his revelation will be Passover, where, as 'Lamb of God' (1:29, 36), he will offer his 'flesh for the life of the world' (6:51)" (Byrne, *Life Abounding*, 131–32). On his "going up" as referring to his future "ascending" to the Father, see Coloe, *God Dwells*, 123.

22. "The synagogue's most important functions were as a place for worship, prayer, and religious study" (Atkinson, "Synagogue," 1262).

from the only God (5:44), the "glory" that Jesus manifested as a basis for believing in him (2:11). His divine glory provides the object for the communal doxological worship that "we observed his glory, glory as of the unique one from the Father, full of a gift of truth" (1:14), the "truth" that includes the divine life eternal that came to be in Jesus as the divine Word (1:3-4).

Jesus then indicated how his healing of the sick man (5:1-18), which pointed to his ability to give divine life eternal, transcended not only Sabbath worship but the rite of circumcision, the practice of which overrides Sabbath observance.[23] If a person receives circumcision, which involves a single member of the body, on the Sabbath without breaking the law of Moses, how can the Jews be angry with Jesus (5:18) because he made a "whole person" well on the Sabbath (7:23)?[24] The Jewish rite of circumcision initiated one into the covenant people of Israel, which enabled him to participate in Jerusalem temple worship. But Jesus told the sick man, whose whole person he healed, to no longer sin (5:14), implicitly by worshiping in the Jerusalem temple. One becomes a true worshiper of God not by being circumcised but by worshiping in Spirit and truth (4:23-24). Thus, the ritual worship of Christian baptism, by which the whole person is born from above/again from water and the Spirit (3:3-5), transcends the ritual worship of Jewish circumcision by enabling one to worship for the divine life eternal that Jesus gives.

Jesus, the new temple, cried out in the Jerusalem "temple" as he was teaching (cf. 7:14) and accused the Jews of not knowing that his origin is from the God who sent him, the "true" God they do not know (7:28). He thus implicitly accused them of not being "true" worshipers who worship the Father in Spirit and truth (4:23). Jesus then taught how the true worship for divine life eternal based on believing in him transcends the water libation ceremony of the feast of Tabernacles:[25] "On the last day, the great day

23. Circumcision, the removal of the foreskin from the penis, "had a unique place in the worship and practice of the people of Israel. . . . It was a requirement of God's covenant (Gen. 17:9-14), along with sabbath observance and food laws. . . . It was the most significant boundary marker which distinguished Jew from Gentile, those within the covenant from those outside" (Bevere, "Circumcision," 256).

24. "The circumcision rule, then, overrides the Sabbath. On the *a fortiori* principle, if, the Sabbath notwithstanding, the law requires an operation (circumcision) on a single member of the human body (the lesser case), how much more (v. 23) should it require the restoration of the whole person to full health (the greater)?" (Byrne, *Life Abounding*, 134-35).

25. The feast of Tabernacles "begins with the Water Libation Ceremony. At the dawn of each day a procession accompanied by blasts of the shofar moves down to the pool of Siloam to gather water in a golden container before returning through the Water Gate. According to the rabbis, this gate marked the source from which the waters of life, issuing from the temple, would flow in the messianic age. . . . This ritual was

of the feast, Jesus stood up and cried out, saying, 'If anyone thirsts, let him come to me and drink'" (7:37).[26] This recalls Jesus' declaration that the one who "drinks" his blood has life eternal, and Jesus will raise him on the "last day" (6:54; cf. 6:39, 40, 44, 53, 56), which is anticipated by this "last day," the great one, of this feast of Tabernacles.[27] It also recalls Jesus' declaration to the Samaritan woman that whoever "drinks" from the living water he will give (4:10) will never thirst for eternity; the water he will give will become within that person a fountain of water springing up to divine life eternal (4:14).

Jesus continued the teaching that he cried out on the last day of Tabernacles (7:37): "The one who believes in me, as the Scripture says, 'From the belly of him will flow rivers of living water'" (7:38). This alludes to several texts of Scripture associated with the feast of Tabernacles: God brought "water" out of the rock in the wilderness and brought down "waters" as "rivers" (LXX Ps 77:16), and he struck the rock and "waters flowed" (LXX Ps 77:20). And "living water" will come out of Jerusalem (LXX Zech 14:8), "water" from under the Jerusalem temple (LXX Ezek 47:1).[28] And it recalls Jesus' declaration that "the one who believes in me will never thirst, ever" (6:35), in other words, the one who drinks the living water Jesus gives and who believes in Jesus as the new temple for true worship will have divine life eternal.[29]

---

linked with the giving of rain in the wilderness" (Brown, *Gift*, 150).

26. For the reasons to take the words "and drink" as the conclusion of 7:37 rather than the introduction to 7:38—"and let drink the one who believes in me," see Coloe, *God Dwells*, 126. "The participle 'Whoever believes in me' is best understood as referring not to someone *being invited* to 'come and drink,' but to a person who has *already* done so, never to thirst again [cf. 6:35]" (Michaels, *John*, 465; emphases original).

27. "The 'great' day in the Johannine Gospel is the day of Jesus' resurrection, with a promise that the believer will share this resurrection experience. Because of these textual links to the resurrection of the believer and Jesus, the 'last day, the great day' has a particular Johannine eschatological perspective. . . . The eschatological emphasis within verses 37–39 is not foreign to the celebration of the feast. Indeed the text states explicitly, 'on the last day of the feast.' Even as the verses look to 'the hour' for the fulfillment of their meaning, the feast itself offers an eschatological perspective which must interplay with 'the hour'" (Coloe, *God Dwells*, 129).

28. "John 6 had taken up the manna in the wilderness from Exod. 16 (cf. also Ps. 78.24) and now John 7 takes up Exod. 17.6, and the rehearsal of this incident in Ps. 78.16, 20 (Ps. 77.16, 20 LXX) employs two of the same terms as here, 'rivers' (ποταμοί) and 'flow' (ῥέω), in its description of the emerging water. . . . It looks, then, as though the Fourth Gospel here in its water imagery may well be associating the flow of water out of the rock from Exod. 17 and Ps. 78 with the flow of water out of the Jerusalem temple from Zech. 14, which had already been linked with the Festival of Tabernacles" (Lincoln, *John*, 256).

29. "The imagery of drinking that Jesus employs here draws upon the ritual of

That rivers of living water will flow from the belly of "him" (7:38) carries a double meaning. First, it refers to the believer, who receives the living water of divine life eternal. The living water Jesus gives will become in the believer not only "a fountain of water springing up to life eternal" (4:14), but "from the belly of him will flow rivers of living water." Secondly, it refers to Jesus as the source for the believer of the living water symbolic of the Spirit. This is confirmed, as it is explained that Jesus said this about the Spirit, whom those believing in him were going to receive, for the Spirit had "not yet" been given, because Jesus was "not yet" glorified (7:39; cf. 2:4; 7:6, 8, 30). That Jesus was not yet "glorified" by God means that he was not yet "exalted" through his death and resurrection (3:14) and given the "glory" that makes him a worthy object of worship (1:14). When believers receive the Spirit from the glorified Jesus, they become a channel of the Spirit that enables the true worship in Spirit and truth (4:23-24) for divine life eternal, which transcends the Jewish worship at the feast of Tabernacles.[30]

Jesus the Bridegroom Calls an Adulteress to True Worship (7:53—8:11)

That each one left the Jerusalem temple and went to his own "house" (7:53) reminds the audience of Jesus' accusation that the temple has become a "house" of trade rather than a place of true worship as the "house" of the Father (2:16).[31] And that Jesus left the Jerusalem temple mount and went to the "mount" of olives (8:1) recalls that the place for true worship is neither on the "mountain" in Samaria nor in Jerusalem (4:20-21). Rather, true wor-

---

Tabernacles. . . . The ritual evokes the vision of Ezekiel 47:1-12, where the prophet sees water flowing down from the temple, in all four directions and in ever-increasing volumes until it becomes a great river, flowing down to the sea, and bringing life and fertility in every aspect to a hitherto barren land. Jesus has, of course, already identified himself with the temple—or, more accurately, has indicated his own body as the replacement of the Jerusalem temple (2:21)" (Byrne, *Life Abounding*, 138-39).

30. "Clearly, 'living water' is nothing other than 'eternal life' (see also 4:14), and just as clearly 'the Spirit' is the source of eternal life" (Michaels, *John*, 467). "While Jesus himself has received the Spirit, as reported by the Baptist (1:32-33), and while he could say to the Samaritan woman that the hour for 'worship in Spirit and in truth' was already at hand (4:23-24), in the more regular view of the gospel the gift of the Spirit to believers follows upon Jesus' hour of 'glorification': the moment, that is, of his expiry upon the cross when he breathes out the Spirit upon the community represented by the Beloved Disciple (19:30; cf. 20:22-23)" (Byrne, *Life Abounding*, 140).

31. Although it was omitted early on in the manuscript tradition, there is strong internal evidence for considering the story in 7:53-8:11 original to the Fourth Gospel, as it fits quite well into its narrative context. See Heil, "Jesus and the Adulteress," 182-91; Heil, "Rejoinder," 361-66.

shipers will worship the Father in Spirit and truth (4:23-24). But early in the morning Jesus again arrived in the Jerusalem temple, and all the people came to him, and, sitting down, he was teaching them (8:2). Whereas Jesus had "stood up" on the last day, the great day, of the feast of Tabernacles (7:37) for his "teaching" (7:14, 28) which pointed to his giving of the Spirit for true worship (7:37-39; cf. 4:23-24), he was now "sitting down" as he was "teaching" all the people in the Jerusalem temple. This prepares the audience for how Jesus, the new temple (2:21), will teach a related but different aspect regarding true worship.[32]

Then the scribes and the Pharisees, who did not believe in Jesus (7:48) and were trying to arrest him (7:32, 45), led a woman caught in adultery and made her stand in the middle (8:3). Similar to the adulterous Samaritan woman (4:18) who served as a representative of the idolatrous worship of the Samaritan people (4:22), this Jewish adulteress represented the false worship of the Jewish people in the Jerusalem temple within the context of the feast of Tabernacles.[33] Testing him, so that they might have a charge against him, they asked him whether he concurred with the Mosaic law that commanded such women to be stoned, but he bent down and was writing with his finger on the ground (8:4-6). When they persisted in asking him, he straightened up and said to them, "Let the one without sin among you be the first to throw a stone at her" (8:7). Then again bending down he wrote on the ground (8:8). They then went away one by one beginning with the elders, implicitly admitting to a sinfulness that associated them with the adultery/idolatry of the woman (8:9a).

When Jesus was left alone with the adulterous/idolatrous woman (8:9b), he straightened up and asked her if anyone has condemned her to death (8:10). After she replied that no one had condemned her, Jesus said, "Neither do I myself condemn you. Go, and from now on no longer sin" (8:11).[34] Jesus had previously told the royal official to "go [πορεύου], your

---

32. One of ceremonies conducted during the feast of Tabernacles, the rite of facing the temple, was concerned with true worship: "At cockcrow of each of the seven days of the feast the men proceed to the east gate of the temple. At sunrise they turn and face the temple and recite, 'Our fathers when they were in this place turned with their backs to the temple of the Lord and their faces to the east, but for us, our eyes were turned toward the Lord.' This ritual greeting the light of the new day affirmed that YHWH is the one true God to whom all honor, glory, and obedience is due" (Brown, *Gift*, 150).

33. "In several prophetical books (e.g., Jer. 2-3; Ezek. 16; 23; Hos. 1-4) and Lamentations, adultery is employed as a metaphor for breach of covenant. In Ezek. 16, e.g., Jerusalem is personified as Yahweh's wife whose 'adulterous' behavior consists of giving worship to deities other than Yahweh" (Day, "Adulteress," 23).

34. "Instead of Jesus being judged and vindicated, the woman is judged and vindicated, and her accusers are judged, just as Jesus' accusers are judged and found wanting

son will live" (4:50), meaning that he will recover from his sickness, but also implying that he will live eternally. As the metaphorical bridegroom (2:9; 3:29) who provided an abundance of good wine for the celebratory worship of divine life eternal (2:1–11), Jesus similarly told the adulteress to "go" (πορεύου), indicating that he has saved her from death, but also implying that Jesus, as her true bridegroom, offers her divine life eternal. This is confirmed by his exhortation for her to "no longer sin," echoing what he said in the Jerusalem temple to the man he had healed (5:14), which implied no longer sinning through adulterous/idolatrous worship in the temple but to worship for the divine life eternal that Jesus, the new temple and the true bridegroom, gives.[35]

Jesus the New Temple Teaches the Truth for True Worship (8:12–59)

Again Jesus spoke to "them" (cf. 7:6, 16, 31), to those whom he had been teaching about true worship within the context of the feast of Tabernacles, when he said, "I am the light of the world; the one who follows me will never walk in the darkness, but will have the light of the life" (8:12).[36] That Jesus is the light of the "world" reminds the audience that he is a worthy object of true worship as the Lamb of God who takes away the sin of the "world" (1:29), the savior of the "world" (4:42), and the one who gives the eucharistic bread that is his flesh for the life of the "world" (6:51). The one who follows him as the light will never walk in "the darkness," because the light shines on in "the darkness," for "the darkness" has not overcome it (1:5). And the one who follows him as the one who teaches about true worship will have

---

in the temple discourse as a whole. And just as her story ends with a stoning that never materialized, so too does the temple discourse itself (see 8:59)" (Michaels, *John*, 500).

35. "His entire concern is to rescue the woman from her terrible plight and set her free for a new direction of life" (Byrne, *Life Abounding*, 144).

36. Another ritual performed during the feast of Tabernacles was the ceremony of light: "Four menorahs are placed at the center of the court of the women. To the sounds of Ps 120–134, celebrations under these lights last most of the night each of the seven days of the feast. The temple then also becomes the beacon that looks back to God's guidance in the wilderness through the pillar of fire and forward to the pillar's expected return in the age of the Messiah" (Brown, *Gift*, 150). "Jesus offers a light surpassing the wilderness cloud, for Jesus is the *logos* who has already been described as a light and life for all people and a light that the darkness could not extinguish (cf. 1:4–5). The tabernacling presence of God that formerly nourished, refreshed, and guided Israel, is once more dwelling in Israel's midst offering bread (ch. 6), water and light (chs. 7 and 8)" (Coloe, *God Dwells*, 136). That Jesus spoke these words while in the temple treasury "provides a reminder of its setting at the Feast of Tabernacles, since the temple treasury was next to the Court of Women, in which the light celebration took place" (Lincoln, *John*, 267).

"the light of the life," because "the life" that came to be in him was "the light" for human beings (1:4), offering divine life eternal to those who worship him. These are among the words that Jesus, the new temple for true worship (2:21), spoke while teaching in the treasury in the Jerusalem temple (8:20).

Jesus spoke again to "them" (cf. 7:6, 16, 31; 8:12), to those whom he has been teaching about true worship within the context of the feast of Tabernacles, when he warned that in their "sin," their failure to believe in him, they "will die," that is, be deprived of divine life eternal (8:21). It is to those who believe in his name that Jesus gives authority to become children of God (1:12) and thus share in divine life eternal.[37] But Jesus is the Lamb of God who takes away the "sin" of the world (1:29). Accordingly, he offers to take away their sin of unbelief, as he warns that they will die in their sins unless they believe that "I am" (8:24), that he is a worthy object of worship as the one who "is" from God (6:46), who now "is" in the bosom of the Father (1:18), and who from the beginning "was" with God and "was" God (1:1-2). When they crucify him, they will lift up/exalt him to be worshiped as the divine Son of Man, and thus they will know that "I am" (8:28; cf. 3:14).[38]

Jesus then challenged the many Jews who had begun to believe in him to truly be his disciples (8:30-31) in order to know the "truth," the "truth" that will free them (8:32) from the sin (8:34) of unbelief and enable them to become true worshipers who worship the Father in Spirit and "truth" (4:23-24), as believers who share in divine life eternal (1:12). But they are trying to kill Jesus, who told them the "truth" he heard from God (8:40). Their father is neither Abraham nor God (8:39-41) but the devil, who does not stand in "truth," because "truth" is not in him (8:44). But because Jesus himself speaks the "truth," they do not believe him (8:45-46). If they would believe him, they could become those who worship the Father in Spirit and "truth," the "truth" that came to be through Jesus Christ (1:17), in whom came to be divine life eternal (1:3-4).

---

37. "Failure to believe, on the other hand—the essence of 'sin' in the Fourth Gospel—entails separation from this source of life and ensures that physical death will mean eternal death ('you will die in your sin[s]')" (Byrne, *Life Abounding*, 147-48).

38. "Jesus, whom John pointed out as the Lamb of God who takes away the sin of the world (1:29), is here presenting himself in this divine role. He bears God's name ('I am'; cf. Exod 3:14-16) not in a static sense but in the function of a divine reaching out to an alienated world in reconciliation. If his present adversaries cannot grasp this saving revelation they stand in peril of consigning themselves to eternal loss" (Byrne, *Life Abounding*, 149). A variant of the Hebrew for this phrase [I am] "was used in the Festival of Tabernacles as an oblique way of referring to YHWH and thus avoiding saying the sacred name.... Jesus' use of the phrase 'I Am' as a term of self-designation would have been both striking and offensive to his opponents" (Coloe, *God Dwells*, 137-38).

Whereas Jesus "honors," with the connotation of truly worships, his Father, the still unbelieving Jews "dishonor" Jesus (8:49) and thus fail to engage in the true worship that includes the worship of him along with the Father (5:23). Jesus does not seek his own "glory" (8:50) and thus does not make himself an object of worship. If he would "glorify" himself, his "glory" is nothing; it is his Father who "glorifies" him (8:54), thus making him an object of true worship. This recalls and reaffirms for the audience the communal act of doxological worship of Jesus: "We have observed his glory, glory as of the unique one from the Father" (1:14). If the unbelieving Jews would keep his word (8:51), truly become believers (cf. 4:41, 50; 5:24), and worship him, they would never taste eternal death (8:52), but rather have divine life eternal.

According to Jewish tradition Abraham was the first to celebrate the feast of Tabernacles.[39] In accord with the joy that was to accompany that feast (Lev 23:40; Deut 16:14) and the tradition that Abraham was given a vision of the future messianic age, Abraham "exulted" to see Jesus' day, and he saw it and "rejoiced" (8:56; cf. 3:29).[40] Jesus then solemnly declared to the unbelieving Jews that before Abraham came to be "I am" (8:58), indicating that he is an object of a joyful worship that transcends the joyful worship associated with the feast of Tabernacles.[41] No one dared to throw a stone at the adulterous/idolatrous woman (8:7). Although the unbelieving Jews picked up stones to throw at Jesus, he hid and went out of the Jerusalem temple of false worship (8:59), as the new temple (2:21) of the true worship for divine life eternal.[42]

---

39. "The book of Jubilees, written in Hebrew and probably completed around 160 BCE, names Abraham as the first to celebrate Tabernacles" (Coloe, *God Dwells*, 139).

40. "The notion that Abraham foresaw Christ's coming seems to have been a familiar one to Christians well before the Gospel of John was written" (Michaels, *John*, 530).

41. "[I]t is clear that the formula [I am] in the Greek Bible as in the Hebrew is interchangeable with 'I am the Lord,' or 'I am God'" (Michaels, *John*, 534).

42. "Recalling Ezekiel's vision of a similar departure of the divine Presence (Shekinah; Ezek 10:18–19; 11:23), the Light that has shone for a time in the temple, eclipsing its light, has now gone out" (Byrne, *Life Abounding*, 157). "The departure of one who has consistently during this feast affirmed his relationship with the Father and so revealed himself as the tabernacling presence of Israel's God acts as a judgment on Israel's cult. As their ancestors once 'turned their backs to the Temple' (Ezek 8:16), now 'the Jews' turn from the true Temple of God. Jesus, the enfleshed glory 'as of the only son' is driven from his Father's House" (Coloe, *God Dwells*, 143).

Jesus the Light of Divine Life Eternal Heals the Man Born Blind (9:1–41)

As Jesus, the temple for true worship (2:21), left the Jerusalem temple (8:59), he saw a man blind from birth (9:1), which implicitly deprived him from worshiping in the temple.[43] "Born blind" (9:2), he exemplifies one who must be "born" from above/again from water and the Spirit (3:3, 5), in order to "see" the kingdom of God (3:3), one who must be "born" of God (1:13) to become a child of God as a believer (1:12) and thus share in divine life eternal. His being born blind was not a punishment due to sin, but so that the "works" of God might be "manifested" in him (9:3). This recalls that one doing the "truth" comes to the light, so that his "works" might be "manifested" that they have been done in God (3:21), enabling one to worship in Spirit and "truth" (4:23–24). Jesus and the man must do the works of God who sent Jesus while it is "day" and the light is available, since the "night" symbolic of the darkness of unbelief is coming when no one can work (9:4; cf. 3:2). Against the background of the light of the Tabernacles feast Jesus is the light of the world (9:5; 8:12), the light of divine life eternal for the man born blind.[44]

Jesus then spat on the ground and made clay from the spittle and anointed the blind man's eyes with the clay (9:6). That Jesus made clay from the "spittle" alliteratively and conceptually suggests a connection to the "Spirit" that remains upon Jesus and with which he baptizes (1:32–33), as the word "Spirit" also means breath, the source of the "spittle."[45] The man born blind is thus not only being physically healed but spiritually born from above/anew (3:3) from water and the "Spirit [πνεύματος]/spittle [πτύσματος]" (3:5) in a ritualistic act suggestive of the sacrament of Christian baptism. This is confirmed as Jesus, the one "sent" by God (9:4), told him to wash in the water of the pool of Siloam, which is interpreted "sent" (9:7), and from which water was drawn during the feast of Tabernacles. Then the blind man went away and washed and came back "seeing" (9:7),

---

43. "Jewish regulations very likely restricted his entry into the temple and participation in regular worship" (Bennema, *Encountering Jesus*, 136).

44. "Although the tone and the outcome are very different, the story of the man born blind remains part of the long sequence centered upon the feast of Tabernacles. At the feast Jesus has revealed himself publicly to be Light of the world (8:12). But the world, in the shape of the authorities, has refused to come to the Light and the Light, publicly at least, has 'gone out' (8:59). In the face of that public refusal and departure of the Light, chapter 9 dramatizes one person's coming to the Light in faith and discipleship" (Byrne, *Life Abounding*, 158).

45. BDAG, 832.

indicating that he is on the way to "seeing" the kingdom of God (3:3) and thus sharing in divine life eternal by being reborn in baptism.[46]

Jesus made the clay and opened the eyes of the man born blind on a Sabbath (9:14). This recalls and reaffirms how he transcended the practice of the ritual of circumcision which could be performed on the Sabbath by making a whole person, the man he healed on the Sabbath (5:9-18), well (7:23). This indicated how the ritual worship of the sacrament of Christian baptism, by which the whole person is born from above/again from water and the Spirit (3:3-5), transcends the ritual worship of Jewish circumcision as well as the Sabbath worship by enabling one to worship for the divine life eternal that Jesus gives. That the man born blind was now able to see physically because he "washed" in the water of the pool of Siloam is repeated an emphatic three times (9:7, 11, 15), suggesting his rebirth in baptism to "see" spiritually the kingdom of God (3:3) and share in divine life eternal.

Ironically, the Jewish authorities invited the man born blind to "give glory to God" and thus perform an act of worship by agreeing with them that Jesus is a sinner (9:24) rather than one who is from God. Instead, the man told them, "In this is the amazing thing, that you do not know where he is from, yet he opened my eyes!" (9:30). This recalls Jesus' statement that the Father will show him greater "works" than these (5:20a), including the "works" of God that Jesus performed in opening the eyes of the man born blind (9:3-4), "so that you may be amazed" (5:20b; cf. 7:21). The man then declared, "We know that God does not listen to sinners, but if someone is a worshiper of God [θεοσεβής] and does his will, he listens to that one" (9:31).[47] This indicates that Jesus, who does the will of God (4:34; 5:30; 6:38), is not only the temple for true worship (2:21) and an object of true worship (1:14, 49; 4:42; 6:69), but also himself a true worshiper of God (cf. 4:23-24).

The parents of the man born blind feared the Jews, for the Jews had agreed that if someone confessed Jesus to be the Christ, he would be expelled

---

46. "This destination [pool of Siloam] is significant. As noted earlier, during the feast of Tabernacles water was drawn daily from this pool and carried in procession to the temple, an acknowledgment of the pool's life-giving role for the population of Jerusalem. Even more significant is the popular etymology of the pool's name as meaning 'sent' (v. 7b). What brings about the blind man's cure is not mere contact with the waters of the pool but the fact that he goes to wash there because he was 'sent' by the One who has been himself sent from the Father on a life-giving mission to the world" (Byrne, *Life Abounding*, 161). "Siloam's waters, like the 'water and Spirit' of which Nicodemus was told (3:5), will give the man born blind another birth, and therefore new eyes" (Michaels, *John*, 547). See also Grigsby, "Washing," 227-35.

47. "John 9:31: 'If anyone is a *worshiper of God* [θεοσεβής] and does his [God's] will, God listens to him'" ("θεοσεβής," *EDNT* 2.142; emphasis original).

from the synagogue (9:22). Accordingly, when the man born blind fearlessly insisted that Jesus was from God (9:32-33), the Jews emphatically "threw him outside [ἐξέβαλον αὐτὸν ἔξω]" (9:34). Jesus heard that they "threw him outside," implying outside of the synagogue, so that now he was deprived of worship not only in the temple but in the synagogue. Jesus, who will never "throw outside" one who comes to him (6:37), found the man and invited him to worship Jesus, when he asked him, "Do you believe in the Son of Man?" (9:35). This recalls that everyone who believes in the Son of Man may have life eternal (3:15). After Jesus identified himself as the Son of Man (9:36-37), the man said, "I do believe, Lord," and he "worshiped" him (9:38). The man born blind exemplifies for the audience how one reborn from water and the Spirit in baptism (3:3-5) becomes a true "worshiper" who "worships" in the Spirit and truth (4:23-24) for divine life eternal.[48]

Jesus Lays Down His Life in Sacrificial Worship for Divine Life Eternal (10:1-21)

Against the background of the light ceremony during the feast of Tabernacles Jesus declared that "I am the light of the world" and that the one who follows him will never walk in the darkness, but will have the light of divine life eternal (8:12; cf. 1:3-5). Still within the context of the feast of Tabernacles there is a shift in metaphors for Jesus' self-identity as the giver of divine life eternal. Jesus solemnly declared that "I am the gate of the sheep" (10:7), that is, of those who follow him as the "shepherd" (10:2-5). He emphatically repeats that "I am the gate" and if anyone enters through him, he will be saved (10:9). This means having divine life eternal through

---

48. "The man's twofold response of a verbal confession and a non-verbal act of worship is the climax of the story.... The man's understanding of Jesus progresses from 'the man called Jesus' (9:11), to 'a prophet' (9:17), to 'a man from God' (9:33), to the climactic 'Lord' (9:38)" (Bennema, *Encountering Jesus*, 142). "In worshiping Jesus the formerly blind man is acknowledging in him the presence of God, ironically fulfilling the injunction brusquely thrust upon him 'to give glory to God' (v. 24)" (Byrne, *Life Abounding*, 167). "Blind 'from birth' (v. 1), he has had his sight restored, signaling nothing less than a new birth. Like the rebirth of which Jesus told Nicodemus (3:5), it is a birth 'from water,' water from the pool of Siloam 'sent' (v. 7) from above. In that sense he was 'baptized,' so to speak, and as a result 'put out of the synagogue' (vv. 22, 34). Now he has confessed Jesus as 'Lord' and worshiped him' (v. 38). His is a classic case study in Christian conversion... the man born blind 'worshiped' Jesus—worshiped him, we may safely conclude, 'in Spirit and truth' (see 4:23, 34)" (Michaels, *John*, 569-70). See also Holleran, "Seeing the Light," 5-26, 354-82.

Jesus, as he goes on to declare that "I myself came that they may have life and have it abundantly" (10:10).[49]

Jesus provides the abundant divine life eternal (10:10) as the "good" (καλός) shepherd who lays down his life for the sheep (10:11, 15).[50] This resonates with the declaration that Jesus has kept the abundant "good" (καλόν) wine symbolic of divine life eternal until now (2:10). As the divine bridegroom, Jesus has kept the good wine until now in contrast to every human being who first "serves" or "lays down" (τίθησιν) the good wine (2:10). Analogously, as the divine good shepherd, Jesus must first "lay down" (τίθησιν) his life in an act of self-sacrificial worship before he can provide divine life eternal. Because Jesus is the good shepherd who lays down his life "for" (ὑπέρ) the sheep, he can give his flesh in eucharistic worship "for" (ὑπέρ) the divine life eternal of the world (6:51). That Jesus is the good shepherd who lays down his life in self-sacrificial worship enables him to be the sacrificial Lamb of God who takes away the sin of the world (1:29), and who thus is also an object of worship.[51]

As the good shepherd, Jesus lays down his life, so that he may take it up again (10:17). No one takes it from him, but he himself lays it down on his own (10:18a). This recalls and resonates with Jesus' declaration, "Destroy this temple and in three days I will raise it up" (2:19). He was speaking about the temple of his body (2:21), about himself as the personified place for

---

49. While there is "a change from the 'light/blindness' motifs in the preceding chapter, we are still within the ambit of the feast of Tabernacles. In fact, the discourse that Jesus gives in 10:1–21, contrasting himself as the good shepherd with others who break in and ravage the flock, is really a reflection upon the preceding episode. Where the authorities have browbeaten, abused, and eventually cast out the man born blind, Jesus has sought out this 'lost sheep' and brought him into the community of faith" (Byrne, *Life Abounding*, 169).

50. "This 'abundant life' should therefore not be viewed (as it has been in some Christian circles) as a 'deeper' or 'victorious' life gained by a second work of grace subsequent to conversion. It is simply a way of speaking of 'eternal life' in the classic Johannine sense of a life that is not merely endless in duration, but new life, a qualitatively different relationship to God" (Michaels, *John*, 585n71). "The 'shepherd' image, whether applied to God or to human rulers, has an important prehistory in the Scriptures of Israel that the present sequence reflects and develops in many ways. The outstanding passage in this respect is Ezekiel 34. Addressing the neglect and abuse of the people by rulers who, on the model of David, were meant to be their 'shepherds,' YHWH describes himself as the 'Shepherd' who will gather, heal, and feed the scattered flock and set up a true Davidic shepherd who will rule with integrity and justice" (Byrne, *Life Abounding*, 169).

51. "But that this shepherd shows his love for the sheep in the ultimate sacrifice, by deliberately dying for them (10:11), bursts the bounds of the shepherd and sheep image. The shepherd's willingness to lay down his life for the sheep (10:11) may connect him with the lamb (1:29)" (Keener, *John*, 1.814).

true worship. Because he has "authority" to lay his life down, and he has "authority" to take it up again (10:18b), he can give "authority" for believers to become children of God and share in divine life eternal (1:12). That this commandment he received from his Father (10:18c) resonates with his doing the will of the God who sent him (4:34; 5:30; 6:38). His laying down his life as an act of sacrificial worship in accord with God's will thus reaffirms that he is a true worshiper of God (9:31). Jesus, then, is not only the temple for true worship and an object of worship, but a true worshiper of God through his self-sacrificial act of worship as the good shepherd who lays down his life for the sheep (10:11, 15).

The Jewish Feast of Dedication and the Worship of the Consecrated Jesus (10:22-42)

Then came the Jewish feast of Dedication in Jerusalem (10:22), which celebrated the consecration of the temple and altar for sacrifice after they were desecrated by idolatrous worship.[52] Jesus was walking in the temple in the portico of Solomon (10:23). This recalls that he had expelled the sacrificial animals from this temple (2:14-15) and indicated that he would be the new personified temple for true worship (2:19-22; cf. 1:14, 51).[53] Although the Jews' question to Jesus is often interpreted as "how long will you keep us in suspense?," literally it asks "how long will you take away our life [ψυχήν]?" (10:24). It thus stands in ironic contrast to Jesus' declaration that he is the good shepherd who performs an act of sacrificial worship by laying down his "life" (ψυχήν) for the sheep (10:11, 15), to whom he thereby gives divine life eternal (10:28). Rather than "taking away" the life of the Jews, Jesus is the sacrificial Lamb of God who "takes away" the sin of the world (1:29). He is thus not only the temple for true worship and a true worshiper, but is himself an object of worship for divine life eternal.

To the Jews who picked up stones so that they might stone him (10:31), Jesus replied that he has shown them many good works from the Father (10:32). These include the healings that indicate his ability to give divine life eternal (4:46-54; 5:1-47; 9:1-41). These "good" (καλά) works recall that Jesus provided the "good" (καλόν) wine symbolic of divine life eternal (2:10),

---

52. The feast of Dedication or Hanukkah was a "celebration in remembrance of the restoration of the Jerusalem temple and the consecration of the new altar in 165 or 164 BCE under Judas Maccabeus (1 Macc 4:36-61)" (Burnett, "Dedication," 335).

53. "The setting in the portico of the ruler (King Solomon) who had built the prototype of the present temple also prepares the way for Jesus' self-presentation as the One whom the Father has sent to replace the function of the temple in the world (cf. 2:13-22)" (Byrne, *Life Abounding*, 177).

and that he is the "good" (καλός) shepherd who lays down his life for the sheep (10:11, 15), thereby giving them divine life eternal (10:28). He then asked for which of these good works do they want to stone him (10:32). But they replied that they want to stone him for blasphemy, because he is making himself God (10:33; cf. 5:18), and thus usurping the role of God as the object of true worship in the rededicated temple.

But Jesus pointed out that the scriptural word of God addresses human beings as "gods" (10:34-35; cf. LXX Ps 81:6). And so he asked how they can say that he, as the one whom God consecrated and sent into the world as the personified Word of God (1:14), blasphemes because he said that he is the Son of God (10:36). As the one whom the Father "consecrated" (ἡγίασεν) as the new temple, Jesus transcends the worship of the feast of Dedication, which commemorated how they "consecrated" (ἡγίασαν) the courts of the rededicated temple (1 Macc 4:48). As the one whom God "consecrated" or "made holy," Jesus is an object of worship not only as the "holy one" (ἅγιος) of God (6:69) but as the Son of God (1:49). Those who hear the voice of the Son of God will live (5:25) the divine life eternal the Father gave to the Son (5:26). Jesus did not make himself God (10:33). Rather, the Father is in him and he is in the Father (10:38), so that he and the Father are one (10:30). The worship of Jesus as the Son of God who gives divine life eternal is the worship of the Father who consecrated him (cf. 5:23).[54]

Summary on 5:1—10:42

Rather than breaking the Sabbath (5:18) with his life-giving words to the sick man (5:8-9), Jesus has transcended the Sabbath worship by revealing himself as the divine Son worthy of worship together with God the Father (5:23), as those who give to believers divine life eternal (5:24).

Just as the overabundance of bread Jesus provided (6:1-13) was a sign pointing to his ability to give his flesh in the bread of the eucharistic meal, so the overabundance of good wine he provided (2:1-10) was a sign pointing to his ability to give his blood in the wine of the eucharistic meal. Whoever

---

54. "Jesus, speaking during the feast commemorating the reconsecration of the altar and temple, describes himself as the Consecrated and Sent One.... The very word central to the celebration of this feast of Dedication is now applied to Jesus" (Coloe, *God Dwells*, 153). "The fact that mention of 'consecration' stands before that of 'sending' into the world implies the preexistence of the Son.... Jesus' refusal to state simply 'Yes, I am the Messiah' (cf. v. 24) is now fully understandable. In view of his origins and the nature of his mission, the title 'Son of God' (v. 36c) is far more appropriate. Jesus has not 'made himself out to be God' (v. 33d). He enjoys divine status by virtue of his eternal filial relationship and union with the Father" (Byrne, *Life Abounding*, 180).

not only "eats" the eucharistic bread that is the flesh of Jesus (6:51), but continually "feeds on" his flesh and continually "drinks" his blood in eucharistic worship has divine life eternal (6:54). Whereas the ancestors of the Jews ate but died during the Exodus event commemorated by the Passover feast, Jesus is the bread that came down from heaven, so that whoever feeds on this bread will live forever (6:58). Thus, the bread/flesh and blood/wine Jesus provides in the meal of eucharistic worship for divine life eternal through his sacrificial death as the Passover Lamb transcends the miraculous but non life-giving food of the Exodus event commemorated in the meal of the Passover feast of the Jews.

Believing in the words Jesus has spoken in his bread of life discourse (6:26–59), the words that are "Spirit" and are "life" (6:63), enables one to eat the flesh of the Son of Man and drink his blood in eucharistic worship to have "life" within him (6:53). Whoever feeds on his flesh and drinks his blood has "life" eternal (6:54). Believing in Jesus' words that are "Spirit" and "life," and eating his flesh and blood that are "true" food and "true" drink (6:55), enables one to be a "true" worshiper who worships in "Spirit" and truth (4:23–24), the truth that came to be in Jesus (1:17), in whom had come to be divine "life" eternal (1:3–4). The Passover feast of the Jews, which included the eating of a sacrificial Passover lamb, commemorated an eating of bread/manna that did not give life eternal. But the new Passover worship of Jesus as "the Holy One of God" (6:69), the Lamb of God (1:29, 36), whose sacrificial flesh/bread and blood/wine are to be eaten and drunk by believers in their eucharistic worship, gives them divine life eternal.

Jesus indicated how his healing of the sick man (5:1–18), which pointed to his ability to give divine life eternal, transcended not only Sabbath worship but the rite of circumcision, the practice of which overrides Sabbath observance. If a person receives circumcision, which involves a single member of the body, on the Sabbath without breaking the law of Moses, how can the Jews be angry with Jesus (5:18) because he made a "whole person" well on the Sabbath (7:23)? The Jewish rite of circumcision initiated one into the covenant people of Israel, which enabled him to participate in Jerusalem temple worship. But Jesus told the sick man, whose whole person he healed, to no longer sin (5:14), implicitly by worshiping in the Jerusalem temple. One becomes a true worshiper of God not by being circumcised but by worshiping in Spirit and truth (4:23–24). Thus, the ritual worship of Christian baptism, by which the whole person is born from above/again from water and the Spirit (3:3–5), transcends the ritual worship of Jewish circumcision by enabling one to worship for the divine life eternal that Jesus gives.

That rivers of living water will flow from the belly of "him" (7:38) carries a double meaning. First, it refers to the believer, who receives the living water of divine life eternal. The living water Jesus gives will become in the believer not only "a fountain of water springing up to life eternal" (4:14), but "from the belly of him will flow rivers of living water." Secondly, it refers to Jesus as the source for the believer of the living water symbolic of the Spirit. This is confirmed, as it is explained that Jesus said this about the Spirit, whom those believing in him were going to receive, for the Spirit had "not yet" been given, because Jesus was "not yet" glorified (7:39; cf. 2:4; 7:6, 8, 30). That Jesus was not yet "glorified" by God means that he was not yet "exalted" through his death and resurrection (3:14) and given the "glory" that makes him a worthy object of worship (1:14). When believers receive the Spirit from the glorified Jesus, they become a channel of the Spirit that enables the true worship in Spirit and truth (4:23-24) for divine life eternal, which transcends the Jewish worship at the feast of Tabernacles.

Jesus had previously told the royal official to "go, your son will live" (4:50), meaning that he will recover from his sickness, but also implying that he will live eternally. As the metaphorical bridegroom (2:9; 3:29) who provided an abundance of good wine for the celebratory worship of divine life eternal (2:1-11), Jesus similarly told the adulteress to "go" (8:11), indicating that he has saved her from being stoned to death (8:3-10), but also implying that Jesus, as her true bridegroom, offers her divine life eternal. This is confirmed by his exhortation for her to "no longer sin," echoing what he said in the Jerusalem temple during the feast of Tabernacles to the man he had healed (5:14), which implied no longer sinning through adulterous/idolatrous worship in the temple but to worship for the divine life eternal that Jesus, the new temple and the true bridegroom, gives.

According to Jewish tradition Abraham was the first to celebrate the feast of Tabernacles. In accord with the joy that was to accompany that feast (Lev 23:40; Deut 16:14) and the tradition that Abraham was given a vision of the future messianic age, Abraham "exulted" to see Jesus' day, and he saw it and "rejoiced" (8:56; cf. 3:29). Jesus then solemnly declared to the unbelieving Jews that before Abraham came to be "I am" (8:58), indicating that he is an object of a joyful worship that transcends the joyful worship associated with the feast of Tabernacles. No one dared to throw a stone at the adulterous/idolatrous woman (8:7). Although the unbelieving Jews picked up stones to throw at Jesus, he hid and went out of the Jerusalem temple of false worship (8:59), as the new temple (2:21) of the true worship for divine life eternal.

Ironically, the Jewish authorities invited the man born blind to "give glory to God" and thus perform an act of worship by agreeing with them that Jesus is a sinner (9:24) rather than one who is from God. Instead, the man told them, "In this is the amazing thing, that you do not know where he is from, yet he opened my eyes!" (9:30). This recalls Jesus' statement that the Father will show him greater "works" than these (5:20a), including the "works" of God that Jesus performed in opening the eyes of the man born blind (9:3-4), "so that you may be amazed" (5:20b; cf. 7:21). The man then declared, "We know that God does not listen to sinners, but if someone is a worshiper of God and does his will, he listens to that one" (9:31). This indicates that Jesus, who does the will of God (4:34; 5:30; 6:38), is not only the temple for true worship (2:21) and an object of true worship (1:14, 49; 4:42; 6:69), but also himself a true worshiper of God (cf. 4:23-24).

The parents of the man born blind feared the Jews, for the Jews had agreed that if someone confessed Jesus to be the Christ, he would be expelled from the synagogue (9:22). Accordingly, when the man born blind fearlessly insisted that Jesus was from God (9:32-33), the Jews emphatically "threw him outside" (9:34). Jesus heard that they "threw him outside," implying outside of the synagogue, so that now he was deprived of worship not only in the temple but in the synagogue. Jesus, who will never "throw outside" one who comes to him (6:37), found the man and invited him to worship Jesus, when he asked him, "Do you believe in the Son of Man?" (9:35). This recalls that everyone who believes in the Son of Man may have life eternal (3:15). After Jesus identified himself as the Son of Man (9:36-37), the man said, "I do believe, Lord," and he "worshiped" him (9:38). The man born blind exemplifies for the audience how one reborn from water and the Spirit in baptism (3:3-5) becomes a true "worshiper" who "worships" in the Spirit and truth (4:23-24) for divine life eternal.

As the good shepherd, Jesus lays down his life, so that he may take it up again (10:17). No one takes it from him, but he himself lays it down on his own (10:18a). This recalls and resonates with Jesus' declaration, "Destroy this temple and in three days I will raise it up" (2:19). He was speaking about the temple of his body (2:21), about himself as the personified place for true worship. Because he has "authority" to lay his life down, and he has "authority" to take it up again (10:18b), he can give "authority" for believers to become children of God and share in divine life eternal (1:12). That this commandment he received from his Father (10:18c) resonates with his doing the will of the God who sent him (4:34; 5:30; 6:38). His laying down his life as an act of sacrificial worship in accord with God's will thus reaffirms that he is a true worshiper of God (9:31). Jesus, then, is not only the temple for true worship and an object of worship, but a true worshiper of God through his self-sacrificial act of worship as the good shepherd who lays down his life for the sheep (10:11, 15).

To the charge of making himself God (10:33) Jesus pointed out that the scriptural word of God addresses human beings as "gods" (10:34–35; cf. LXX Ps 81:6). And so he asked how they can say that he, as the one whom God consecrated and sent into the world as the personified Word of God (1:14), blasphemes because he said that he is the Son of God (10:36). As the one whom the Father "consecrated" as the new temple, Jesus transcends the worship of the feast of Dedication, which commemorated how they "consecrated" the courts of the rededicated temple (1 Macc 4:48). As the one whom God "consecrated" or "made holy," Jesus is an object of worship not only as the "holy one" of God (6:69) but as the Son of God (1:49). Those who hear the voice of the Son of God will live (5:25) the divine life eternal the Father gave to the Son (5:26). Jesus did not make himself God (10:33). Rather, the Father is in him and he is in the Father (10:38), so that he and the Father are one (10:30). The worship of Jesus as the Son of God who gives divine life eternal is the worship of the Father who consecrated him (cf. 5:23).

6

Jesus' Sacrificial Worship for Divine Life Eternal Glorifies God (11:1—12:50)

With Worship Jesus Raised Lazarus from the Dead for the Glory of God (11:1–46)

When Jesus heard that Lazarus from Bethany, the brother of Martha and Mary, was sick (11:1–3), he declared, "This sickness is not unto death but for the glory of God, so that the Son of God may be glorified through it" (11:4). That this sickness is for the glory of God means that it will be an occasion for giving glory to or glorifying God (cf. 9:24) as an object of worship. But this sickness will also be an occasion for God to glorify Jesus as the Son of God through it, so that he also may be an object of worship. Jesus previously stated that if he glorifies himself, his glory is nothing; it is his Father who glorifies him (8:54). But that Jesus will be glorified as the Son of God through this sickness resonates with his being lifted up/exalted by God in his crucifixion, so that everyone who believes in him may have divine life eternal (3:14–15).[1] This sickness will not cause eternal death, but it is for the sake of the mutual glorification and thus worship of both the Father and the Son for divine life eternal.[2]

    1. "The title 'Son of God' occurs in the gospel particularly in contexts where Jesus presents himself as one with the Father in giving life (3:16–18; 5:19–29; 10:36; 11:25–27; 20:31)" (Byrne, *Life Abounding*, 185n3). "Jesus in fact rarely uses the full term, 'Son of God'... A likely reason for 'Son of God' here is the wordplay between 'the glory *of God* (τοῦ θεοῦ) and 'the Son *of God* (τοῦ θεοῦ) being 'glorified'" (Michaels, *John*, 616n10).

    2. "Jesus' glorification in this narrative is inextricably linked to his death and exaltation (cf. 7.39; 12.16, 23, 28; 13.31–2)" (Lincoln, *John*, 319). "Jesus' 'glorification,' like his 'exaltation' or 'lifting up' (3:14; 8:28; 12:32–33), comes to realization paradoxically in his death on the cross (see 12:23–24).... and consequently in his 'glorification'—for 'the glory of God'" (Michaels, *John*, 616). "Since the death of Jesus is ultimately for

When Jesus arrived in Bethany (11:17-18) after the death of Lazarus (11:14), Martha said to him, "Lord, if you had been here, my brother would not have died" (11:21). This indicates to the audience that Martha believed that Jesus could have prevented the death of Lazarus, as he prevented the death of the royal official's sick son (4:46-53). But her faith is even greater than that, as she goes on to say, "But even now I know that whatever you ask God, God will give you" (11:22). This reminds the audience that Jesus is a true "worshiper of God" (θεοσεβής) who does God's will (4:34; 5:30; 6:38), so that God listens to him (9:31). Her statement thus amounts to an implicit request for Jesus to offer an intercessory prayer of petition for God to do something beneficial in regard to the death of her brother. Although she does not dare to ask explicitly for the restoration of the life of Lazarus, her hopeful request implies that and leaves it open as a distinct possibility.[3]

Jesus' revelation to Martha, "I am the resurrection and the life; the one who believes in me, even if he dies, will live" (11:25), affirms his role in bringing Lazarus and every believer who dies physically to divine life eternal on the last day (11:23-24). His further revelation that everyone who lives and believes in him will never die (11:26) indicates that although believers will die physically, they will not experience an eternal death, but rather share in divine life eternal. After Jesus asked her if she believes this (11:26), she replied with an affirmative "yes, Lord" (11:27). She then added a further confession of faith as an act of worship, worshiping Jesus as the giver of divine life eternal: "I myself have come to believe that you are the Christ, the Son of God, the one coming into the world" (11:27). This affirms that Jesus is the resurrection and the life, as it recalls the pronouncement that Jesus, the Christ through whom the gift of truth came to be (1:17), the Word with the glory of the unique Son from the Father (1:14), was "coming into the world" as the true light (1:9) of divine life eternal (1:3-4).[4]

---

the life of the world (6:51), the illness of Lazarus, which remotely brings it about, is not a sickness leading to death but something ordered to the life-giving glory of God" (Byrne, *Life Abounding*, 185).

3. Martha does not express "a specific hope (that her brother be raised), but an open-ended, generalized confidence that God can and will do something more" (Byrne, *Life Abounding*, 190).

4. Martha's worship of Jesus as the one coming into the world as the Christ and Son of God surpasses the reference to him, among those who were miraculously fed, as the one coming into the world as the prophet (6:14). Moloney ("John 11.1—12.8," 514) claims that Martha "does not acknowledge Jesus' self-revelation in vv. 25–6 as the resurrection and the life." But when Jesus asked her, "Do you believe this?" (11:26), she replied, "Yes, Lord," before giving a full confession of her faith (11:27). "Her emphatic 'yes, Lord,' her confident 'I myself have come to believe,' and the threefold title she confers, indicate considerable advance from her opening words. Moreover, while we may think Martha need not assume the raising of her brother, the Johannine evangelist has

When Mary came to the place where Martha had met Jesus (11:30) and saw him, "she fell at his feet" in a gesture of worship and echoed the words of Martha indicating the belief that Jesus had the power to prevent Lazarus from dying, "Lord, if you had been here, my brother would not have died" (11:32; cf. 11:21). Her gesture, focused upon the feet of Jesus, links her to an even more dramatic act of worship, as it recalls that Mary "anointed the Lord with perfumed oil and dried his feet with her hair" (11:2; cf. 12:3). Her devotional act of worship coincides with and complements that of her sister Martha. Together these sisters indicate to the audience that Jesus is a worthy object of worship as the "Lord" who not only has the life-giving power to prevent death (11:21, 32) but the divine power to act in a life-giving way in the immediate aftermath surrounding a recent death (11:22).[5]

To Jesus' request that the stone be taken away from the tomb of Lazarus, Martha replied, "Lord, by now there will be an odor, for it is the fourth day" (11:39). Although Martha worshiped Jesus as the one who will give believers divine life eternal on the last day (11:24-27), she did not yet believe that Jesus can restore to life one who has been dead for four days. Her concern with the odor of death accentuates its stark human reality. Jesus said to her, "Did I not tell you that if you believe, you will see the glory of God?" (11:40). He thus promised Martha, who affirmed that she believed in him as the giver of divine life eternal on the last day (11:27), that if she continues to believe, she will see the glory of God now. This recalls Jesus' pronouncement that the illness of Lazarus "is not toward death but for the glory of God, so that the Son of God may be glorified through it" (11:4). That Martha will "see the glory of God" will make her a participant in the prologue's communal act of doxological worship—"we observed his glory, glory as of the unique one from the Father" (1:14).[6]

---

depicted Jesus as the one who can do precisely that, making present in the here-and-now the eschatological events of God's future (e.g., 3.18-21; 5.24-25)" (Lee, "Martha and Mary," 203).

5. On Mary's gestures directed to the feet of Jesus as the posture of worship, see Barker, *King*, 341. "Mary kneels at Jesus' feet (verse 32), suggesting a posture of devotion or worship" (Hylen, *Imperfect Believers*, 82). Martha and Mary "act in counterpart to confess the faith of the believing community. Martha's confession is in *word*, in the 'I believe' of her response to Jesus' self-disclosure, while Mary's is in *deed*, in the anointing of his feet, with all its implications of dedication and love" (Lee, "Martha and Mary," 209-10; emphases original).

6. "Despite recognizing Jesus' true identity in 11:27, she may not have fully understood the significance of Jesus' revelation in 11:25-26 or its realized dimension. She probably believes that Jesus is able to provide resurrection life beyond death, but only then—on the last day. Alternatively, Martha's newfound or deepened belief may have cringed in the face of reality—a body that had been rotting for four days. Whatever causes her to make this remark, Jesus encourages her to continue to believe (11:40)"

Once "they lifted [ἦραν] the stone" from the tomb, Jesus "lifted [ἦρεν] his eyes upward" in a prayer of thanksgiving, "Father, I thank you that you have listened to me" (11:41; cf. 6:11, 23).[7] This reinforces for the audience how Jesus is a true worshiper of God as one who does God's will, so that God "listens" to him (9:31). Jesus' prayer, with its implicit petition for God to restore the life of Lazarus, answered Martha's implicit request for his prayer, when she told him that "even now I know that whatever you ask God, God will give you" (11:22).[8] Jesus continued his prayer: "I myself [ἐγώ] have known that you always listen to me, but on account of the crowd standing around I said this, so that they may believe that you yourself [σύ] sent me" (11:42). Jesus prayed so that the crowd may be among those who "believe" in him to have divine life eternal (3:16), for God "sent" his Son into the world, so that the world may be saved through him (3:17). Jesus thus prayed that the raising of Lazarus would result in believers who share in the divine life eternal he now provides as the one who is "the resurrection and the life" (11:25).[9]

Jesus' dramatic command to "loosen" (λύσατε) Lazarus from the bindings of his burial clothes and thus set him free from the bounds of death after four days (11:44) serves as a counter symbol for Jesus' raising of his own body (2:21) in three days to be the temple for true worship after his command to "destroy" (λύσατε) it (2:19).[10] Jesus' prayer for believers (11:42) was effective, as many of the Jews who had come to Mary and observed the things he did believed in him (11:45). They thus saw the glory of God which Jesus promised Martha that she would see, if she believed (11:40). That they believed as they "observed" (θεασάμενοι) the glory of God in the raising of Lazarus, so that the Son of God may be glorified (11:4), reaffirms for

---

(Bennema, *Encountering Jesus*, 148). "She has not grasped the meaning of the earlier word of revelation (vv. 25–26): that Jesus *is* 'the resurrection and the life,' who will display this truth symbolically by raising her brother from the dead" (Byrne, *Life Abounding*, 197; emphasis original).

7. The prayer of Jesus is thus linked to the raising of Lazarus through the wordplay involving the verb "lift." Jesus "lifted" his eyes in prayer as they "lifted" the stone from the tomb. For more on this deliberate wordplay, see Michaels, *John*, 642.

8. "The opening words of the prayer in v 41b assume that Jesus has already prayed concerning Lazarus and his recall to life" (Beasley-Murray, *John*, 194). "Jesus' thanksgiving at just this moment *is* in effect his petition to the Father" (Michaels, *John*, 643; emphasis original).

9. "In heeding the Son's cry and coming forth, Lazarus anticipates all who will rise at the general resurrection. Alongside this future reference, however, his present coming back to life signifies the power of Jesus to be for believers here and now 'the resurrection and the life' (v. 25)" (Byrne, *Life Abounding*, 198).

10. That these are the only occurrences of this verbal form (λύσατε), with its contrasting meanings, enhances this connection.

the audience the basis of their communal worship of Jesus—"we observed [ἐθεασάμεθα] his glory, glory as of the unique one from the Father" (1:14). "But some of them went to the Pharisees and told them the things Jesus had done" (11:46). This sets an ominous tone, as the Pharisees (7:32, 45) were among those Jews trying to kill Jesus (5:18; 7:1, 19, 25; 8:37, 40).[11]

The High-Priestly Self-Sacrificial Worship of Jesus for the Children of God (11:47-57)

The chief priests and the Pharisees were concerned that if they allowed Jesus to continue to perform signs (11:47), all will believe in him (cf. 7:31; 8:30; 10:42; 11:45), and the Romans will come and "take away" (ἀροῦσιν) both their "place" (τόπον), the temple, and their nation (11:48).[12] But, ironically, Jesus, who ordered the sellers to "take away" (ἄρατε) the animals they were selling for sacrificial worship in the Jerusalem temple (2:16), will replace it with his risen body, the new personified place for true worship (2:21). Indeed, Jesus is the sacrificial Lamb of God who "takes away" (αἴρων) the sin of the world (1:29), thus enabling not only the Jewish nation but all people to engage in true worship. Although salvation is from the Jews (4:22), the "place" (τόπος) where it is necessary to worship (4:20) is not in the Jerusalem temple (4:21). True worshipers will worship the Father in the Spirit and truth that Jesus embodies (4:23-24; cf. 1:14, 17, 32-33), the Jesus who is also an object of worship as truly the savior not only of the Jews but of the whole world (4:42).

Caiaphas, who was high priest that year (11:49), declared that it would be better for them that one man die for the people and the whole nation not perish (11:50). This accords with the sacrificial nature of the Jewish high priesthood. According to Leviticus 16, it was the duty of the high priest to sacrifice one animal in atonement for his own sins and another in atonement for all the sins of the people. This was to occur each year on the day of atonement. That Caiaphas was high priest that "year" (ἐνιαυτοῦ) recalls the high priest's duty to offer the sacrifices of atonement: "This shall be an everlasting statute for you, to make atonement for the people of Israel once in the year [ἐνιαυτοῦ] for all their sins" (LXX Lev 16:34). Caiaphas thus

---

11. "Some report back to the Pharisees what has happened, and it will now become unmistakably clear that the raising of Lazarus precipitates the coming of Jesus' hour, to which the whole action of the plot has been moving" (Lincoln, *John*, 329).

12. "The phrase ὁ τόπος ('the place') refers to the Temple (cf. 4:20; Matt 24:15; Acts 6:13; 21:28), so intimately associated with the existence of Israel as a nation" (Moloney, *John*, 343).

knows the value of sacrificing one animal for the sake of many people and transfers this idea to the sacrifice of the one man Jesus for the benefit of the whole nation.

But, as the good shepherd, Jesus assumes the sacrificial duty of a new and unique kind of high priest who sacrifices himself, the Lamb of God (1:29, 36), for the "sheep" who believe in him: "I am the good shepherd. The good shepherd lays down his life for the sheep" (10:11). When Caiaphas declared that it would be beneficial if one man died for the people (11:50), "he did not say this of himself, but being high priest that year he prophesied that Jesus was going to die for the nation" (11:51). This not only indicates that his statement was not from himself but from God as a prophecy, but it also emphasizes that the one man to die is not Caiaphas himself but Jesus.[13] That Caiaphas did not say this "of himself" (ἀφ' ἑαυτοῦ) contrasts Jesus' emphatic insistence that he will sacrifice himself as the good shepherd: "The Father loves me because I lay down my life in order to take it up again. No one takes it from me, but I lay it down of myself [ἀπ' ἐμαυτοῦ]" (10:17-18). In contrast to Caiaphas, Jesus will perform a unique high priestly act of worship by sacrificing himself as an expiatory victim, the Lamb of God, for his people.

Caiaphas advised that it would be better for them that one man die for the people than that the whole nation perish (11:50), but the universalizing and unifying effects of the sacrificial death of Jesus as the good shepherd-high priest will far surpass this narrow nationalism. Jesus had proclaimed that he has other sheep that do not belong to this fold, that is, all, Jew or Gentile, who are not yet believers. These also he must lead, and they will hear his voice, and there will be "one sheep herd [ποίμνη], one shepherd [ποιμήν]" (10:16).[14] Whereas Caiaphas wants to sacrifice Jesus so that the whole Jewish nation "not perish" (μὴ ἀπόληται), Jesus, by sacrificing himself, will give all his sheep, his believing Jewish and Gentile followers (10:26-27), divine life eternal, and they "shall never perish" (οὐ μὴ ἀπόλωνται) for eternity (10:28). Whereas Caiaphas was high priest for only "that year" (11:49), the effects of the unique high priestly self-sacrificial worship of Jesus last "for eternity."

When Caiaphas unwittingly prophesied that Jesus was going to die not only for the nation but also for gathering into one the dispersed children

---

13. "This means not that he is actually a 'prophet,' but that on one memorable occasion he 'prophesied,' that is, he spoke for God. Although the comment links Caiaphas's ability to prophesy to his being 'Chief Priest of that year,' there is no hard evidence that Jewish priests or high priests necessarily had the gift of prophecy" (Michaels, *John*, 652).

14. Brown's translation (*John*, 387).

of God (11:51-52), he confirmed for the audience the universalizing and unifying effects of the high priestly sacrificial death of Jesus. The "children of God" are all those who receive Jesus and believe in his name (1:12). Their description as "dispersed" assimilates them to the "other sheep," future believers who do not yet belong to the fold, but who will be united into "one sheep herd, one shepherd" (10:16). In contrast to the chief priests and Pharisees, who "gathered" (συνήγαγον) the Sanhedrin to save the Jewish nation from the Gentile Romans (11:47-48), Jesus will die so that he might "gather" (συναγάγῃ) into one believing and worshiping community the dispersed children of God, both Jews and Gentiles (11:52). For anyone who confesses Jesus to be the Christ and then is expelled "from the synagogue" (ἀποσυνάγωγος), a Jewish gathering for worship (9:22), Jesus will provide a new communal and universal gathering for worship.

On the level of Caiaphas's own consciousness as high priest he advised the chief priests and Pharisees, concerned to preserve their Jewish "nation" (11:48), that it would be better for them that one man die for the Jewish people as the chosen "people" of God than that the whole "nation," the Jewish people as a political entity, perish (11:50). But on an ironic deeper level for the audience, the level of the self-sacrifice of Jesus as the unique high priest, Caiaphas unconsciously advised that one man die for the "people" as the new community of believers and true worshipers composed of Jews and Gentiles. The whole "nation" will not perish, because believing Jews will now be part of the universal people of God. Jesus' dying "for" (ὑπέρ) the people parallels his laying down his life "for" (ὑπέρ) the sheep (10:11, 15), that is, those who believe in him (10:26-27). Caiaphas prophesied that Jesus was going to die not only for the Jewish nation but also to gather into one the dispersed children of God (11:51-52), including the audience as those who are to compose a new unified community of true worshipers.[15]

The Passover of the Jews was near (cf. 2:13; 6:4), when many went up to Jerusalem from the country before the Passover, so that they might "purify" (ἁγνίσωσιν) or make themselves holy in order to engage properly in the worship of the Passover feast (11:55).[16] But in ironic contrast, Jesus declared that the Father "consecrated" (ἡγίασεν) or made him holy (10:36), so that he is worthy to be an object of worship as the "Holy One" (ἅγιος) of God (6:69), who has the words of divine life eternal (6:68). In the Jerusalem temple they

---

15. Heil, "Unique High Priest," 731-35. On the irony, see Duke, *Irony*, 88.

16. "Self-purification in order to celebrate the Passover was mandated in Scripture (see Num 9:6-12; 2 Chr 30:17-18)" (Michaels, *John*, 661). "Ironically, the purification they are seeking belongs to the past. It will be replaced by the more efficacious purification that Jesus will effect by dying at Passover as the Lamb of God" (Byrne, *Life Abounding*, 201).

were wondering if Jesus would come to the feast (11:56). Whereas the chief priests and Pharisees, determined to kill him (11:53), had given "commandments" (ἐντολάς) that he should be identified and arrested (11:57), Jesus received the "commandment" (ἐντολήν) from his Father to lay down his life in an act of high priestly sacrificial worship and take it up again (10:18). Jesus replaced the sacrificial worship in the temple (2:14-22) as the new sacrificial Passover Lamb of God who takes away the sin of the world (1:29), thus purifying believers, making them holy for true worship.[17]

The Anointing of Jesus at Bethany as an Act of Worship (12:1-11)

After three notices that the Passover was vaguely "near" (2:13; 6:4; 11:55), it was now precisely very near. Indeed, only six days before Passover Jesus came to Bethany, where Lazarus was, whom Jesus had "raised" from the dead (12:1).[18] This recalls and reinforces for the audience Jesus' ability to "raise" the destroyed temple (2:19) of his body (2:21) to become the new personified temple for true worship. They made for him a "dinner" there (12:2), suggestive of a festive banquet in celebration of Jesus' raising of Lazarus.[19] In what can be understood as a celebratory response to her seeing the life-giving glory of God (11:40) in the raising of Lazarus, Martha was serving (12:2). That Lazarus was one of those "reclining" with him (12:2) associates him with those "reclining" at the previous festive meal, those to whom Jesus gave bread (6:11) as a sign that the living bread of divine life eternal for the world that he will give is his sacrificial flesh (6:51) as the Passover Lamb of God (1:29, 36).[20] Lazarus thus represents those who will be given divine life eternal as a result of the self-sacrificial death of Jesus.[21]

17. "Through his unique sacrificial death Christ has not only made the normal sacrifices of the temple cult unnecessary, but he has also exposed their real meaning. The same holds of the purity he gives his own: it is more than ritual purity" ("ἁγνός," *NIDNTTE* 1.138).

18. "The time reference 'six days before the Passover' (cf. 11:55) significantly places Jesus' ensuing passion within the context of that important festival, which may intend to remind the reader that Jesus is the paradigmatic sacrificial lamb" (Köstenberger, *John*, 359).

19. The term for "dinner" (δεῖπνον) here generally refers to "an elaborate dinner celebration" (BDAG, 215). "The 'dinner' may have been arranged to welcome Jesus back from his sojourn and celebrate with him the raising of Lazarus" (Michaels, *John*, 664).

20. "Festive meals were held in the evening and were eaten in a reclining position" (Wanke, "δεῖπνον," 281).

21. The presence of Lazarus as one of those reclining at the dinner for Jesus is to "underline the role of Lazarus as representative of all for whom Jesus is going to die"

Mary previously "fell at the feet" of Jesus in an act of devotional, supplicatory worship and declared, "Lord, if you had been here, my brother would not have died" (11:32), thus acknowledging Jesus' power to prevent death. In what can be understood as a celebratory response to Jesus' restoration of the life of Lazarus as a sign that he can give divine life eternal, Mary complemented her previous gesture of worship, as she anointed "the feet of Jesus" with very precious ointment and dried "his feet" with her hair (12:3; cf. 11:2). In contrast to the concern that "by now there will be an odor [ὄζει]" of death when the tomb of Lazarus was opened (11:39), "the house was filled with the fragrance [ὀσμῆς] of the ointment" (12:3) in symbolic correspondence to resurrection from death and Jesus' ability to give divine life eternal.[22] Mary thus anointed the body of Jesus (2:21), the personified temple that will be destroyed, but that Jesus will raise (2:19) in and through his act of worship in sacrificing himself as the Passover Lamb of God (1:29, 36), to be the new temple for true worship.[23]

Judas the Iscariot, who was going to "betray" or "give over [παραδιδόναι]" (12:4; cf. 6:64, 71) Jesus to death to be the good shepherd who lays down his life as the sacrificial Passover Lamb of God, objected that the ointment could have been sold and the money given to the poor (12:5). That he said this not because he "cared for" the poor (12:6) characterizes him as a hired man who, in contrast to the good shepherd, does not "care for" the sheep (10:13). That he was a "thief" who stole money (12:6) recalls Jesus' statement that "a thief comes only to steal and slaughter and destroy; I myself came so that they may have life and have it abundantly" (10:10). Jesus then indicated that Mary recognized the uniqueness of this occasion (12:8), as he declared that she kept the ointment for the day of his burial preparation (12:7).[24] This confirms that she, as an act of devotional, celebratory

---

(Byrne, *Life Abounding*, 202).

22. "The stench of death has now given way to the 'fragrance' of eternal life" (Michaels, *John*, 666). "But the Johannine Jesus, in summoning Lazarus from the tomb demonstrates that he alone can eliminate the obscene odor of death and decay. By contrast, the home of the Bethany family is flooded with the scent of life in Mary's anointing.... The Johannine Jesus explicitly connects this profligate fragrance to his own death and burial (12:7) and, by implication, his resurrection, to which the raising of Lazarus symbolically points" (Lee, "Five Senses," 124–25). See also Giblin, "Mary's Anointing," 560–64.

23. "Six days before the final solemn Passover, when the Temple of Jesus's body will be destroyed and a new Temple raised up, Mary anoints Jesus' feet in preparation for this final transcending moment" (Coloe, "Anointing," 117). "Her caressing of Jesus' feet is the ritual adoration directed to the one who, in the Johannine view, replaces the temple as the locus of true worship (2:13–22; 4:19–26)" (Lee, *Flesh and Glory*, 210).

24. For ἐνταφιασμοῦ in 12:7 as "preparation for burial," see BDAG, 339.

worship, anointed his body (2:21) in preparation for its destruction as the temple which he will raise (2:19) to be the new temple for true worship.[25]

A large crowd of the Jews learned that Jesus was there and came not only because of Jesus, but that they might also see Lazarus whom he had raised from the dead (12:9). Lazarus is thus further associated with Jesus as the one who can not only raise from the dead but give divine life eternal. This reaffirms for the audience that Lazarus represents all those believers who will be given divine life eternal as a result of the self-sacrificial death of Jesus as the Passover Lamb of God.[26] On account of Lazarus many of the Jews were going away and believing in Jesus (12:11). Consequently, the chief priests "resolved" to kill Lazarus also (12:10), just as they had "resolved" to kill Jesus (11:53). They are determined to kill both Jesus and Lazarus whom he raised as a sign that he will raise his own body to be the personified new temple for the true worship of God (2:19-21) for divine life eternal.

The Worship of Jesus as the King of Israel as He Entered Jerusalem (12:12-16)

The next day, and thus five days before Passover (cf. 12:1), the large crowd (12:9) that had come to the feast heard that Jesus was coming to Jerusalem (12:12). In celebration of his coming, they took festive branches of palm trees and went out to meet him (12:13).[27] Jesus had raised Lazarus so that the crowd might believe that God sent Jesus (11:42) and thus that they might see the life-giving glory of God (11:40). When in the presence of the crowd he commanded Lazarus to come out of the tomb, Jesus "cried out [ἐκραύγασεν]" (11:43). In appropriate correspondence the crowd with the palm branches "cried out" (ἐκραύγαζον) with an act of celebratory worship: "Hosanna! Blessed is the one coming in the name of the Lord [LXX Ps 117:25], the King of Israel!" (12:13).[28] In contrast to the crowd (6:2, 5) who were going to seize Jesus and make him "king" (6:15), this crowd praised

---

25. "With this act of devotion, Mary . . . recognizes that in raising Lazarus Jesus has been willing to go to his own death and that therefore the day for his burial preparation has already arrived" (Lincoln, *John*, 339). See also Lee, *Flesh and Glory*, 197–211.

26. "As the first beneficiary of Jesus' costly death, Lazarus is . . . once more standing in for all who receive the gift of life from Jesus" (Byrne, *Life Abounding*, 202).

27. "Since the regaining of Jerusalem and the rededication of the temple at the time of the Maccabees, the palm had been associated with national liberation and functioned as a symbol for Israel. Here too the palm branches serve a similar purpose for the crowd, who treat Jesus as a national hero" (Lincoln, *John*, 343).

28. "The Hebrew expression 'Hosanna,' or 'Save now' . . . has become here an expression of praise to God" (Michaels, *John*, 676). See also BDAG, 1106.

God and worshiped Jesus as the "King of Israel," reaffirming Nathanael's confessional worship of Jesus: "You are the King of Israel!" (1:49).

Jesus implicitly acknowledged their worship of him as the King of Israel, but he clarified the nature of his kingship. He found a young donkey and sat upon it in accord with God's scriptural plan (12:14): "Do not fear, daughter Zion. Behold, your king is coming, sitting upon the colt of a donkey [cf. LXX Zech 9:9; LXX Zeph 3:14-15]" (12:15). Jesus is coming into Jerusalem not as a military warrior king mounted on a warhorse but, in accord with the scriptural citation, in the humility of "sitting" (καθήμενος) upon the colt of a donkey, recalling the lowliness of the man born blind, who was "sitting" (καθήμενος) and begging (9:8).[29]

The disciples of Jesus "remembered" the Scripture that "zeal for your house will consume me [cf. LXX Ps 68:10]" (2:17), indicating that Jesus would be killed for restoring the house of his Father as a place for true worship (2:14-16). After Jesus was raised from the dead, his disciples "remembered" that he had said that he would raise his dead body (2:21) to be the new personified temple (2:19) for true worship. Similarly, the disciples did not understand Jesus' triumphal entry into Jerusalem at first, but when he was "glorified," that is, lifted up/exalted in crucifixion (3:14; 8:28), they "remembered" that these things were written about him and that they did these things for him (12:16).[30] These "remembrances" provide the audience with complementary "commemorations" for worship. In their communal worship they may commemorate that Jesus is not only the personified temple for true worship but worthy to be worshiped as the King of Israel (1:49; 12:13), because he was glorified by God to be an object of worship as the King who gave his life in an act of self-sacrificial worship for divine life eternal.

---

29. "The fulfillment of this prophecy confirms that Jesus is a king . . . but a king, the nature of whose rule differs sharply from that of contemporary rulers who rule by fear and impressive display of power" (Byrne, *Life Abounding*, 208). "Here the Jerusalem crowd's acclamation is put in the appropriate perspective by the portrayal of Jesus seated on the donkey's colt rather than leading armed resistance on a warhorse" (Lincoln, *John*, 347).

30. "Experience of his glorification led them to 'remember' this gesture and see it as the fulfillment of the text from Zechariah. They could then understand it as a corrective to the messianic reception he was receiving from the crowd, a revelation of the true nature of God's rulership in Israel" (Byrne, *Life Abounding*, 209).

The Worship by the Greeks and the Hour for the Son of Man to be Glorified (12:17-36)

The crowd who went out to meet Jesus and worship him (12:13) did so because they heard the testimony of the crowd (12:18) who was with Jesus when he called Lazarus from the tomb and raised him from the dead (12:17). The alarmed Pharisees then declared to one another that "the world has gone [ἀπῆλθεν] after [ὀπίσω] him" (12:19). But this exaggeration stands in ironic contrast to the fact that many of his disciples "went away" (ἀπῆλθον) to what lay "behind" (ὀπίσω) them and no longer walked with him (6:66). Indeed, the "world" hates Jesus (7:7) and the "world" did not know him (1:10). Nevertheless, God did not send him into the "world" so that he might condemn the "world," but so that the "world" might be saved through him (3:17). Jesus is thus a worthy object of worship as the savior of the "world" (4:42).[31]

In ironic contrast to the speculation that Jesus might be going to the diaspora among the Greeks to teach the Greeks (7:35), among those going up to Jerusalem so that they might "worship" (προσκυνήσωσιν) at the feast (12:20) were some Greeks, who wanted to "see" (ἰδεῖν) Jesus (12:21). This implies that they wanted to see him in order to worship him, as it recalls that when Jesus told the man he healed of his blindness that "you have seen" (ἑώρακας) the Son of Man (9:35) in Jesus (9:37), he "worshiped" (προσεκύνησεν) him (9:38). It also accords with Jesus' pronouncement that the hour is coming when "you will worship" (προσκυνήσετε) not in Jerusalem (4:21) but in the Spirit and truth that Jesus embodies (4:23-24). When Philip and Andrew, two disciples with Greek names, informed Jesus that the Greeks wanted to see him (12:22), he declared that the hour has come for the Son of Man to be "glorified" (12:23), and thus given the glory by God that makes him a worthy object of worship not only by the Greeks but by all in the audience.[32]

Jesus' solemn pronouncement that unless a grain of wheat falls into the ground and dies, it remains alone, but if it dies, it produces much "fruit"

---

31. "As the arrival of 'the Greeks' in the very next scene will show, Jesus is indeed beginning to draw people to himself as 'Savior of the world' (3:16-17; 4:42)" (Byrne, *Life Abounding*, 210).

32. "While these 'Greeks' have come up to worship in the temple along with the mass of other Passover pilgrims, their interest in Jesus marks them out as forerunners of all from the Gentile world who, after his death and resurrection, will come to 'worship' not in the Jerusalem temple but in the One (Jesus) who replaces that temple as the locus of God's presence on earth. Their worship will be that 'worship in sprit and truth' about which Jesus spoke to the Samaritan woman (4:20-24)" (Byrne, *Life Abounding*, 211-12).

(12:24) refers to how the death of Jesus will produce much "fruit" by bringing people to believe in order to have divine life eternal. It recalls and resonates with Jesus' declaration that the Samaritans who are coming to believe in him (4:39–42) indicate that the divine reaper is gathering "fruit" for life eternal (4:36).[33] As the good shepherd who lays down his "life" (ψυχήν) for the sheep (10:11), all those who believe in him, so that they may have life eternal (10:10), Jesus serves as the model for his declaration that the one loving his "life" (ψυχήν) destroys it, and the one hating his "life" (ψυχήν) in this world guards it for life eternal (12:25). If anyone would serve Jesus, he is to follow him, and where he is his servant will be. If anyone would serve Jesus by following his example of laying down his life as an act of self-sacrificial worship, the Father will honor him with the gift of divine life eternal (12:26).

After stating that he was now deeply troubled, Jesus queried whether he should pray for the Father to save him from this hour. But he decided against it, since it was to be glorified (12:23) that he came to this hour (12:27). Accordingly, he prayed, "Father, glorify your name." Then in answer to his prayer a voice came from heaven, "I have glorified and I will again glorify" (12:28). In glorifying his own name the Father at the same time glorifies Jesus, who came in the name of his Father to do the works he does (5:43; 10:25). In the raising of Lazarus from the dead the Father "has glorified" both himself and Jesus, since the illness of Lazarus was not unto death but "for the glory of God, so that the Son of God might be glorified through it" (11:4; cf. 11:40). And he "will again glorify" his name and Jesus when Jesus is lifted up/exalted through his crucifixion (3:14; 8:28).[34] That the crowd thought the voice from heaven was theophanic thunder but others that of an angel (12:29) confirms that the prayer of Jesus received a divine answer.[35]

But Jesus told them that the divine answer to his prayer was not for his sake but for theirs (12:30). He declared that "when I am lifted up/exalted

---

33. "Jesus' death has just been implied through the notion of glorification. Like the martyr's death but on a greater scale it will produce 'much fruit'—a worldwide community participating in the salvation and life it achieves" (Lincoln, *John*, 349).

34. "Aside from God's (presumably private) words to John (1:33), it is the *only* time God speaks in the entire Gospel. On the assumption that the glorification of God's name is the same as the glorification of Jesus himself, 'the Son of man' (v. 23), it appears that the promise, 'I will glorify again,' refers to Jesus' 'hour' now at hand" (Michaels, *John*, 694; emphasis original).

35. "In the biblical tradition thunder is a widespread signal of the presence of God, and angels regularly feature as instruments of divine communication. Both interpretations on the part of the crowd could signal an awareness that a theophany had taken place, that they were hearing some divine ratification of Jesus' prayer, albeit without full understanding" (Byrne, *Life Abounding*, 215–16).

[ὑψωθῶ], I will draw all to myself" (12:32; cf. 3:14; 8:28) to be both the personified place (1:14, 51; 2:19, 21) and object of worship through his self-sacrificial death on the cross (12:33). Jesus thus likened himself to the house/temple of God that in the last days "will be lifted up/exalted" (ὑψωθήσεται) and all nations shall come to it (LXX Isa 2:2).[36] That "I will draw [ἑλκύσω] all to myself" complements how it is the Father who "draws" (ἑλκύσῃ) people to come to Jesus that he may raise them to divine life eternal on the last day (6:44).[37] The crowd questioned the identity of the Son of Man who is to be "lifted up/exalted" (12:34), and thus "glorified" (12:23) to be the place and object of worship. This recalls that after Jesus identified himself as the Son of Man to the man he healed of his blindness (9:35-37), the man believed and worshiped him (9:38).

Jesus then appealed for this questioning crowd to believe in and thus worship him as the Son of Man who is the light of life eternal (1:3-4), that they may become sons of light (12:36). This recalls and resonates with becoming children of God and thus sharing in divine life eternal through believing in the name of Jesus (1:12). As the Son of Man to be "lifted up/exalted" (3:14; 8:28; 12:32, 34) and thus "glorified" (12:23) through his act of self-sacrificial worship, his death on the cross, Jesus becomes both the personified place and object of true worship for divine life eternal.

The Worship of Jesus as the One to Save the World for Divine Life Eternal (12:37-50)

Despite the many signs Jesus did, many did not believe (12:37) in fulfillment of God's will as spoken by the prophet Isaiah (12:38; cf. LXX Isa 53:1). They could not believe because again Isaiah said (12:39), "He blinded their eyes and hardened their heart, so that they might not see with their eyes and understand with their heart and turn, and I will heal them" (12:40; cf. LXX Isa 6:10). This implies that there is still hope that they will see with their

36. "The 'lifting up' of Jesus in death (12:33) fulfills the prophecy that the eschatological Temple would be lifted up and be a source of in-gathering for the nations (Isa 2:2-3)" (Coloe, *God Dwells*, 177). "The lifting up of the Temple in the last days exalts it above all other temples (Isa 2:2). This demonstrates the unworthiness of all competing temples. Likewise, the lifting up of Jesus exalts him above all other temples, including the Jerusalem Temple. He therefore replaces the Jerusalem Temple as the proper locus for true worship (John 4:21, Isa 66:23). As such, he becomes the place where the nations come to be instructed in the way of the Lord (Isa 2:3). As a result, they can worship 'in truth' (John 4:22-24)" (Hoskins, *Temple*, 157).

37. "Jesus has been lifted up on the cross and to glory, back to the Father's presence, where he was before (6:62). He draws men and women into that communion with the Father that he himself enjoys" (Morgan-Wynne, *Cross*, 155).

"eyes" and believe if they "turn," that is, repent and convert. Indeed, as he illustrated with the man born blind, Jesus has the divine power to heal their eyes, so that they might believe and worship him (9:1-41). As he stated, "For judgment I came into the world, so that those not seeing may see and those seeing may become blind" (9:39). And that "I will heal them" recalls that Jesus has the divine life-giving power to heal (4:47), which indicates his power to give divine life eternal.[38]

Isaiah said this because he saw beforehand the life-giving divine "glory" of Jesus (12:41; cf. LXX Isa 6:3).[39] Nevertheless, many did believe in him, but they did not "confess," that is, publicly worship him, so that they would not be put out of the synagogue, the Jewish gathering for worship (12:42; cf. 9:22). They were thus unwilling to abandon one of their customary places of worship for a worship focused upon Jesus, the new temple for true worship (2:19-21). Jesus will give his life in self-sacrificial worship as the unique high priest (11:51) to "gather" the dispersed children of God into one (11:52) to be a unified community of true worship. Those who believed but did not worship Jesus loved the "glory of human beings," which amounts to false worship, rather than the "glory of God" (12:43), the "glory of God" that believers are to see in the raising of Lazarus back to life (11:40). His illness was not unto death but for the "glory of God," so that the Son of God, Jesus, might be "glorified" through it (11:4), and thus become an object of true worship for divine life eternal.[40]

The one who sees, believes, and thus worships Jesus (cf. 9:35-38), sees, believes, and thus worships the Father who sent him (12:44-45). Jesus has come into the world as the light (12:46; cf. 1:9) of divine life eternal (1:3-5), so that he might save the world (12:47; cf. 3:17). The Father has given Jesus a "commandment" (ἐντολήν) regarding what he should say and what he should speak (12:49). Jesus knows that his Father's "commandment" (ἐντολή) is life eternal and this is what he reveals to believers from his Father (12:50). This recalls and resonates with the "commandment" (ἐντολήν) which Jesus received from his Father that he has the divine authority to lay down his life in an act of self-sacrificial worship and take it up again (10:18),

---

38. "For the evangelist, the invitation is still to be extended to those in the darkness of blindness to believe and be healed (cf. also v. 46)" (Lincoln, *John*, 358).

39. "The allusion would seem to be to the prophet's vision of divine glory as described earlier in Isaiah 6 (vv. 1-5): since Christ as preexistent Logos shared the glory of God (1:1, 14; 17:5), all visions of God's glory were also visions of the glory of Christ" (Byrne, *Life Abounding*, 219).

40. "While it is true that 'whoever believes has eternal life,' there is no genuine belief without public confession—and perhaps by implication, Christian baptism" (Michaels, *John*, 713).

so that those who believe and worship both him and the Father who sent him may have divine life eternal (10:10-11, 15).[41]

Summary on 11:1—12:50

To Jesus' request that the stone be taken away from the tomb of Lazarus, Martha replied, "Lord, by now there will be an odor, for it is the fourth day" (11:39). Although Martha worshiped Jesus as the one who will give believers divine life eternal on the last day (11:24-27), she did not yet believe that Jesus can restore to life one who has been dead for four days. Her concern with the odor of death accentuates its stark human reality. Jesus said to her, "Did I not tell you that if you believe, you will see the glory of God?" (11:40). He thus promised Martha, who affirmed that she believed in him as the giver of divine life eternal on the last day (11:27), that if she continues to believe, she will see the glory of God now. This recalls Jesus' pronouncement that the illness of Lazarus "is not toward death but for the glory of God, so that the Son of God may be glorified through it" (11:4). That Martha will "see the glory of God" will make her a participant in the prologue's communal act of doxological worship—"we observed his glory, glory as of the unique one from the Father" (1:14).

Once "they lifted the stone" from the tomb, Jesus "lifted his eyes upward" in a prayer of thanksgiving, "Father, I thank you that you have listened to me" (11:41; cf. 6:11, 23). This reinforces for the audience how Jesus is a true worshiper of God as one who does God's will, so that God "listens" to him (9:31). Jesus' prayer, with its implicit petition for God to restore the life of Lazarus, answered Martha's implicit request for his prayer, when she told him that "even now I know that whatever you ask God, God will give you" (11:22). Jesus continued his prayer: "I myself have known that you always listen to me, but on account of the crowd standing around I said this, so that they may believe that you yourself sent me" (11:42). Jesus prayed so that the crowd may be among those who "believe" in him to have divine life eternal (3:16), for God "sent" his Son into the world, so that the world may be saved through him (3:17). Jesus thus prayed that the raising of Lazarus would result in believers who share in the divine life eternal he now provides as "the resurrection and the life" (11:25).

When the high priest Caiaphas unwittingly prophesied that Jesus was going to die not only for the nation but also for gathering into one the

---

41. "The Father's 'command' from the start pointed Jesus first toward death ('I lay down my life'), but then toward life ('that I might receive it back again,' 10:17)" (Michaels, *John*, 717).

dispersed children of God (11:51–52), he confirmed for the audience the universalizing and unifying effects of the high priestly sacrificial death of Jesus. The "children of God" are all those who receive Jesus and believe in his name (1:12). Their description as "dispersed" assimilates them to the "other sheep," future believers who do not yet belong to the fold, but who will be united into "one sheep herd, one shepherd" (10:16). In contrast to the chief priests and Pharisees, who "gathered" the Sanhedrin to save the Jewish nation from the Gentile Romans (11:47–48), Jesus will die so that he might "gather" into one believing and worshiping community the dispersed children of God, both Jews and Gentiles (11:52). For anyone who confesses Jesus to be the Christ and then is expelled "from the synagogue," a Jewish gathering for worship (9:22), Jesus will provide a new communal gathering for worship.

On the level of Caiaphas's own consciousness as high priest he advised the chief priests and Pharisees, concerned to preserve their Jewish "nation" (11:48), that it would be better for them that one man die for the Jewish people as the chosen "people" of God than that the whole "nation," the Jewish people as a political entity, perish (11:50). But on an ironic deeper level for the audience, the level of the self-sacrifice of Jesus as the unique high priest, Caiaphas unconsciously advised that one man die for the "people" as the new community of believers and true worshipers composed of Jews and Gentiles. The whole "nation" will not perish, because believing Jews will now be part of the universal people of God. Jesus' dying "for" the people parallels his laying down his life "for" the sheep (10:11, 15), that is, those who believe in him (10:26–27). Caiaphas prophesied that Jesus was going to die not only for the Jewish nation but also to gather into one the dispersed children of God (11:51–52), including the audience as those who are to compose a new unified community of true worshipers.

The Passover of the Jews was near (cf. 2:13; 6:4), when many went up to Jerusalem from the country before the Passover, so that they might "purify" or make themselves holy in order to engage properly in the worship of the Passover feast (11:55). But in ironic contrast, Jesus declared that the Father "consecrated" or made him holy (10:36), so that he is worthy to be an object of worship as the "Holy One" of God (6:69), who has the words of divine life eternal (6:68). In the Jerusalem temple they were wondering if Jesus would come to the feast (11:56). Whereas the chief priests and Pharisees, determined to kill him (11:53), had given "commandments" that he should be identified and arrested (11:57), Jesus received the "commandment" from his Father to lay down his life in an act of high priestly sacrificial worship and take it up again (10:18). Jesus replaced the sacrificial worship in the temple (2:14–22) as the new sacrificial Passover Lamb of God who takes away the sin of the world (1:29), thus purifying believers, making them holy for true worship.

Mary had previously "fell at the feet" of Jesus in an act of devotional, supplicatory worship and declared, "Lord, if you had been here, my brother would not have died" (11:32), thus acknowledging Jesus' power to prevent death. It what can be understood as a celebratory response to Jesus' restoration of the life of Lazarus as a sign that he can give divine life eternal, Mary complemented her previous gesture of worship, as she anointed "the feet of Jesus" with very precious ointment and dried "his feet" with her hair (12:3; cf. 11:2). In contrast to the concern that "by now there will be an odor" of death when the tomb of Lazarus was opened (11:39), "the house was filled with the fragrance of the ointment" (12:3) in symbolic correspondence to resurrection from death and Jesus' ability to give divine life eternal. Mary thus anointed the body of Jesus (2:21), the personified temple that will be destroyed, but that Jesus will raise (2:19) in and through his act of worship in sacrificing himself as the Passover Lamb of God (1:29, 36), to be the new temple for true worship.

The disciples of Jesus "remembered" the Scripture that "zeal for your house will consume me [cf. LXX Ps 68:10]" (2:17), indicating that Jesus would be killed for restoring the house of his Father as a place for true worship (2:14–16). After Jesus was raised from the dead, his disciples "remembered" that he had said that he would raise his dead body (2:21) to be the new personified temple (2:19) for true worship. Similarly, the disciples did not understand Jesus' triumphal entry into Jerusalem at first, but when he was "glorified," that is, lifted up/exalted in crucifixion (3:14; 8:28), they "remembered" that these things were written about him and that they did these things for him (12:16). These "remembrances" provide the audience with complementary "commemorations" for worship. In their communal worship they may commemorate that Jesus is not only the personified temple for true worship but worthy to be worshiped as the King of Israel (1:49; 12:13), because he was glorified by God to be an object of worship as the King who gave his life in an act of self-sacrificial worship for divine life eternal.

In ironic contrast to the speculation that Jesus might be going to the diaspora among the Greeks to teach the Greeks (7:35), among those going up to Jerusalem so that they might "worship" at the feast (12:20) were some Greeks, who wanted to "see" Jesus (12:21). This implies that they wanted to see him in order to worship him, as it recalls that when Jesus told the man he healed of his blindness that "you have seen" the Son of Man (9:35) in Jesus (9:37), he "worshiped" him (9:38). It also accords with Jesus' pronouncement that the hour is coming when "you will worship" not in

Jerusalem (4:21) but in the Spirit and truth that Jesus embodies (4:23-24). When Philip and Andrew, two disciples with Greek names, informed Jesus that the Greeks wanted to see him (12:22), he declared that the hour has come for the Son of Man to be "glorified" (12:23), and thus given the glory by God that makes him a worthy object of worship not only by the Greeks but by all in the audience.

Jesus declared that "when I am lifted up/exalted, I will draw all to myself" (12:32; cf. 3:14; 8:28) to be both the personified place (1:14, 51; 2:19, 21) and object of worship through his self-sacrificial death on the cross (12:33). Jesus thus likened himself to the house/temple of God that in the last days "will be lifted up/exalted" and all nations shall come to it (LXX Isa 2:2). That "I will draw all to myself" complements how it is the Father who "draws" people to come to Jesus that he may raise them to divine life eternal on the last day (6:44). As the Son of Man to be "lifted up/exalted" (3:14; 8:28; 12:32, 34) and thus "glorified" (12:23) through his act of self-sacrificial worship, his death on the cross, Jesus becomes both the personified place and object of true worship for divine life eternal.

Many did believe in Jesus, but they did not "confess," that is, publicly worship him, so that they would not be put out of the synagogue, the Jewish gathering for worship (12:42; cf. 9:22). They were thus unwilling to abandon one of their customary places of worship for a worship focused upon Jesus, the new temple for true worship (2:19-21). Jesus will give his life in self-sacrificial worship as the unique high priest (11:51) to "gather" the dispersed children of God into one (11:52) to be a unified community of true worship. Those who believed but did not worship Jesus loved the "glory of human beings," which amounts to false worship, rather than the "glory of God" (12:43), the "glory of God" that believers are to see in the raising of Lazarus back to life (11:40). His illness was not unto death but for the "glory of God," so that the Son of God, Jesus, might be "glorified" through it (11:4), and thus become an object of true worship for divine life eternal.

The one who sees, believes, and thus worships Jesus (cf. 9:35-38), sees, believes, and thus worships the Father who sent him (12:44-45). Jesus has come into the world as the light (12:46; cf. 1:9) of divine life eternal (1:3-5), so that he might save the world (12:47). The Father has given Jesus a "commandment" regarding what he should say and what he should speak (12:49). Jesus knows that his Father's "commandment" is life eternal and this is what he reveals to believers from his Father (12:50). This recalls and resonates with the "commandment" which Jesus received from his Father that he has the divine authority to lay down his life in an act of self-sacrificial worship and take it up again (10:18), so that those who believe and worship both him and the Father who sent him may have divine life eternal (10:10-11, 15).

7

Jesus' Farewell Teaching about the Worship for Divine Life Eternal (13:1—17:26)

At Meal before Passover Jesus Washed Disciples' Feet and Predicted Betrayal (13:1-38)

Whereas a previous dinner given for Jesus took place six days before Passover (12:1), the feast of the Passover was drawing even closer (cf. 12:12) when Jesus participated in another dinner (13:2) "before the feast of the Passover" (13:1). Jesus knew that "the hour," which previously had not yet come (2:4; 7:30; 8:20), had now come (cf. 12:23, 27) for him to pass from this world back to the Father (cf. 1:1-18). He loved "his own" in the world "to the end," that is, to the end of his life as well as to the uttermost.[1] This reminds the audience that, as the good shepherd, Jesus will lay down his life in love for "his own" sheep (10:3-4, 11-12, 15), an act of self-sacrificial worship that will establish him as *the* Passover Lamb of God (1:29, 36), and thus also as an object of worship.[2] Although the devil had put into the heart of Judas that he should "betray" or "give over [παραδοῖ]" (13:2; cf. 6:64, 71;

---

1. "Jesus loves 'his own' in the world 'to the end' (εἰς τέλος) both in the qualitative sense of having loved them to the uttermost and also in the sense of loving them to the 'end' of his life" (Byrne, *Life Abounding*, 228). See also Moloney, *Love*, 105.

2. "Jesus' love for his disciples ('the Twelve' in particular) has been expressed in the first half of the Gospel in his choice of them as 'his own,' signaled metaphorically by the image of 'the shepherd of the sheep' summoning 'his own sheep' by name and leading them out of the courtyard (10:3). The expressions 'his own sheep' and 'all his own' (10:4) in that passage, and 'his own' in the present one, stand in apparent contrast to the principle stated in the beginning that Jesus 'came to what was his own, and his own did not receive him' (1:11). Yet that negative verdict, as we have seen, was immediately qualified by the notice that some of 'his own' *did* in fact 'receive him' (1:12)" (Michaels, *John*, 721; emphasis original).

12:4) Jesus as a sacrificial victim (cf. 11:50-52), Jesus knew that the Father "had given" (ἔδωκεν) all things into his hands, as the one who had come out from God and was going back to be again "with God" (13:3; cf. 1:1-2).

Jesus rose from the dinner and "laid down" (τίθησιν) his outer garments, and "taking up" (λαβών) a towel, he girded himself (13:4). This action symbolizes the self-sacrificial death and resurrection of Jesus, the good shepherd, who declared: "This is why the Father loves me, because I myself lay down [τίθημι] my life, so that I may take it up [λάβω] again. No one takes it from me, but I myself lay it down [τίθημι] on my own. I have authority to lay it down [θεῖναι], and I have authority to take it up [λαβεῖν] again" (10:17-18).[3] This prepares the audience to understand that what Jesus is about to do indicates that his self-sacrificial death is an act of supreme love, love to the uttermost (13:1), for his own.

Jesus then put "water" in the washbasin and began to "wash" the feet of the disciples and dry them with the towel (13:5). This adds another aspect to the Gospel's theme of sacramental worship with regard to baptism. Not only must one be born from above/again from "water" and the Spirit in the sacrament of baptism to see and enter the Kingdom of God (3:3-5), but once one has "washed" one is able to see and worship Jesus, as exemplified by the man born blind. After he "washed" in the pool of Siloam (9:7, 11, 15), which alludes to the sacrament of baptism, he was able to see and worship Jesus (9:35-38). By "washing" the feet of the disciples with "water," Jesus further developed the baptismal significance of being born from above/again from "water" and the Spirit. He performed a ritual act of loving hospitality that symbolically welcomed them into the "house," the communal household, of his Father (2:16-17), so that they may worship in Spirit and truth (4:23-24) in the new "temple" that he will establish when he raises his destroyed body from the dead (2:19-21).[4]

When Mary anointed the "feet" of Jesus and "dried" his "feet" with her hair (12:3; cf. 11:2) as a preparation for his burial (12:7), the house was filled with the fragrance of the ointment (12:3), symbolically indicative of his resurrection, in contrast to the concern about the odor of death at the raising of Lazarus (11:39). In a complementary contrast to Mary's ritual

---

3. "Already there are hints that this act symbolizes Jesus' coming death" (Lincoln, *John*, 367). See also Coloe, *Household of God*, 131; Moloney, *John*, 378; Michaels, *John*, 724-25.

4. "Culturally, and within the Jewish religious traditions about Abraham, there is evidence to suggest that a first-century community would understand the Johannine footwashing primarily as a gesture of hospitality and welcome. Footwashing also had a cultic purpose, for it was necessary to wash one's feet before entering the precincts of the Temple" (Coloe, *Household of God*, 133). See also Coloe, "Welcome," 400-15; Thomas, *Footwashing*, 29-60.

anointing of his feet and drying them, Jesus began to ritually wash the "feet" of his disciples and "dry" them (13:5). The Jesus who was honored with an act of reverential worship in preparation for his death performed a very humiliating act of hospitable service indicative of the act of worship he would perform by the self-sacrifice of his life as the Passover Lamb before being raised from the dead. His rather humiliating and unusual act of hospitable, loving service for his disciples thus underscored how he loved his own in the world to the end of his life as well as to the uttermost (13:1).[5]

Peter objected to Jesus washing his feet (13:6-7) and said to him, "You will never wash my feet for eternity [εἰς τὸν αἰῶνα]" (13:8). Ironically, Peter unwittingly indicates to the audience that Jesus' washing of the feet of his disciples is oriented to their participation in divine life eternal.[6] This is confirmed as Jesus replied that unless he washes the feet of Peter, he will have no "share" (μέρος) with Jesus (13:8).[7] He will thus not be able to participate in the worship for divine life eternal in the new communal household or temple into which Jesus' ritual washing of feet welcomes the disciples. Peter then pleaded that Jesus wash his hands and head as well (13:9). But Jesus replied that the one who has "bathed" (λελουμένος), that is, has been "baptized," has no need except to have his feet washed, and then he is completely "clean [καθαρός]" (13:10), ritually purified to share in worship with Jesus.[8] All of the baptized and washed disciples are thus ritually and cultically "clean" except for the one (Judas) who is going to "betray" or "give over" Jesus (13:11; cf. 13:2) to a sacrificial death.

Jesus instructed his disciples that if he, as their Lord and teacher, washed their feet (13:12-13), then they ought to wash the feet of one another (13:14). They are to metaphorically wash the feet of one another by

5. "Slaves washed their masters' feet after a journey, wives the feet of their husbands, disciples the feet of their teachers" (Michaels, *John*, 726). "There is no parallel in extant ancient literature for a person of superior status voluntarily washing the feet of someone of inferior status" (Byrne, *Life Abounding*, 229). See also Lincoln, *John*, 367; Köstenberger, *John*, 405.

6. The same phrase, "for eternity" (εἰς τὸν αἰῶνα), refers to divine life eternal in 4:14; 6:51, 58; 8:51, 52; 10:28; 11:26.

7. "The term μέρος . . . has the force in similar contexts elsewhere of lot, share, inheritance, with particular reference to a person's eschatological destiny . . . Here, then, its reference is to the share in or solidarity with Jesus that enables one to share his destiny" (Lincoln, *John*, 368). See also BDAG, 634.

8. The same verb for "bathe" (λούω) refers to baptism in Heb 10:22; see Heil, *Hebrews*, 281; Heil, *Worship*, 176. A cognitively related verb (ἀπολούω) refers to baptism in 1 Cor 6:11. The cognate noun "bath" (λουτρόν) refers to baptism in Eph 5:26; Titus 3:5. On the meaning of ritually clean or cultically pure for καθαρός, see BDAG, 489. Previously in John baptism (3:22-24) was very closely related to, if not synonymous with, ceremonial "purification" or "cleansing [καθαρισμοῦ]" (3:25).

loving one another to the extent that Jesus demonstrated in literally washing their feet as a symbolic anticipation of his self-sacrificial death for them (cf. 13:7). The "model" or "pattern" (ὑπόδειγμα) Jesus gave them to imitate (13:15) refers to his exemplary self-sacrificial death that he has enabled them to imitate by washing their feet as an act of supreme love.[9] It also refers to the model or prototype they are to copy in order to have a share with Jesus (13:8) in becoming the new temple, the communal household, of true worship.[10] By imitating Jesus' model, his act of self-sacrificial worship in laying down his life for them, the disciples, as well as the audience, in laying down their lives, whether literally or metaphorically, by loving one another will participate in true worship for divine life eternal.[11]

Jesus' solemn pronouncement that a "slave" (δοῦλος) is not greater than his lord nor one sent greater than the one who sent him (13:16) recalls that whoever would serve Jesus is to follow him, and where Jesus is there his "servant" (διάκονος) will be (12:26). To be a slave or servant of Jesus one must follow and be with him as he lays down his life in an act of self-sacrificial worship by which he will illustrate that the one who loves his life destroys it, and the one who hates his life in this world guards it for divine life eternal (12:25). Just as the Father will honor anyone who serves Jesus in this self-sacrificial way (12:26), so the disciples who understand and do these things are blessed by God (13:17) to have a share with Jesus in his act of supreme love, his true self-sacrificial worship for divine life eternal.

Jesus' statement, "I am not speaking about *all* of you; I know those whom I have chosen" (13:18), recalls that not *all* of his disciples are clean, as he knew Judas was going to "betray" or "give him over" to a sacrificial

---

9. According to Culpepper ("Johannine *hypodeigma*," 142–43), ὑπόδειγμα is used in Jewish literature "to exhort the faithful to mark an exemplary death." See LXX 2 Macc 6:28, 31; 4 Macc 17:22–23; Sir 44:16. "We might paraphrase Jesus' words this way: 'By acting in this way, I enable you to act the same'" (Léon-Dufour, *To Act*, 127). See also Burridge, *Imitating Jesus*, 343–45; Bennema, "Mimesis in John 13," 261–74.

10. "In the OT background it appears that παράδειγμα and ὑπόδειγμα are interchangeable.... Moses is shown the pattern (παράδειγμα) of the heavenly tabernacle and its furniture, which he is to make (Exod 25:9). David gives Solomon the model (παράδειγμα) of the Temple he is to build (1 Chr 28:11, 12, 18, 19). Similarly, Ezekiel is shown a vision of the Temple as the model (ὑπόδειγμα) of the new house of God (42:15)" (Coloe, *Household of God*, 137).

11. "In welcoming disciples into his Father's household, Jesus proleptically draws them into his own divine sonship within his Father's household. What is acted out here in symbol will be realized at the cross. In his life and death Jesus is the Temple of his Father's presence. In the post-resurrection time the disciples, as children of the Father, will continue to be the dwelling place of God in history. Jesus is now the ὑπόδειγμα or prototype of the future house/hold of God, which his disciples will become through their having a part (μέρος) in his hour" (Coloe, *Household of God*, 137).

death (13:11), even though he was one of the twelve whom "I have chosen" (6:70). The Scripture (Ps 41[LXX 40]:10) to be fulfilled thus refers to Judas: "The one feeding on my bread lifted up his heel against me" (13:18). That he "lifted up" (ἐπῆρεν) his heel for a metaphorical malicious kick against Jesus characterizes his betrayal as an offense against the intimacy of his meal fellowship with Jesus.[12] But, ironically, it contributed to the divine necessity for Jesus as the Son of Man to be "lifted up/exalted [ὑψωθῆναι]" in crucifixion (3:14), so that everyone who believes in him might have divine life eternal (3:15). And that Judas did this as the one "feeding on" my "bread" ironically contributed to the establishment of the Eucharist. It made it possible for Jesus to give his flesh for the life of the world as the living "bread" (6:51); the one "feeding on" this "bread" in the Eucharist will live for eternity (6:58).[13]

Jesus was telling his disciples this now before it happens, so that when it happens they may "believe" that "I am" (13:19), that Jesus is the divine Word that in the beginning "was" with God and "was" God (1:1-2), and now is the divine revelation of God. When Judas metaphorically "lifts up" his heel (13:18) to "betray" and thus "give over" Jesus to his sacrificial death, it will enable the Jews to "lift up/exalt/glorify" Jesus in crucifixion as the Son of Man, so that they will know that "I am" (8:28), and thus that Jesus is a divine object of worship. And if the Jews, the disciples, and the audience then "believe" and thus worship Jesus as the divine "I am," they will not die in their sins (8:24); they will have divine life eternal.

Then Jesus solemnly pronounced: "The one receiving the one I send receives me, and the one receiving me receives the one who sent me" (13:20). This resonates with Jesus' previous solemn pronouncement that the "one sent" is not greater than the one who "sent" him (13:16). The one Jesus sends refers to a disciple he sends to imitate his model of supreme love indicative of his self-sacrificial worship (13:15). Anyone who "receives" one whom Jesus sends to love as an act of self-sacrificial worship "receives" and thus

12. Lifting up of the heel implied a malicious kick according to BDAG, 895. "To turn away and lift one's heel against a person is a notable gesture of insult and contempt in the Mediterranean culture" (Byrne, *Life Abounding*, 233n18). "The quotation speaks of rebellion and open disdain on the part of a trusted friend or family member, exactly the opposite action and attitude in the washing of one another's feet" (Michaels, *John*, 740). "One who has had his feet washed by Jesus in what was meant to be a sign of continued fellowship is now said to raise the heel of his foot against Jesus in contempt of the invitation to fellowship" (Lincoln *John*, 373).

13. "Instead of the verb for 'to eat' in Ps. 40.10 LXX and in Mark 14.18, John substitutes the synonym (τρώγω) he consistently used earlier in the bread of life discourse (cf. 6.54, 56-8)" (Lincoln, *John*, 373). And "the scriptural text as quoted by John has changed the plural 'loaves' of the LXX to the singular 'loaf'" (Byrne, *Life Abounding*, 234n19), so that it accords with the singular "bread" in John 6:51, 58. See also Moloney, *John*, 381; Menken, "Translation of Ps 41:10," 61-79.

believes in Jesus who loved as an act of self-sacrificial worship. This recalls that to those who "received" and believed in the name of Jesus he gave the authority to become children of God (1:12). And anyone who receives and thus believes in Jesus receives the God who "sent" him, the God who "sent" his Son so that the world might be saved through him (3:17). For God so loved the world that he gave his unique Son, who loved his own to the uttermost as an act of self-sacrificial worship (13:1), so that everyone who believes in him and worships like him may have divine life eternal (3:16).[14]

Confirming that he is the one who would "lift up his heel" against Jesus after "feeding on my bread" (13:18), Judas took the piece of bread Jesus gave him (13:26-27) and went out to "betray" and thus "give over" Jesus (13:30; cf. 13:2, 21) to his sacrificial death. Jesus then declared that now he as the Son of Man is "glorified" and God is "glorified" in him (13:31). This recalls Jesus' previous declaration that the hour has come for the Son of Man to be "glorified" (12:23), so that the Greeks may see (12:21) and worship him (cf. 9:35-38). That the Son of Man is "glorified" makes him an object of worship, and that God is "glorified" in him means that worship of the Son of Man is worship of God. Not only is God "glorified" and thus worshiped in the Son of Man, but "God will glorify him in him, and glorify him at once" (13:32), so that worship of God is worship of the Son of Man. Judas set in motion the divine necessity for the Son of Man to be "lifted up/exalted/glorified" in his sacrificial death (3:14), so that everyone who believes in and thus worships him may have divine life eternal (3:15).[15]

In view of his imminent departure from them (13:33), Jesus gave his disciples a new commandment that they should love "one another," just as he has loved them, they are also to love "one another" (13:34). This confirms and clarifies that his previous instruction that they ought to wash the feet of "one another" (13:14) was a symbolic model for how they are to love one another as Jesus loved them to the end of his life and to the uttermost

---

14. Anyone "who 'receives' (or welcomes) the disciples and accepts their message actually 'receives' (in faith) Jesus himself, and therefore God the Father, because Jesus represents the Father.... The disciples, like Jesus, will be 'sent,' and Jesus, like the Father, will take on the role of Sender" (Michaels, *John*, 744). The disciples will be effective witnesses "when they understand how the footwashing discloses its meaning and when they reproduce in their love for each other the sacrificial love of Jesus that it embodies" (Byrne, *Life Abounding*, 234).

15. "The sense, then, is that God is glorified in Jesus but also enables Jesus to be glorified in God by participating in the divine glory" (Lincoln, *John*, 387). "To paraphrase: 'the Son of man is glorified'—*in* his death; 'and God is glorified in him'—that is, *in his death*; 'and God will glorify him in him'—again, *in his death*; and he will immediately glorify him'—in that *his death* is imminent" (Michaels, *John*, 756-57; emphases original).

(13:1)—by laying down his life for them. This new "commandment" thus accords with the "commandment" Jesus received from his Father, that he has the divine authority to lay down his life and the divine authority to take it up again (10:18). The Father gave Jesus this "commandment" (12:49) and Jesus knows that his "commandment" is divine life eternal (12:50). As the hallmark for being a disciple of Jesus (13:35), the fulfillment of this new commandment for the disciples to love one another as Jesus loved them coincides with the divine commandment for him to lay down his life for them in an act of supreme love.[16]

After Jesus told Peter that he could not follow him now but that he would follow later (13:36), Peter nevertheless exuberantly promised, "I will lay down my life for you!" (13:37). Jesus' reply, "your life for me you will lay down" (13:38), carries a double meaning. It is a skeptical question, since Peter cannot follow Jesus now. But it is also a promise of how Peter will follow Jesus later (cf. 21:18-19). Jesus then solemnly pronounced that Peter in fact would deny him three times (13:38). Peter's promise accords with the new commandment for disciples to love in the way that Jesus loved them (13:34), that is, by laying down his life for them. But before Peter will be able to lay down his life for others, he must be among the sheep for whom Jesus, as the good shepherd, lays down his life (10:11, 15) in love as an act of self-sacrificial worship. Then Peter, the rest of the disciples, and the audience will be able to fulfill the new commandment by imitating the way Jesus loved them. They will be able to lay down their lives in love for one another in acts of sacrificial worship for divine life eternal (10:10; 12:50).[17]

---

16. Jesus "has already given them an exemplary paradigm of such love when he washed their feet. If they follow his example, they will be loving one another with the same self-sacrificial love with which he has loved them.... The commandment is 'new' not so much in the sense of adding any ethical content to the commandment of love already in place (Lev 19:18; cf. Mark 12:19-31 and parallels). It is new in the sense of being required in the new situation following Jesus' departure to the Father" (Byrne, *Life Abounding*, 240).

17. "Ironically, then, in asserting he will lay down his life for Jesus, Peter is depicted as believing himself capable of the sort of love just depicted in v. 34, the love Jesus has for his followers. He has not understood the crucial distinction between 'now' and 'later' in Jesus' words. Not until Jesus' hour has been completed and his love demonstrated in death will Peter have the resources for living out Jesus' model" (Lincoln, *John*, 388).

The Spirit of Truth Will Enable Worship for Divine Life Eternal (14:1-31)

Although Jesus himself was "troubled" at the prospect of being betrayed (13:21), since the devil had put into the "heart" of Judas that he should betray him (13:2), and although he was "troubled" in view of the approaching hour of his death (12:27), he encouraged his disciples not to let their "heart" be "troubled" (14:1) because of his imminent departure (13:33). Rather, they are to continue to believe in God and to believe in him (14:1), since in the "household" (οἰκίᾳ) of his Father (14:2), the communal household of believers that is to replace the "house" (οἶκον) of his Father, the temple in Jerusalem (2:16), there are many "dwellings" (14:2).[18] These "dwellings" or "abidings" (μοναί) refer, then, not to spatial "rooms" for believers in the heavenly house of the Father, but to various divine interpersonal relationships, which enable believers to function as the communal household of true worship that replaces worship in the Jerusalem house/temple.[19]

One of the many interpersonal "dwellings" within the Father's household is that of the Spirit whom John saw come down and "remain" or "dwell" (μένον) upon Jesus, enabling him to baptize with the Holy Spirit (1:33). This provides the basis for the household's sacramental worship, as it enables a believer to be born from above/again from water and the Spirit in the sacrament of baptism (3:3, 5). The Samaritans asked Jesus to "remain" or "dwell" (μεῖναι) with them and he "remained" (ἔμεινεν) there two days (4:40), which resulted in more of them believing (4:41) and in their declaration to the Samaritan woman, as well as to the audience, that Jesus is a worthy object of worship. Indeed, they confess that they know that he is "truly the savior of the world" (4:42). This exemplifies what it means that the hour is now here for true worshipers to worship in the Spirit that "dwells" upon Jesus (1:33) and in the truth that he embodies (4:23-24; cf. 1:14, 17). And

---

18. "In chapter 2 the image of Temple shifted to a single person, Jesus (2:21). In chapter 14 this movement continues and extends beyond one person to a group of people in a household or familial relationship. Chapter 14 develops this personal and relational understanding even further with the shift from the word οἶκος to οἰκίᾳ. . . . Whereas in 2:16 the initial reference was to the οἶκος in the sense of a building, here in chapter 14, through the change of the word to οἰκία there is a continuation of the movement begun in 2:21 to understand the phrase, 'my Father's house,' not as a building but as a quality of personal relationships" (Coloe, *God Dwells*, 161-62). See also McCaffrey, *House*, 31.

19. "The father's house is no longer heaven, but God's household or family" (Gundry, "My Father's House," 70).

whoever eats the flesh of Jesus and drinks his blood in the sacrament of the Eucharist "remains" or "dwells" (μένει) in Jesus and Jesus in him (6:56).[20]

Jesus went on to query that if there were not many such dwellings oriented to worship in his Father's household, would he have told them that he is going to "prepare" (ἑτοιμάσαι) a "place" (τόπον) for them (14:2).[21] "And if I go and prepare [ἑτοιμάσω] a place [τόπον] for you, I will come again and take you to myself, so that where [ὅπου] I am you also may be" (14:3). The "place" Jesus is going to prepare, the place "where" (ὅπου) he is (12:26), refers to his relationship with the Father to whom he is going (13:1), and "where" (ὅπου) he is going (13:33, 36). It is the "place where" (τόπος ὅπου) it is now necessary to worship (4:20), the metaphorical place that transcends all geographical places for worship (4:21), including and especially the "place" (τόπον) for worship in Jerusalem (11:48; cf. 2:13-21).[22]

In ironic contrast to his own people who did not "accept" (παρέλαβον) him (1:11), Jesus will come again and "accept" or "take" (παραλήμψομαι) his disciples "to myself [πρὸς ἐμαυτόν]" (14:3). This develops his declaration that when he is lifted up/exalted through his act of self-sacrificial worship by dying on the cross (12:33), "I will draw all to myself [πρὸς ἐμαυτόν]" (12:32). Jesus then added that "where I am going you know the way" (14:4), recalling that "he is going to God" (13:3). That "you know" the way resonates with his statement that if "you know" these things, blessed are you if you do them (13:17). This refers to the model he has given them to wash one another's feet as he washed their feet (13:14-16) in anticipation of his act of self-sacrificial worship in loving them to the uttermost (13:1). Jesus' "way" of going to the Father, then, is the "way" of self-sacrificial worship by dying on the cross as an act of supreme love for his own. It will prepare the

---

20. "While μοναί can mean the physical chambers within a house, and so at one level be understood as many rooms within a physical Temple building, the shift from building to personal relationships suggested by the phrase 'in my Father's house' requires a similar shift in understanding what the evangelist means by 'dwellings' (μοναί).... Chapters 14 and 15 use derivatives of μένω and μονή to describe a variety of interpersonal relationships between the Father, Jesus, Paraclete, and believers. The relationships are usually described with the translation 'abiding,' or 'dwelling.' These various relationships are appropriately introduced by the phrase 'many dwellings' (μοναὶ πολλαί)" (Coloe, *God Dwells*, 162).

21. "While Jesus has not explicitly given such an assurance to the disciples, it is perhaps implicit in statements about his 'going away' (12:26; 13:33, 36-37)" (Byrne, *Life Abounding*, 242n40).

22. There is scriptural precedent for "preparing a place" for worship in LXX 2 Chr 3:1, which refers to the house of the Lord (temple) for worship in Jerusalem that Solomon began to build in the "place" (τόπῳ) which David had "prepared" (ἡτοίμασεν). See also Coloe, *God Dwells*, 164-67.

"place where" they in the household of his Father (14:2) may offer their own self-sacrificial worship by loving one another as Jesus loved them (13:34).

Thomas asked how they can know the way, since they do not know where he is going (14:5). Jesus' reply implicitly answered his question: "I am the way and the truth and the life; no one comes to the Father except through me" (14:6). Jesus embodies "the way" of self-sacrificial worship by dying on the cross in love for others as "the way" to the Father. "The way" that Jesus embodies is also "the truth" that he embodies as the one through whom the gift of "the truth" came to be (1:17), the "unique one" who is full of a gift of divine "truth" (1:14). This entails the truth that God so loved the world that he gave his Son, the "unique one," to sacrifice his life in love so that everyone who believes in him may have "life eternal" (3:16), which is "the life." "The way" to the Father's divine life eternal Jesus embodies as the one the Father loved for laying down his life (10:17) in an act of self-sacrificial worship. In response the Father raised him from his self-sacrificial death so that he is the resurrection and "the life" (11:25), the embodiment of divine life eternal.[23]

No one comes "to the Father" (πρὸς τὸν πατέρα) except through Jesus (14:6). This confirms that when Jesus comes and takes his disciples "to myself [πρὸς ἐμαυτόν]" (14:3), he will at the same time be taking them to his Father. His relationship with the Father is thus the "place" he will prepare for them (14:2) through his act of self-sacrificial worship in dying for them, the "place where" it is necessary to worship (4:20) the Father in Spirit and truth (4:23-24), which they may do by offering their own self-sacrificial worship in imitation of Jesus (13:15, 34). That no one comes to the Father except "through me" (δι' ἐμοῦ) resonates with Jesus' pronouncement that he is the metaphorical "door" or "gate" for the "sheep" and if anyone comes in "through me" (δι' ἐμοῦ), "he will be saved, and will come in and go out and find pasture" (10:9).[24] This means that through Jesus' self-sacrificial worship by laying down his life as the good shepherd (10:11) one may come to the Father and thereby be saved, a synonym for having divine life eternal (10:10; cf. 3:15-16).

Jesus climaxed his exchange with Philip regarding the unity of Jesus and the Father (14:7-9) with the declaration that the Father "dwelling" (μένων) in Jesus does his works (14:10). This exemplifies another one of the many "dwellings" (μοναί), the divine interpersonal relationships, within

---

23. "Jesus is the way to the Father because in him is to be found the revelation of the true reality of God ('truth'), which, when appropriated through faith, communicates a share in the divine '(eternal) life'" (Byrne, *Life Abounding*, 243).

24. That these are the only two occurrences in John of the phrase "through me" enhances this connection.

the household of the Father which facilitate its worship (14:2). That Jesus is in the Father and the Father is in him (14:10-11) and that he is going to the Father (14:12) establishes him as an object, along with the Father, of supplicatory worship for the disciples, as well as the audience. Whatever they ask for in their petitionary prayers in the name of Jesus, he will do, so that, in turn, the Father, the ultimate object of worship, may be "glorified" in the Son (14:13). Indeed, since God will give to Jesus whatever he asks him (11:22; cf. 9:31), whatever they ask Jesus in his name he will do (14:14). The worship of praying to Jesus as the Son amounts to the worship of glorifying God as the Father.

Jesus then declared that if his disciples love him, they will keep his commandments (14:15), including especially his new commandment that they love one another in the way that he has loved them (13:34), that is, as an act of self-sacrificial worship. Jesus will then ask the Father and he will send them another "Advocate" or "Paraclete" (παράκλητον), one in addition to Jesus, so that he may be with them for eternity (14:16).[25] This Advocate is the Spirit of truth that "dwells" (μένει) with them and will be in them (14:17), yet another example of the many "dwellings" (μοναί), the divine interpersonal relationships, within the household of the Father which facilitate its worship (14:2). This Spirit of truth, who will be with them for eternity, will thus enable them to become true worshipers who worship the Father in Spirit and truth (4:23-24) for divine life eternal—when Jesus comes to them (14:18), they will live eternally as he lives eternally (14:19).

Jesus went on to say that if anyone loves him, he will keep his "word" (14:23). This refers to the "word" he received from the Father (12:48), the commandment the Father gave him (12:49), the new commandment that they should love one another in the self-sacrificial way that he loved them (13:34). It accords with the commandment he received from his Father that he lay down his life in self-sacrificial worship and take it up again (10:18), the commandment which is life eternal (12:50). The Father will love the one who keeps this word/commandment, and Jesus and the Father will come to him and make a "dwelling" (μονήν) with him (14:23), another one of the many "dwellings" (μοναί), the divine interpersonal relationships, within

---

25. "The phrase 'another advocate' implies that Jesus himself is an 'advocate' for his disciples, presumably by virtue of 'going off to prepare a place' for them with the Father (vv. 2-3). This other 'advocate,' he promises will be 'with you forever' (v. 16), in contrast to Jesus himself, who said he would be 'with you' only 'a short time' (13:33)" (Michaels, *John*, 783-84). "The most likely background for the term [παράκλητος] is in the Jewish Scriptures and Second Temple Judaism with their interest in intercessory figures who functioned as advocates, sometimes in the heavenly court, and whose advocacy could sometimes take the form of counter-accusation" (Lincoln, *John*, 393). See also Byrne, *Life Abounding*, 247.

the household of the Father (14:2) which facilitate its worship. In addition, the Advocate who is the Holy Spirit will teach them everything and remind them of everything Jesus told them (14:26). Such teaching and commemoration will take place within their communal worship as the household of the Father, further facilitating their worship for divine life eternal.[26]

Remain in Jesus the True Vine to Worship for Divine Life Eternal (15:1–17)

Again speaking metaphorically, Jesus identified himself as the "true vine" and his Father as the "vinekeeper" (15:1).[27] Every person/"branch" in Jesus that does not "produce fruit" his Father "cuts off" (αἴρει), and every "branch" that "produces fruit" he "cuts clean" (καθαίρει) so that it might "produce more fruit" (15:2).[28] To "produce more fruit" recalls and resonates with a previous similar metaphor that unless the grain of wheat falling into the earth dies, it remains alone; but if it dies, it "produces much fruit" (12:24). "Producing fruit" means producing believers to have life eternal. In the metaphor of the "harvester" who is gathering "fruit" for life eternal (4:36) the Samaritans represent the "harvest" (4:35), the metaphorical "fruit," who came to believe in Jesus as the savior of the world (4:39–42), so that, as believers, they might have life eternal (3:15–16). When Jesus, as a metaphorical grain of wheat, dies and is lifted up on the cross in an act of self-sacrificial love, he will not remain alone but will draw all people to himself (12:32), potentially producing believers, "fruit," to have divine life eternal.

As among those whom the Father "cuts clean" (καθαίρει) so that they may produce more fruit (15:2), the disciples are already "clean" (καθαροί)

---

26. "The human faculties of memory and insight, and the activity of worship and prayer, are named as the primary moments when the community experiences the gift of the Spirit and, through the stirrings of the Spirit, these cultic moments become the special times of Jesus' presence" (Coloe, *God Dwells*, 176).

27. "The notion of the Father as 'Vinekeeper' is not surprising . . . going back to biblical imagery about Israel as God's vineyard (for example, Ps 80:8–18; Isa 5:1–7; Ezek 15:1–8; 17:5–8; 19:10–14). . . . Jesus is the 'true' Vine in the same sense in which he is 'the true bread from heaven' (6:32), or 'the good Shepherd' (10:11, 14). The point is not to differentiate him from other 'vines' (Israel, for example), but simply to claim him as the very embodiment of what every vine should be—above all, the source of life to its branches" (Michaels, *John*, 801).

28. "The depiction of God's dealing with unproductive and productive branches involves a play on words. Branches that fail to bear fruit are cut off or taken away (αἴρω), while those that bear fruit are enabled to continue to be fruitful by being cut clean or pruned (καθαίρω)" (Lincoln, *John*, 403).

because of the word Jesus has spoken to them (15:3). This recalls that the disciples are "clean" (καθαροί) as those whose feet Jesus washed (13:10) as an example of the self-sacrificial love they are to imitate in accord with the commandment, the word, he has spoken to them that they are to love one another in the self-sacrificial way that he has loved them (13:34).[29] This implies that by loving one another, the disciples will produce more believers, the metaphorical "more fruit" (15:2), by drawing people to themselves in imitation of Jesus, who will draw all people to himself through his death on the cross as an act of self-sacrificial love (12:32).[30]

The disciples are to "remain" in Jesus, the vine, and he in them. Just as the branch is not able to produce fruit by itself unless it "remains" on the vine, so neither can they unless they "remain" in Jesus (15:4). "Remaining" or "dwelling" in Jesus exemplifies another one of the many "dwellings," the divine interpersonal relationships, that facilitate worship in the Father's communal household (14:2). Indeed, eucharistic worship serves as a preeminent way of "remaining" in Jesus. His directive to "remain in me, as I in you [μείνατε ἐν ἐμοί, κἀγὼ ἐν ὑμῖν]" (15:4a) and his declaration that "the one remaining in me and I in him [μένων ἐν ἐμοὶ κἀγὼ ἐν αὐτῷ]—this one produces much fruit" (15:5) recall and resonate with his declaration that "the one who feeds on my flesh and drinks my blood in me remains and I in him [ἐν ἐμοὶ μένει κἀγὼ ἐν αὐτῷ]" (6:56). The one remaining in Jesus with the divine assistance afforded by the Eucharist "produces much fruit" (15:5), future believers to have divine life eternal, but anyone who does not "remain" in Jesus will be discarded as useless for producing such fruit (15:6).

If the disciples "remain" in Jesus, the vine, and his words "remain" in them, they may "ask" for whatever they want in prayer and it will be done for them (15:7). This reaffirms Jesus' promise that whatever they "ask" by praying in his name he will do it (14:13-14). If the words of Jesus remain in them, preeminently his word or commandment that they love one another in the self-sacrificial way that he loved them (cf. 12:47-50; 13:34), they are assured that their prayers will be answered, since their prayers will be in accord with God's will or commandment that they love one another. In other words, they are assured of the divine assistance they pray for to be able to love one another. The Father of Jesus is "glorified" that they "produce much fruit," that is, bring others to believe by loving one another, and thus

---

29. Jesus' "word" is often synonymous with his "commandment." See 12:48-50; 14:23-24. "The wordplay continues, since 'clean' (καθαρός) is a cognate of the earlier verb and evokes both the agricultural imagery (pruned) and the spiritual state of the disciples (clean)" (Lincoln, *John*, 403).

30. "[T]he disciples are to embody love in the world so as to attract their fellow human beings to the Source of that love (cf. 12:32)" (Byrne, *Life Abounding*, 259).

become true disciples of Jesus (15:8; cf. 14:13). In other words, their "producing much fruit" amounts to the ethical worship of glorifying God as true disciples of Jesus—those who have love for one another (13:35).

The disciples are to "remain" in the love of Jesus, who loves them as the Father loves him (15:9). If they keep his commandments, preeminently that they love one another (13:34), they will "remain" in his love as Jesus "remains" in the love of his Father (15:10). Jesus has told them these things so that his "joy" may be in them and their "joy may be fulfilled" (15:11). This recalls how John the Baptist "rejoices with joy" at the sound of Jesus, the "bridegroom" (3:29). Once everyone was coming to be baptized by Jesus and thus becoming believers—the metaphorical "producing of fruit" (3:22–26), John declared that his "joy has been fulfilled" (3:29). Similarly, when the disciples keep the commandment of Jesus to love one another in the self-sacrificial way that he loves them (15:12), so that they "produce much fruit"—believers to have divine life eternal, Jesus' "joy" may be in them and their "joy may be fulfilled."[31]

As the "good shepherd," Jesus "lays down his life for the sheep" (10:11, 15). But "the sheep" for whom Jesus "lays down his life" in an act of self-sacrificial worship are his "friends," those whom he loves (cf. 11:5, 11), as no one has greater love than this (15:13).[32] The disciples are no longer "slaves" (15:15) but the "friends" of Jesus if they do what he commands them (15:14)—love one another as he loves them. They thus, like Jesus, "remain" in the "household" for eternity (8:35).[33] He chose and appointed them that they may go and "produce fruit and your fruit may remain," so that whatever they in prayer ask the Father in his name he will give them (15:16; cf. 14:13-14; 15:7). They are to "produce fruit"—future believers—by loving one another (15:17). Accordingly, their "fruit" may "remain" in Jesus as the true vine (15:4, 5, 6, 7) and in his love (15:9, 10). And their "fruit," as believers, may "remain" (μένῃ) within the many "dwellings" (μοναί), the divine interpersonal relationships (14:10, 17, 23, 25), within the household of the Father (14:2), the household of communal worship for divine life eternal.

31. "But the joy of these disciples, as of the readers of the Gospel, is a shared joy. It is shared with Jesus, for it is his joy to begin with, and by implication with each other, but its ultimate 'fulfillment' is yet to come" (Michaels, *John*, 811).

32. "'Friend' (φίλος) has the particular sense in Greek of 'one who is loved,' which the English word 'friend' does not quite capture" (Byrne, *Life Abounding*, 258n93). "When the sheep metaphor is dropped, Jesus' 'sheep' become 'his friends,' those whom he loves and cares about" (Michaels, *John*, 812).

33. "The image of the vine and the branches (15:1–8), situated within passages that describe abiding within the divine household (14:1–31; 15:9–17), invites disciples into a union with Jesus that will draw them into his own abiding as Son in the household of the Father for eternity (8:35)" (Coloe, *Household of God*, 165).

The Spirit of Truth Will Guide the Disciples for Self-Sacrificial Worship (15:18–16:33)

As the world hated Jesus, so it hates his disciples (15:18), since they are not of the world, as Jesus chose them out of the world (15:19). The disciples are to remember the word Jesus spoke to them that "a slave is not greater than his lord" (15:20a; cf. 13:16). This recalls the reason they are to imitate his act of self-sacrificial love for them, exemplified and anticipated by his washing of their feet (13:12–15). If they persecuted Jesus despite his life-giving love (cf. 5:16), they will also persecute his disciples despite their love for others (15:20b). Indeed, they will put disciples out of the synagogue (16:2a), a public place for Jewish worship, implicitly for publicly confessing their faith and worship of Jesus as the Christ (cf. 9:22; 12:42). In fact, everyone who kills disciples will think he is offering worship to God (16:2b). But ironically, by killing disciples, they will enable them to literally imitate Jesus' laying down of his life in self-sacrificial love as an act of the true worship of God.

Jesus had promised that the Father will give the disciples another Advocate to be with them for eternity (14:16), the Spirit of truth (14:17). This Advocate, the Holy Spirit, will teach them everything, remind them of everything Jesus told them (14:26), and testify about Jesus (15:26). When that one comes, the Spirit of truth, he will guide the disciples in all truth and prepare them for the future, as he "will announce" to them the things that are coming (16:13). Because he "will announce" to them what he will receive from Jesus (16:14), that is, he "will announce" to them everything that Jesus and the Father have (16:15), that one "will glorify" Jesus (16:14) as an object of worship. This recalls the Samaritan woman's declaration that when the Christ comes, that one "will announce" everything to us (4:25), preeminently everything involving the true worship of the Father in Spirit and truth (4:23–24). As the other Advocate, the Spirit of truth will thus guide the disciples in all truth, enabling them to be true worshipers who worship the Father in Spirit and truth by imitating Jesus' self-sacrificial worship.

Jesus developed the worship theme of petitionary prayer (cf. 14:13–14; 15:7, 16) as he promised his disciples that when he sees them again (16:22) whatever they "ask" the Father in his name he will give them (16:23). Although they have not yet "asked" anything in his name, they are to "ask" and they will receive, so that their "joy may be fulfilled" (16:24). This implies that they are to pray for divine assistance to love one another. It recalls that Jesus told them that if they keep his commandments (15:10), especially that they love one another in the self-sacrificial way that he loves them (15:12), his joy may be in them and their "joy may be fulfilled" (15:11).³⁴ In the future they will "ask" in his name (16:26) but the Father himself who loves them (16:27) will answer, as Jesus is leaving the world and going back to the Father (16:28). Although they will have trouble in the world, they are to take courage since Jesus has conquered the world (16:33; cf. 15:18) through his self-sacrificial love (12:25, 31; 14:30-31; 16:11) which they are to imitate with the assistance they receive from their petitionary prayer.³⁵

The Prayer of Jesus for Glorification, the Disciples, and All Believers (17:1-26)

Jesus addressed a prayer of thanksgiving to the "Father" (11:41) before the raising of Lazarus from the dead. Rather than praying to the "Father" to save him from the hour of his death (12:27), he prayed, "Father, glorify your name." Then in answer to his prayer came a voice from heaven, "I have glorified and again I will glorify" (12:28). After he "spoke these things," recalling "these things I have spoken" (14:25; 15:11; 16:1, 4, 6, 25, 33) in his farewell discourse to his disciples, he raised his eyes to heaven and prayed, "Father, the hour has come; glorify your Son, so that the Son may glorify you" (17:1; cf. 13:31). He thereby prayed that the Father "glorify" the Son, thus establishing the Son as an object of worship, by raising him from the dead to divine life eternal, so that the Son may in turn "glorify" the Father as an object of worship by extending divine life eternal to those who believe and worship both the Father and the Son. This is confirmed as Jesus continued his prayer, stating that to all those believers whom the Father gave him (cf. 6:37, 39) he may give life eternal (17:2; cf. 3:14-17).

Continuing his prayer, Jesus declared, "Now this is the eternal life, that they know you, the only true God, and the one whom you sent, Jesus Christ" (17:3).³⁶ Those who experience divine life eternal are those who "know,"

---

34. "Prayer 'in his name' will be answered because it is the prayer of those who know him, and do not have to be told what he would want" (Michaels, *John*, 847). "As Jesus' authorized representatives who pray in accord with what he himself represents, they will find their requests answered by the Father, who has given to Jesus and will continue to give to them. Such praying is both the way to and part of the joy they have been promised" (Lincoln, *John*, 425).

35. "Although the disciples will not have the physical presence of Jesus in the time to come, their union with him will be so complete that their prayers to the Father will be as assured of response as his own prayer had been. The Father will respond to their prayer 'in his name' in the sense of responding as though Jesus were the one making the prayer" (Byrne, *Life Abounding*, 274).

36. "Like the narrative asides, the definition of eternal life is for the reader's benefit, despite being addressed to God" (Michaels, *John*, 860).

by believing and worshiping, the Father as the only "true" God (cf. 7:28), recalling that "true" worshipers are those who worship the Father in Spirit and truth (4:23-24), the truth embodied by Jesus and his self-sacrificial love as the way to the Father (14:6). And they are those who also "know," by believing and worshiping, the one whom the Father sent, Jesus Christ, the Jesus Christ through whom came to be the gift of the truth (1:17), the truth of divine life-giving love. The Jesus Christ whom the Father "sent" is the Son God "sent" into the world (3:17), for God so loved the world that he gave his unique Son, so that everyone who believes and thus worships him exalted on the cross through self-sacrificial love may have life eternal (3:14-16). Thus, knowing by believing and worshiping both the only true God and the Jesus Christ whom he sent is to have divine life eternal.[37]

In his prayer Jesus acknowledged that he "glorified," and thus offered true worship to, the Father on earth by "completing the work" which the Father gave him to do (17:4). This recalls Jesus' declaration that his food is to do the will of the God who sent him and to "complete his work" (4:34). Jesus did the will of God and completed his work by bringing people to believe in order to have divine life eternal (6:39-40) through his self-sacrificial love, an act of true worship that glorified God. Jesus then repeated and developed his initial prayer (17:1): "And now you glorify me, Father, with yourself with the glory which I had with you before the world was" (17:5). Jesus thus prayed for the Father to return him, after his self-sacrificial death, to the divine status, the divine glory, he had in the beginning when he, as the Word, was with God and was God (1:1-2). This reaffirms the basis for the prologue's communal act of doxological worship of the Word who became flesh and dwelt among us: "We observed his glory, glory as of the unique one from the Father" (1:14).

Regarding the disciples whom the Father gave him as believers out of the world, Jesus acknowledged in his prayer to the Father that "they have kept your word" (17:6). This is the same as the word or commandment of Jesus (17:7; cf. 12:49) to love one another in the self-sacrificial way he loves them (13:34; 15:12) for divine life eternal (12:50). Since the disciples received the words the Father gave Jesus, they have known that Jesus truly came from the Father and have believed that the Father sent Jesus (17:8), thus indicating that they have divine life eternal (3:16-17; 17:3). Jesus

---

37. "'Knowing' here is tantamount to believing. Beyond intellectual knowledge it has the Semitic overtones of commitment to another person in relationship. The sense is not that one knows God, on the one hand, and Jesus, on the other, quite independently of each other. Rather, one appropriates the true revelation of God in and through the person and work of Jesus. To know God in this sense is to be drawn already into the 'eternal life' of the divine communion of love" (Byrne, *Life Abounding*, 282).

prays for them as believers the Father has given him (17:9) and as those in whom "I have been glorified" (17:10). By keeping his word/commandment that they love one another in the self-sacrificial way he loves them, which amounts to self-sacrificial worship, the disciples have "glorified" and thus offered true worship to Jesus.

After Jesus prayed that the Holy Father keep the disciples united as they are united (17:11) and keep them from the evil one (17:15), he prayed that the "Holy" Father "consecrate" or "make holy" the disciples in the truth, and the word of the Father is truth (17:17), which is the word/commandment of Jesus to love one another as he loves them for life eternal.[38] This will liken the disciples to Jesus whom the Father "consecrated" and sent into the world (10:36). Indeed, as the Father sent Jesus into the world, so Jesus sent them into the world (17:18): "And for them I consecrate myself, so that they also may be consecrated in truth" (17:19). Jesus consecrates himself "for" his disciples by laying down his life "for" them (10:11, 15) as an act of self-sacrificial love (15:13) and worship, so that they also may be consecrated in the truth of life-giving love.[39] By loving one another in the self-sacrificial way Jesus loves them for life eternal, the disciples, like Jesus, become true worshipers who worship the Father in Spirit and truth (4:23–24), the divine truth of life-giving love embodied in Jesus as the truth and the life (14:6).

Jesus prayed that all believers may be united in the unity he shares with the Father, so that "the world may believe that you sent me" (17:20–21), and thus have life eternal (3:16–17). Jesus has given believers the "glory" the Father gave him, the glory of divine life eternal through self-sacrificial love, "so that they may be one as we are one" (17:22) in a communion of divine love (17:23).[40] Jesus' prayerful "I desire" is that believers may be with him, "so that they may see my glory, which you gave me because you loved me before the foundation of the world" (17:24).[41] This refers to the glory of Jesus as the Word who was with God and was God (1:1–2), the basis for the communal doxological worship that "we observed his glory, glory

---

38. "The prologue portrayed Jesus as God's word, the Logos (cf. 1.1–2, 14), and earlier in the farewell section Jesus proclaimed himself to be the truth (14.6)" (Lincoln, *John*, 438).

39. "A reference here to the Son's self-sacrificial death is guaranteed by the phrase ὑπὲρ αὐτῶν [for them], the preposition ὑπέρ being almost invariably used in the Fourth Gospel with reference to dying for the sake of others" (Byrne, *Life Abounding*, 286n181).

40. "The world cannot see, or 'know,' a merely 'spiritual' unity or indwelling of the disciples in each other, or in the Father and the Son, but it can recognize the love believers have for each other as a sign of God's love for them" (Michaels, *John*, 878).

41. "The change of verb from 'ask' to 'desire' (θέλω) serves as a reminder that Jesus' will is one with that of the Father and therefore underscores the efficacy of his prayer" (Lincoln, *John*, 439).

as of the unique one from the Father, full of a gift of truth" (1:14). Jesus concluded his prayer with the desire that the life-giving love with which the Father loved him, as well as he himself, may be in the disciples (17:26). With Jesus, the embodiment of the truth of self-sacrificial, life-giving love in them, disciples may thus become true worshipers of the Father in Spirit and truth (4:23-24).[42]

Summary on 13:1—17:26

When Jesus put "water" in the washbasin and began to "wash" the feet of the disciples and dry them with the towel (13:5), he added another aspect to the Gospel's theme of sacramental worship with regard to baptism. Not only must one be born from above/again from "water" and the Spirit in the sacrament of baptism to see and enter the Kingdom of God (3:3-5), but once one has "washed" one is able to see and worship Jesus, as exemplified by the man born blind. After he "washed" in the pool of Siloam (9:7, 11, 15), which alludes to the sacrament of baptism, he was able to see and worship Jesus (9:35-38). By "washing" the feet of the disciples with "water," Jesus further developed the baptismal significance of being born from above/again from "water" and the Spirit. He performed a ritual act of loving hospitality that symbolically welcomed them into the "house," the communal household, of his Father (2:16-17), so that they may worship in Spirit and truth (4:23-24) in the new "temple" that he will establish when he raises his destroyed body from the dead (2:19-21).

Jesus instructed his disciples that if he, as their Lord and teacher, washed their feet (13:12-13), then they ought to wash the feet of one another (13:14). They are to metaphorically wash the feet of one another by loving one another to the extent that Jesus demonstrated in literally washing their feet as a symbolic anticipation of his self-sacrificial death for them (cf. 13:7). The "model" or "pattern" Jesus gave them to imitate (13:15) refers to his exemplary self-sacrificial death that he has enabled them to imitate by washing their feet as an act of supreme love. It also refers to the model or prototype they are to copy in order to have a share with Jesus (13:8) in becoming the new temple, the communal household, of true worship. By imitating Jesus' model, his act of self-sacrificial worship in laying down his

---

42. "From the Father's love for the Son (15:9) comes the Son's love for the disciples (13:34; 15:12) and their love for one another (13:34-35; 15:12, 17). His prayer is that the Father's love for him might be 'in them' as well, and in that sense, consequently, he can add 'and I in them,' for (as we have seen throughout the farewell discourse) the concrete expression of 'indwelling' (14:20; 15:1-8) is love" (Michaels, *John*, 882).

life for them, the disciples, as well as the audience, in laying down their lives, whether literally or metaphorically, by loving one another will participate in true worship for divine life eternal.

Jesus' statement, "I am not speaking about *all* of you; I know those whom I have chosen" (13:18), recalls that not *all* of his disciples are clean, as he knew Judas was going to "betray" or "give him over" to a sacrificial death (13:11), even though he was one of the twelve whom "I have chosen" (6:70). The Scripture (Ps 41[LXX 40]:10) to be fulfilled thus refers to Judas: "The one feeding on my bread lifted up his heel against me" (13:18). That he "lifted up" his heel for a metaphorical malicious kick against Jesus characterizes his betrayal as an offense against the intimacy of his meal fellowship with Jesus. But, ironically, it contributed to the divine necessity for Jesus as the Son of Man to be "lifted up/exalted" in crucifixion (3:14), so that everyone who believes in him might have divine life eternal (3:15). And that Judas did this as the one "feeding on" my "bread" ironically contributed to the establishment of the Eucharist. It made it possible for Jesus to give his flesh for the life of the world as the living "bread" (6:51); the one "feeding on" this "bread" in the Eucharist will live for eternity (6:58).

In view of his imminent departure from them (13:33), Jesus gave his disciples a new commandment that they should love "one another," just as he has loved them, they are also to love "one another" (13:34). This confirms and clarifies that his previous instruction that they ought to wash the feet of "one another" (13:14) was a symbolic model for how they are to love one another as Jesus loved them to the end of his life and to the uttermost (13:1)—by laying down his life for them. This new "commandment" thus accords with the "commandment" Jesus received from his Father, that he has the divine authority to lay down his life and the divine authority to take it up again (10:18). The Father gave Jesus this "commandment" (12:49) and Jesus knows that his "commandment" is divine life eternal (12:50). As the hallmark for being a disciple of Jesus (13:35), the fulfillment of this new commandment for the disciples to love one another as Jesus loved them coincides with the divine commandment for him to lay down his life for them in an act of supreme love.

One of the many interpersonal "dwellings" within the Father's household is that of the Spirit whom John saw come down and "remain" or "dwell" upon Jesus, enabling him to baptize with the Holy Spirit (1:33). This provides the basis for the household's sacramental worship, as it enables a believer to be born from above/again from water and the Spirit in the sacrament of baptism (3:3, 5). The Samaritans asked Jesus to "remain" or "dwell" with them and he "remained" there two days (4:40), which resulted in more of them believing (4:41) and in their declaration to the Samaritan woman, as well as to the audience, that Jesus is a worthy object of worship. Indeed, they confess that they know that he is "truly the savior of the world" (4:42). This exemplifies what it means that the hour is now here for true worshipers to worship in the Spirit that "dwells" upon Jesus (1:33) and in the truth that he embodies (4:23–24; cf. 1:14, 17). And whoever eats the flesh of Jesus and drinks his blood in the sacrament of the Eucharist "remains" or "dwells" in Jesus and Jesus in him (6:56).

Jesus climaxed his exchange with Philip regarding the unity of Jesus and the Father (14:7–9) with the declaration that the Father "dwelling" in Jesus does his works (14:10). This exemplifies another one of the many "dwellings," the divine interpersonal relationships, within the household of the Father which facilitate its worship (14:2). That Jesus is in the Father and the Father is in him (14:10–11) and that he is going to the Father (14:12) establishes him as an object, along with the Father, of supplicatory worship for the disciples, as well as the audience. Whatever they ask for in their petitionary prayers in the name of Jesus, he will do, so that, in turn, the Father, the ultimate object of worship, may be "glorified" in the Son (14:13). Indeed, since God will give to Jesus whatever he asks him (11:22; cf. 9:31), whatever they ask Jesus in his name he will do (14:14). The worship of praying to Jesus as the Son amounts to the worship of glorifying God as the Father.

As the "good shepherd," Jesus "lays down his life for the sheep" (10:11, 15). But "the sheep" for whom Jesus "lays down his life" in an act of self-sacrificial worship are his "friends," those whom he loves (cf. 11:5, 11), as no one has greater love than this (15:13). The disciples are no longer "slaves" (15:15) but the "friends" of Jesus if they do what he commands them (15:14)—love one another as he loves them. They thus, like Jesus, "remain" in the "household" for eternity (8:35). He chose and appointed them that they may go and "produce fruit and your fruit may remain," so that whatever they in prayer ask the Father in his name he will give them (15:16; cf. 14:13–14; 15:7). They are to "produce fruit"—future believers—by loving one another (15:17). Accordingly, their "fruit" may "remain" in Jesus as the true vine (15:4, 5, 6, 7) and in his love (15:9, 10). And their "fruit," as believers, may "remain" within the many "dwellings," the divine interpersonal relationships (14:10, 17, 23, 25), within the household of the Father (14:2), the household of communal worship for divine life eternal.

Jesus had promised that the Father will give the disciples another Advocate to be with them for eternity (14:16), the Spirit of truth (14:17). This Advocate, the Holy Spirit, will teach them everything, remind them of everything Jesus told them (14:26), and testify about Jesus (15:26). When that one comes, the Spirit of truth, he will guide the disciples in all truth and prepare them for the future, as he "will announce" to them the things that are coming (16:13). Because he "will announce" to them what he will receive from Jesus (16:14), that is, he "will announce" to them everything that Jesus and the Father have (16:15), that one "will glorify" Jesus (16:14) as an object of worship. This recalls the Samaritan woman's declaration that when the Christ comes, that one "will announce" everything to us (4:25), preeminently everything involving the true worship of the Father in Spirit and truth (4:23-24). As the other Advocate, the Spirit of truth will thus guide the disciples in all truth, enabling them to be true worshipers who worship the Father in Spirit and truth by imitating Jesus' self-sacrificial worship.

Jesus developed the worship theme of petitionary prayer (cf. 14:13-14; 15:7, 16) as he promised his disciples that when he sees them again (16:22) whatever they "ask" the Father in his name he will give them (16:23). Although they have not yet "asked" anything in his name, they are to "ask" and they will receive, so that their "joy may be fulfilled" (16:24). This implies that they are to pray for divine assistance to love one another. It recalls that Jesus told them that if they keep his commandments (15:10), especially that they love one another in the self-sacrificial way that he loves them (15:12), his joy may be in them and their "joy may be fulfilled" (15:11). In the future they will "ask" in his name (16:26) but the Father himself who loves them (16:27) will answer, as Jesus is leaving the world and going back to the Father (16:28). Although they will have trouble in the world, they are to take courage since Jesus has conquered the world (16:33; cf. 15:18) through his self-sacrificial love (12:25, 31; 14:30-31; 16:11) which they are to imitate with the assistance they receive from their petitionary prayer.

Jesus prayed that all believers may be united in the unity he shares with the Father, so that "the world may believe that you sent me" (17:20-21), and thus have life eternal (3:16-17). Jesus has given believers the "glory" the Father gave him, the glory of divine life eternal through self-sacrificial love, "so that they may be one as we are one" (17:22) in a communion of divine love (17:23). Jesus' prayerful "I desire" is that believers may be with him, "so that they may see my glory, which you gave me because you loved me before the foundation of the world" (17:24). This refers to the glory of Jesus as the Word who was with God and was God (1:1-2), the basis for the communal doxological worship that "we observed his glory, glory as of the unique one from the Father, full of a gift of truth" (1:14). Jesus concluded his prayer with the desire that the life-giving love with which the Father loved him, as well as he himself, may be in the disciples (17:26). With Jesus, the embodiment of the truth of self-sacrificial, life-giving love in them, disciples may thus become true worshipers of the Father in Spirit and truth (4:23-24).

8

Jesus' Self-Sacrificial Death Produces Divine Life-Giving Worship (18:1—19:42)

As the Unique High Priest Jesus Sacrifices Himself for Divine Life Eternal (18:1-27)

After his prayer (17:1-26) Jesus went out "with his disciples" across the Kidron valley where there was a garden, into which he entered—"he and his disciples" (18:1), the place where Jesus often gathered together "with his disciples" (18:2). The emphasis upon the close union of Jesus with his disciples in this "place" anticipates his preparation of a "place" for them to worship with Jesus in the communal household of his Father (14:2; 4:20). After he prepares this "place" of worship by returning to the Father, "I will come again and take you to myself so that where I am you also may be" (14:3). That Jesus "entered" the garden with his disciples characterizes him as the gate/good shepherd, recalling that whoever "enters" through him will be saved (10:9) and have life eternal (10:10). And he "gathered together" there with his disciples. This anticipates that he will "gather together" into one the dispersed children of God, his sheep (11:52;10:12), by his act of self-sacrificial worship in laying down his life "for" (ὑπέρ) the sheep/people/nation as the good shepherd/high priest, so that they may have divine life eternal (10:11, 15; 11:50-52).

Judas took a cohort of soldiers as well as officers from the chief priests and from the Pharisees (18:3), who wanted to kill Jesus (11:47, 53) because they feared that all will believe in him and then the Romans will come and take away their "place"/temple for worship and their nation (11:48). They came there with lanterns and torches for light and weapons for killing (18:3). This characterizes them as those who walk in the darkness of death rather than believing in Jesus to have the light of divine life eternal (8:12; 12:46). After Jesus went out and asked, "Whom are you seeking?" (18:4), they answered him, "Jesus the Nazorean [τὸν Ναζωραῖον]" (18:5). Ironically, this offers them the opportunity to believe in and worship Jesus. It recalls that Jesus' question to his first followers, "What are you seeking?" (1:38), led to their discovery that he is the Christ (1:41), "the one from Nazareth [τὸν ἀπὸ Ναζαρέτ]" (1:45), whom Nathanael believed in and worshiped as the Son of God and King of Israel (1:49).

Jesus' reply to them, "I am," not only identified him as the Nazorean they are seeking (18:5) to kill but recalls previous "I am" pronouncements indicating that he is the one who offers believers divine life eternal (6:35, 48, 51; 8:12, 24; 10:10–11; 11:25; 14:6). Although Judas, who knew the place and was standing with them, was the one who betrayed or "gave over" (παραδιδούς) Jesus to a sacrificial death (18:2, 5), Jesus, knowing all the things coming upon him (18:4), gave himself up as the good shepherd/high priest who lays down his life "for" (ὑπέρ) others (10:11, 15; 11:50, 51, 52; 15:13) as an act of self-sacrificial worship (10:18). Overawed by Jesus' divinely superior "I am," they "withdrew backwards [ἀπῆλθον εἰς τὰ ὀπίσω] and fell [ἔπεσαν] to the ground" (18:6). This underlines their unbelief, as it recalls and resonates with those disciples who "withdrew backwards" (ἀπῆλθον εἰς τὰ ὀπίσω) and no longer walked with Jesus (6:66). But it also, ironically, places them in a position of worshiping Jesus, as it recalls how Mary "fell" (ἔπεσεν) at the feet of Jesus in a gesture of reverential worship (11:32).

The repetition of Jesus' question regarding whom they are seeking and their repeated reply, "Jesus the Nazorean" (18:7), underline his self-surrender and thus self-sacrificial worship as the good shepherd/high priest. After his emphatic insistence upon his identification and divine status as "I am," Jesus directed them to "let these go [ἄφετε τούτους ὑπάγειν]" (18:8), thus saving his disciples from physical death, reminiscent of his raising of Lazarus from physical death to life with the identical directive, "untie him and let him go [ἄφετε αὐτὸν ὑπάγειν]" (11:44). This indicates how Jesus did not "lose" or "let perish" a single one of those God gave him as believers (18:9; cf. 17:12). Caiaphas, the high priest that year (11:49), prophesied that Jesus was going to die (11:51) for the people so that the whole nation may not "perish" (11:50). As the new and unique high priest, Jesus was to die in an act of self-sacrificial worship not only for the Jewish nation but to gather together into one the dispersed children of God (11:52), all believers, so that they may not "perish" but have divine life eternal (3:16; 6:39–40; 10:28).

Peter cut off the right ear of Malchus, the high priest's servant, a mutilation disqualifying this chief representative of the high priest from assisting in his sacrificial office (18:10; cf. Lev 21:16–23).[1] Peter was thus hindering not only the high priest's sacrifice of Jesus (11:51) but also Jesus' own high-priestly act of self-sacrificial worship. Jesus rejected Peter's violent defense lest it prevent him from "drinking the cup" of suffering and death the Father has given him (18:11).[2] Jesus' willingness to "drink the cup" the Father has given him resonates with his being the good shepherd/high priest who freely sacrifices his own life for the sheep and people of God (10:11–15; 11:50–52), in accord with the command he received from his Father (10:17–18). Drinking the cup of death the Father "has given" him will enable Jesus, as the new and unique high priest, to surpass the high priest Caiaphas by not losing or letting perish a single one of all those believers the Father "has given" him (18:9) so that they may have divine life eternal.

Jesus continued to allow himself to be the sacrificial victim as the band of soldiers, the tribune, and the Jewish officers arrested, bound, and led him before Annas first, for he was the father-in-law of Caiaphas, the high priest of that year (18:12–13). Caiaphas had advised the Jews that it was better for "one man" to die for the people (18:14; cf. 11:49–50). Despite Peter's violent assault of the high priest's servant (18:10), neither he nor any of the other disciples were arrested along with Jesus. This underlines the uniqueness of Jesus as the one high priest who sacrifices himself as the unique victim in contrast to a confusing plurality evident in the Jewish high priesthood. That both Annas and Caiaphas are referred to as high priest (18:19, 24) creates confusion for the audience about who is truly the high priest. This confusion reinforces the singularity of Jesus as the "one man" to die for the people, the one who offers his own life in an act of self-sacrificial worship as the one and only true high priest, the "one" shepherd (10:16) who gathers into "one" God's dispersed children (11:52) to share in divine life eternal (1:12).

After Jesus was arrested, Simon Peter and another disciple "followed" him (18:15). They thus represent the sheep who "follow" the good shepherd rather than another leader (10:4–5, 27). This other disciple was "known" to the high priest (18:15), which associates him with the high priest Caiaphas. But on a deeper level it also associates him with the high priest Jesus, who, as

---

1. "That the narrator discloses the name, Malchus, of this member of the otherwise anonymous group of officers from the chief priests and Pharisees (18:3) further associates him with the high priest whose name, Caiaphas, has also been disclosed (11:49), and thus heightens his importance as a chief representative of the high priest" (Heil, *Blood and Water*, 27). "[T]he proximity to the high priest is highlighted by the Greek word order: not 'he struck the servant of the high priest' but 'he struck *the* of the high priest *servant*,' as though the servant to some degree 'contained' or represented the high priest" (Brodie, *John*, 527; emphases original).

2. The image of the cup one must drink refers to one's destiny determined by God. See BDAG, 857.

the good shepherd, lays down his life for the sheep whom "I know" and who "know" me (10:14). As an ideal representative of the disciples, this other disciple entered the "courtyard" (αὐλή) of the high priest (18:15), which also represents the "sheepfold" (αὐλή) of the good shepherd (10:1, 16). Peter, however, remained standing before the "gate" (18:16), a symbol of Jesus, who had declared, "I am the gate of the sheep" (10:7). It is then emphatically repeated that the other disciple was "known" to the high priest (18:16). This implies that he knows of the necessity for the high priest Jesus to lay down his life in an act of self-sacrificial worship for the divine life eternal of the sheep.

The other disciple went out and brought Peter, as one of the sheep, through the gate into the courtyard/sheepfold of the high priest/good shepherd. The other disciple spoke to the "gatekeeper" in order to bring Peter in (18:16). This placed Peter in the position of being not only a sheep but also a shepherd. Jesus had stated that whoever enters through the gate is shepherd of the sheep. For him the "gatekeeper" opens (10:2–3). As a sheep, Peter numbers among the disciples for whom Jesus, the good shepherd, lays down his life. But as a true shepherd and disciple, Peter must in turn lay down his life as an act of self-sacrificial worship for the sheep (10:11). Just as Jesus washed the feet of his disciples, a gesture symbolic of his self-sacrificial death for them, so they must wash one another's feet (13:14–16). This means they are to love one another as Jesus loved them in accord with the new commandment he gave them (13:34; 15:12, 17). And no one has greater love than to lay down his life in an act of self-sacrificial worship for the divine life eternal of his friends (15:13; 12:50).

Peter was very eager to fulfill the role of both the good shepherd and the disciple who lays down his life when he promised Jesus, "I will lay down my life for you" (13:37). Instead he fulfilled Jesus' prediction that he would deny him thrice (13:38; 18:17–18, 25–27). But, nevertheless, Peter entered the courtyard/sheepfold as one of the sheep for whom the good shepherd/high priest lays down his life. Before Peter, and any member of the audience, can be a disciple/shepherd who lays down his life for his friends (13:14–16, 37; 15:12–13), he must realize the need to be a disciple/sheep for whom the good shepherd and unique high priest Jesus first lays down his own life in an act of self-sacrificial worship for divine life eternal.[3]

---

3. Heil, "Unique High Priest," 735–39.

The Jews and Pilate Enable the Self-Sacrificial Worship of Jesus (18:28—19:11)

While leading Jesus to his death, the Jews were concerned with being able to eat the Passover meal that included the Passover lamb (18:28). This reminds the audience that the self-sacrificial death of Jesus will enable him to become the new Passover Lamb of God (1:29, 36), who gives his flesh to be eaten as the bread of divine life eternal in eucharistic worship (6:50–58).[4] Pilate's reference to Jesus as "this man" (18:29) recalls Caiaphas's reference to Jesus as "this man" who is doing many signs (11:47), the one and only "man" whose sacrificial death not only can save the people (11:50; 18:14), but gather into one the dispersed children of God (11:52), all those who believe, for divine life eternal (1:12).

The Jews told Pilate that if "this one" were not doing evil, "we would not have given him over [παρεδώκαμεν] to you" (18:30). This associates them with Judas, repeatedly identified as the one who "betrayed" or "gave over" (παραδιδούς) Jesus (18:2, 5; cf. 6:64, 71; 12:4; 13:2, 11, 21). But on the deeper level of the divine plan God "gave" (ἔδωκεν) his unique Son over to a self-sacrificial death, so that everyone who believes in him might not perish but might have divine life eternal (3:16). Accordingly, it is not "lawful" or "permitted" (ἔξεστιν) for the Jews to kill anyone (18:31; cf. 5:10), since Jesus will lay down his life on his own in accord with the command he received from his Father (10:18).[5] This is confirmed by the notice that they said this "in order that the word of Jesus might be fulfilled that he said indicating the kind of death he was to die" (18:32; cf. 12:33)—a self-sacrificial death of being "lifted up/exalted" by God (divine passive) in crucifixion so that he might draw all "to myself" as both the personified place and object of true worship (12:32; 14:3).[6]

---

4. "While so scrupulous to safeguard their capacity to consume the paschal lamb of the old order, they are—ironically—bent on bringing about the death of the Lamb who truly takes away the sin of the world" (Byrne, *Life Abounding*, 302).

5. "The point is that now, in saying, 'It is not lawful for us to kill anyone,' the Jewish chief priests have condemned themselves, validating at last Jesus' judgments on them long before at the Tent festival: 'Has Moses not given you the law? And none of you does the law? Why are you seeking to kill me?' (7:19), and 'If you are Abraham's children, you would be doing the works of Abraham. But now you are seeking to kill me' (8:39–40a)" (Michaels, *John*, 918).

6. "Once again, then (cf. 18:9, 27), we are reminded that, while pressing for his death, the authorities are following a divinely ordained script" (Byrne, *Life Abounding*, 303). "For Jesus to draw people 'to himself,' simultaneously means drawing them to God and his true Temple" (Hoskins, *Temple*, 157).

Pilate's words to Jesus, introduced with an emphatic "you," carry a double meaning. On the one hand they continue the denigration of Jesus as "this man" (18:29) with a derisive, incredulous question: "*You* [of all people!] are the King of the Jews?" (18:33). But ironically for the audience Pilate's scornful question can also be heard on a deeper level as an act of worship: "*You* [truly] are the King of the Jews!"[7] This ironic declaration that Jesus is the King of the Jews by the non-Jewish (18:35) Roman governor complements the worship of him as the King of Israel by Jews (1:49; 12:13). Indeed, as the divine King, Jesus is an object of worship not only for Jews and Greeks (12:20-21) but for all people (11:50-52; 12:32). As one whose own nation and chief priests "gave over [παρέδωκάν]" to Pilate for a self-sacrificial death (18:35), Jesus' kingdom is not of this world, otherwise "I would not have been given over [παραδοθῶ] to the Jews" (18:36) by God (divine passive) for a self-sacrificial death. Jesus is thus King in a kingdom not of this world but in the kingdom of God (3:3, 5).

As King, Jesus was born and came into the world, sent by the Father (5:43; 7:28; 8:42; 16:28) to lay down his life in love for others as an act of self-sacrificial worship for divine life eternal (3:16-17; 10:10-18; 12:50; 15:12-13), so that he might testify to the truth. Everyone who is of the truth "hears" his "voice" (18:37), that is, "hears" the "voice" of Jesus as the good shepherd/king and follows him (10:3-5, 16, 27) to have divine life eternal through self-sacrificial love for one another. Pilate, apparently exasperated, muttered to Jesus, "What is truth?" (18:38), an ironic question the audience can answer for themselves.[8] As those who have heard the voice of Jesus as the good shepherd/king so that they are of the truth, believers are to appreciate that the truth to which Jesus testified consists of having divine life eternal through self-sacrificial love of one another. This is the truth by which true worshipers will worship the Father in "Spirit and truth" (4:23-24), in Jesus who is the personification of truth (14:6) as the good shepherd/king who lays down his life in self-sacrificial worship for divine life eternal.[9]

---

7. That these words are introduced by "he said" rather than "he asked" (cf. 18:19) and begin with an emphatic "you" facilitate this double meaning. See also Duke, *Irony*, 189n29.

8. "Pilate's physical and mental ambivalence becomes the ultimate catalyst for audience members to stop the vacillating and make the decision for themselves" (Brown, "Truth," 86). See also Michaels, *John*, 926.

9. "Here, the notion of 'kingship,' while not denied, is subordinated to Jesus' primary mission, which is that of being witness to 'the truth': that is, the revelation of God that exposes and strips away delusion and self-centeredness and draws human beings into the divine communion of love. The Son, who is ever 'with God' (1:1-2, 18), became incarnate for this and entered the world for this: that human beings, who are of the world, might share the (eternal) life of God (3:16)" (Byrne, *Life Abounding*, 305).

In rejecting Pilate's offer to release to them the "King of the Jews" at the Passover (18:39), the Jews facilitated Jesus' self-sacrifice as the new Passover Lamb of God (1:29, 36). In demanding Barabbas instead, who was a "robber" (18:40), they accepted one of the "robbers" representative of those who came before the good shepherd (10:1, 8), rather than "hearing the voice" (18:37; 10:3, 16, 27) of Jesus, the good shepherd/king. After Pilate had Jesus scourged (19:1), in a cruel parody of a royal Roman coronation and investiture the soldiers placed a crown of thorns on Jesus' head and clothed him with an imperial purple garment (19:2). Preceding their slaps, their declaration mimicking the way they would address their own Roman emperor, "Hail, King of the Jews!" (19:3), on the deeper level is an ironic act of worship.[10] From the viewpoint of the audience, Jesus is to be worshiped as the King of Jews, Gentiles, and all people as the good shepherd/king, not of this world (18:36), who lays down his life in self-sacrificial worship to draw all believers (12:32) to divine life eternal with the Father (10:11, 15–18, 27–30).[11]

Pilate again came outside the praetorium and told the Jews he was leading Jesus out to them, so that they may know that he finds no case or cause in him (19:4). But Jesus came outside on his own rather than being led out, depicted as actively wearing, rather than passively clothed with (19:2), the thorny crown and royal purple garment (19:5). This accords with Jesus laying down his own life in self-sacrificial worship as the good shepherd/king (10:11, 16, 17–18).

Having contemptuously referred to Jesus as "this man" (18:29), Pilate declared to the Jews, "Behold [ἰδού], the Man!" (19:5), rather than, as might be expected, "Behold, your King!"[12] This recalls and resonates with John's declaration, "Behold [ἴδε], the Lamb of God who takes away the sin of the world!" (1:29; cf. 1:36), indicating the worthiness of Jesus to be worshiped as the new sacrificial Passover Lamb. It also reaffirms and complements the

---

10. "The soldiers mimic the '*Ave Caesar*' greeting given the Emperor" (Brown, *John*, 875). The undeserved "slap" (ῥάπισμα) the Jewish officer of the high priest gave Jesus (18:22), the new and unique high priest who transcends the Jewish high priesthood, is complemented by the abusive "slaps" (ῥαπίσματα) the Roman soldiers gave Jesus (19:3), who transcends Jewish and Roman kingship as the divine King not of this world.

11. "Yes, he is 'King of the Jews'—though the leaders of that nation will not own it. Moreover, as non-Jews themselves, the soldiers represent the nations of the world ('the Greeks' [12:21]) whom Jesus will 'draw' in allegiance to himself as king when 'lifted up' upon the cross (12:32)" (Byrne, *Life Abounding*, 308).

12. "John's formulation of Pilate's mockery of both Jesus and Jewish notions of kingship employs words used of Israel's very first king ['Behold, the man' in LXX 1 Sam 9:17] and thereby reinforces Jesus' true identity as 'King of the Jews'" (Lincoln, *John*, 466).

statement of the Jewish high priest Caiaphas, who referred to Jesus as the "one man" to die as a sacrificial victim not only for the Jewish nation (11:50) but to gather into one the dispersed children of God (11:52). And it ironically points to Jesus as the "Son of Man" now in the process of being "lifted up/exalted" (3:14; 8:28; 12:32–34) and "glorified" (12:23; 13:31) as both the personified place and object of worship for divine life eternal.[13]

Jesus' allusion to the "authority" that comes from above (19:11) contributes to the Johannine theme of the authority given to Jesus and those who believe in and worship him. Jesus previously prayed for the Father to glorify him so that the Son may glorify the Father, just as the Father has given him "authority" over all people, so that he may give divine life eternal to all whom the Father has given him (17:1–2). As the good shepherd who lays down his life in self-sacrificial worship for the sheep (10:11, 15, 17), and thus obeyed the command he received from his Father, he received authority over his life: "I have authority to lay it down, and I have authority to take it up again" (10:18). This overshadows Pilate's vain assertion of his imperial authority over Jesus' life: "I have authority to release you and I have authority to crucify you" (19:10). That Jesus pointed Pilate to the "authority" that is "from above" (19:11), ultimately from God, then, functions as an appeal for the audience to believe in and worship Jesus who has the "authority" from above to grant them divine life eternal as God's children (1:12).

Jesus' declaration that those who "gave him over" to Pilate to be crucified as a sacrificial victim have a greater "sin" (19:11) brings the audience to a climactic moment. The revelation Jesus gave Pilate inside the praetorium (18:33–38a; 19:1–3, 8–11) invites each member of the audience to make a personal decision to avoid not only Pilate's sin of unbelief but the "greater sin," the greater unbelief, of the individuals who rejected Jesus outside the praetorium (18:28–32, 38b-40; 19:4–7). All members of the audience, then, are called to believe in and worship the Jesus who has given authority to believers to become children of God (1:12) as the self-sacrificial Lamb of God who takes away the "sin" of the world (1:29, 36).[14]

---

13. "Pilate, the Gentile, cannot be made to say *Son of man* outright, for that would not only be historically implausible but violate the sanctity of that title as Jesus' own. Pilate can, however, be permitted to say with plausibility and great sarcasm, 'Behold the man!'—not only a majestic title itself, but one that evokes for perceptive readers a vision of 'heaven opened, and the angels of God ascending and descending upon the Son of man' (1:51)" (Duke, *Irony*, 107; emphasis original). See also Michaels, *John*, 930.

14. On John 18:28—19:11, see Heil, *Blood and Water*, 45–76.

The Self-Sacrificial Worship of Jesus in His Death and Burial (19:12-42)

The Jews warned Pilate that if he releases Jesus, "You are not a friend of Caesar.[15] Everyone who makes himself a king opposes Caesar" (19:12). This recalls and complements the Jews' previous false accusation that Jesus "made himself Son of God" (19:7). Together these two false accusations remind the audience that Jesus is the object of true worship as both the Son of God and the King of Israel (1:49; 11:27; 12:13, 15). The Father has made Jesus the Son of God (10:36) and, rather than man made, his divine kingship is not of this world (18:36).[16] It is not so much that Jesus' kingship "opposes" Caesar or disqualifies one from being a "friend" of Caesar as that it totally transcends the pretentions of worldly power with an authority that comes "from above" (19:11). Indeed, unlike Caesar and all other human kings, Jesus, the good shepherd/king, lays down his life for his "friends" (15:13) in an act of self-sacrificial worship for divine life eternal (10:11, 15, 28). This makes him worthy to be worshiped by the audience as both the divine Son of God and the divine King not only of Israel/Jews but of all human beings.

In another example of Johannine double meaning with purposeful ambiguity (e.g., 7:37-38), when Pilate led Jesus out, either he himself "sat" (ἐκάθισεν as intransitive) or he "sat" (ἐκάθισεν as transitive) Jesus on the elevated "judicial platform" (βήματος) at a place called Stone Pavement, in Hebrew, Gabbatha (19:13).[17] On the surface level Pilate himself sat on the seat of judgment to judge the case of Jesus, but on the deeper ironic level Jesus sat there as *the* Judge. This accords with the Johannine view that the Father has given all judgment to the Son, so that all may honor/worship the Son just as they honor/worship the Father for divine life eternal (5:22-26). The Father gave Jesus authority to exercise judgment, because he is the Son of Man (5:27). In taking his seat on the elevated judicial platform, Jesus is thus in the process of being lifted up/exalted/glorified through his act of self-sacrificial worship as the Son of Man who will draw all to himself

---

15. "It is possible that 'friend of Caesar' is a technical reference to a specific privilege bestowed upon those whose service of the emperor has won formal recognition" (Byrne, *Life Abounding*, 312n64).

16. "The identification of 'Son of God' and 'King' is something the reader understands, for Nathanael paired the two titles right from the start (1:49), and the reader knows full well that Jesus *is* both 'Son of God' and 'King of Israel.' What is not true is that he has 'made himself' either of those things. He is, on the contrary, One 'whom the Father consecrated and sent into the world' (10:36), and 'the One coming in the name of the Lord' (12:13), who speaks and acts *not* 'on his own,' but always at the Father's command" (Michaels, *John*, 939; emphases original).

17. On the transitive and intransitive meanings of καθίζω, see BDAG, 491-92.

(12:32; cf. 3:14–15; 8:28) as both the personified place and object of worship for divine life eternal.[18]

On the surface level Pilate ridiculed the Jews with his judicial pronouncement regarding Jesus, "Behold, your King!" (19:14). But on the deeper level he points to Jesus, the divine King not of this world (18:36), as an object of true worship through his being lifted up/exalted and thus glorified by crucifixion (19:6, 10, 15).[19] This recalls and complements the declaration not only of Pilate, "Behold, the man!" (19:5), alluding to Jesus as the Son of Man to be lifted up/exalted as the "one man" to sacrifice himself for divine life eternal (3:14–15; 8:28; 11:50; 12:32), but of John, "Behold, the Lamb of God" (1:29, 36), alluding to Jesus as the sacrificial Passover Lamb. Jesus is to be worshiped then as the good shepherd/king who sacrificed himself as the Passover Lamb of God. This is indicated by the notice that it was the preparation day for the Passover (19:14), the day the priests in the temple began to slaughter the paschal lambs to be eaten as sacrificial victims in the Passover meal that evening.[20]

Jesus is the divine Judge/King (19:13–14) in the sense that he compels a faith decision. God sent the Son into the world not to judge the world, but that the world might be saved through him. Whoever believes in him is not judged, but whoever does not believe has already been judged (3:17–18). The notice that "the hour was about the sixth" (19:14) recalls the identical notice (4:6) that resulted in the faith decision by the Samaritans that Jesus is truly the savior of the world (4:42). In contrast, at this hour Pilate rejected Jesus as "your" (not "my") king (19:14) and the chief priests disowned their divine King with an idolatrous, "We have no king but Caesar!" (19:15).[21] In contrast to the crowd who "cried out" in worship of Jesus as the King of Israel (12:13), the Jews "cried out" to Pilate, "Take him away, take him away,

---

18. On βῆμα as an elevated judicial platform, see BDAG, 175. The likely meaning of "Gabbatha" is high place or hill, which subtly accents the exalted position of Jesus as Judge/Son of Man (see Lincoln, *John*, 470; Byrne, *Life Abounding*, 313n68).

19. "If—as is generally agreed—the crucifixion is Jesus' 'lifting up' (as in 3:14; 8:28; 12:32), it is just as plausible to think of the presentation, 'Look, your king!' as his 'glorification' (as in 7:39; 11:4; 12:16, 23, 28; 13:31–32; 17:1, 5), for the one is no less ironic than the other" (Michaels, *John*, 943).

20. Keener, *John*, 2.1130–31; Michaels, *John*, 942.

21. "Their cry, 'We have no king but Caesar' (19:15), is idolatrous. It is a choice to reject God's divine sovereignty now manifest before them in Jesus, who alone, and not the emperor, can identify himself as 'I am'" (Coloe, *God Dwells*, 185). "The full force of this repudiation comes home in light of the solid biblical tradition of God as Israel's king" (Byrne, *Life Abounding*, 313). "It is ironically, soberly, and tragically true that for those who do not believe in the kingship not of this world there is indeed 'no king but Caesar' (19:15)" (Heil, *Blood and Water*, 83).

crucify him!" (19:15), ironically making him the Lamb of God who "takes away" the sin of the world (1:29). This invites the audience to make the decision to worship Jesus as their divine King not of this world, who sacrifices himself as the true Passover Lamb to offer the world divine life eternal.

Although the Jews had "given over" Jesus to Pilate (18:30, 35) and Pilate "gave over" Jesus to the Jews to be crucified (19:16) as a sacrificial victim, Jesus will ultimately sacrifice himself. The Jews "accepted" (παρέλαβον) Jesus to be crucified (19:16), reaffirming that his own people did not "accept" (παρέλαβον) him (1:11) by believing in his name (1:12). Jesus actively "came out" on his own rather than passively being led out of the praetorium, boldly wearing the thorny crown and the purple garment of his derided kingship (19:5). He now again actively "came out" on his own to the place of crucifixion, triumphantly carrying the cross of his royal enthronement "for himself" (19:17).[22] He thus continued to demonstrate that he is the good shepherd/king, who allows no one to take his life from him, but lays down his life "on my own" (10:18). By crucifying Jesus in the middle of two others at a place with a Jewish name (19:17), like a king elevated and enthroned between his royal attendants (19:18), the Jews ironically established Jesus as an object of worship, as the divine King not of this world (18:36).[23]

Complementing what Moses with divine authority "wrote" about Jesus (1:45; 5:46), Pilate "wrote" an inscription and placed in on the cross. There was "written," ultimately by God (divine passive), "Jesus the Nazorean, the King of the Jews" (19:19). And it was decisively "written," ultimately by God, in Hebrew, Latin, and Greek (19:20), the three principal languages of the world at that time. The chief priests of the Jews urged Pilate to write instead, "This one said, I am King of the Jews" (19:21). But actually Jesus said that he was the Nazorean with an absolute "I am" (18:5, 6, 8), indicating his divine status, which overawed his arrestors to fall to the ground in an ironic gesture of worship (18:6). Pilate had said Jesus is the King of the Jews (18:33, 37, 39; 19:14, 15), now ironically writing that, as the Nazorean (cf. 1:46), Jesus is the divine King of the Jews. His refusal to the Jews, "What I have written, I have written" (19:22), reinforces that it was divinely, decisively "written"

---

22. "Literally the Greek means: 'He carried the cross for himself' as something that for him had great value. In this way the evangelist wants to show that Jesus did not carry the cross like a man condemned to death, undergoing punishment unwillingly, going to his fate passively, facing torments under compulsion. No. Christ carries the cross 'for himself' as the privileged instrument of his work of salvation, the sign of his triumph and of his sovereignty" (de la Potterie, *Hour*, 93).

23. "Moreover, while not denying the aspect of suffering and degradation, John is more intent on telling the 'other side' of the story: a victory of divine love in which Jesus is exalted upon the cross to reign as King" (Byrne, *Life Abounding*, 315).

that Jesus is the divine King of the Jews, enthroned by his self-sacrificial crucifixion, to be worshiped by the whole world.[24]

Jesus took off his "clothes" (13:4) when he washed the feet of his disciples in order for them to have a "share" (μέρος) with him (13:8) in the divine life eternal that his self-sacrificial death produces. Jesus' clothes represent his life. That Jesus "took off" or "laid down [τίθησιν]" (13:4) his clothes symbolized how he, as the good shepherd/high priest, "lays down [τίθησιν]" (10:11; cf. 10:15) his own life to give divine life eternal to all who become his sheep by hearing, following, believing in, and worshiping him (10:27–28). By taking his "clothes" and making four "shares" (μέρη), a "share" (μέρος) for each soldier, the Roman soldiers who crucified Jesus (19:23) ironically anticipated how Jesus' death, as an act of self-sacrificial worship, will offer a share in divine life eternal to individual persons—even those who are Gentiles.[25]

The Roman soldiers' concern not to divide Jesus' tunic, "seamless, woven from above as a whole" (19:23), alludes to a rich biblical background in which the divinely determined and unified clothing of the high priest represents the unity of his people.[26] Just as Jesus had indicated to Pilate that divine authority comes "from above [ἄνωθεν]" (19:11), that Jesus' seamless tunic is woven "from above" (ἄνωθεν) indicates that its emphasized unity (both "seamless" and "woven as a whole") has a divine origin (see also 3:3, 7, 31). Although there has been "division" (σχίσμα) among the Jewish people regarding Jesus (7:43; 9:16; 10:19), the Gentile soldiers, by deciding, "Let us not divide [σχίσωμεν] it" (19:24), symbolically promoted the unity that Jesus' self-sacrificial death as the unique high priest will effect. The soldiers' desire not to divide the dying Jesus' seamless tunic woven from above as a

---

24. "The repeated accent on 'writing,' and what 'was written' (vv. 19–20), gives the notice an authoritative quality, almost comparable to the authority of Scripture (2:17; 6:31, 45; 8:17; 10:34; 12:14, 16; 15:25), or the Gospel of John itself (20:30–31)" (Michaels, *John*, 950). "Those drawn to the truth will see in the inscription a proclamation of true kingship, in which Jesus reigns from the cross, drawing to himself an allegiance of all who are on the side of truth (12:32). The multiple-language inscription announces the universal scope of that allegiance" (Byrne, *Life Abounding*, 316).

25. "John would have the reader see in Jesus' crucifixion, in the distribution of his garments among the soldiers, the graphic consummation of that which Jesus anticipated in John 13. In his crucifixion, then, Jesus fulfills his promises by laying down his garments (i.e., his life) so that he might proffer life. Not only this, one sees in the distribution of these garments that this life is given not only to the Jews but also to the Gentiles" (Schuchard, *Scripture*, 129).

26. Although not a tunic, which was an undergarment, the robe of the high priest is described as an undergarment worn under the ephod (Exod 28:31; 36:29), and this allows for the symbolic correspondence with the tunic of Jesus. For further details to this background, see Heil, "Unique High Priest," 742–43; Coloe, *God Dwells*, 201–6.

"whole" (ὅλου), a symbol of unity, corresponds to the high priest Caiaphas's advice to preserve the unity of the "whole" (ὅλον) nation by putting the one man Jesus to death (11:50).

But, as the unique high priest who surpasses the Jewish high priest, Jesus will die not just for the unity of the nation but to gather into one the dispersed children of God (11:52), all believers (cf. 1:12) dispersed throughout the world. By not dividing his unified tunic (19:23), the soldiers advanced the goal of Jesus as the good shepherd/high priest to unify all into a believing, worshiping community (10:15-16; 17:11, 20-23). What the Gentile soldiers did with the clothing of the crucified Jesus ironically advanced the divine plan recorded in Jewish Scripture with Jesus as the speaker: "They distributed my clothes among themselves, and for my clothing they cast lots [Ps 22 (LXX Ps 21):19]" (19:24). The soldiers shared the clothes of Jesus among themselves (19:23), which points to individual Gentiles appropriating the divine life eternal Jesus' death will effect. And they cast lots for his seamless tunic, which demonstrates how Gentiles will preserve and participate in the unity and universality of the believing, worshiping community established by Jesus' death, his act of self-sacrificial worship, as the unique high priest.

Whereas, "on the one hand" (μέν), the four male Gentile soldiers "then did these things" with the clothing of the dying Jesus (19:24), "meanwhile" or "on the other hand" (δέ), there were four Jewish women and a male disciple standing by the cross of the dying Jesus (19:25-26).[27] The soldiers shared the clothing of Jesus and vied for his tunic as anonymous individuals. But the women are named and identified by their relation to Jesus and others. The first two are related to Jesus as members of his family—his mother and his mother's sister. The third and fourth are both specifically named Mary—one identified in relation to Clopas as his wife, and the other, Mary Magdalene, identified in relation to the people of Magdala, a city on the Sea of Galilee (19:25). And the disciple is identified as the one whom Jesus loved (19:26; cf. 13:23). Thus the self-sacrificial death of Jesus establishes a believing, worshiping community that is to be unified, universal (Jews and Gentiles, men and women), and familial.

The crucified Jesus invited his mother and the beloved disciple to see and accept one another in a new familial relationship based on his self-sacrificial death. He exhorted his mother to see and accept a new maternal relationship with the beloved disciple, "Woman, behold, your son!" (19:26). And in turn he urged the disciple whom he loved to see and accept a new

27. "The Greek construction μέν . . . δέ links the soldiers in 19:24b with those associated with Jesus who stood near the cross" (Köstenberger, *John*, 547). See also BDAG, 629-30.

filial relationship with the mother of Jesus, "Behold, your mother!" (19:27). The one introduced as "his [Jesus'] mother [μήτηρ αὐτοῦ]" (19:25), and then referred to more generally as "the mother" (τὴν μητέρα; τῇ μητρί), addressed as "woman" (19:26; cf. 2:4), now becomes "your [the beloved disciple's] mother [μήτηρ σου]" (19:27).[28] The beloved disciple then took her to "his own" (19:27). He thus formed a new familial community of believers and household of worship, composed of family members and disciples (cf. 2:12), originating and resulting "from" (ἀπ') that "hour," the hour of Jesus' death as an act of self-sacrificial worship (19:27).[29]

The disciple whom Jesus loved embodies and represents all those disciples for whom Jesus demonstrates his great love by laying down his life for them in an act of self-sacrificial worship as "his own [τοὺς ἰδίους]" (13:1), his friends (15:12-13), his "sheep" (10:11, 15). The beloved disciple took the mother of Jesus "to his own [εἰς τὰ ἴδια]" (19:27) to give birth to a new family of faith and household of worship, which reverses the inadequate faith of each of the other disciples who was to scatter "to his own [εἰς τὰ ἴδια]" (16:32). Although Jesus came "to his own" (εἰς τὰ ἴδια) people who did not accept him (1:11), the beloved disciple took the mother of Jesus, the model of authentic faith (2:1-5), "to his own," that is, to believing disciples whom Jesus loves.[30] The "hour" of the "woman" whose sorrow turns to joy when she gives birth to a child (16:21) has arrived with the "hour" of Jesus' death as an act of self-sacrificial worship, when the "woman" who is his mother symbolically "gives birth" to a new son, the beloved disciple, who serves as a model for every member of the audience.[31]

With the arrival of the "hour" of his death Jesus invited the woman who is his mother to complete the initial family of faith and household of

---

28. "Although called 'mother,' her physical maternity has had no function in the narrative so far. Her motherhood is to function in a different symbolic way. When she is introduced by the narrator she is called ἡ μήτηρ αὐτοῦ (19:25, cf. 2:1). When the narrator changes to give us Jesus' perspective, she is not called his mother but the mother (τὴν μητέρα). Jesus speaks to the mother (19:26). The use of the definite article gives this title a universal significance" (Coloe, God Dwells, 187).

29. The preposition ἀπό can indicate both origin and cause, facilitating the double meaning; BDAG, 105-7.

30. "His own" (τὰ ἴδια) "has come to stand for the intimate circle of believers whom Jesus has 'loved unto the end' (13:1). It is, then, in the name of that community and as their representative that the disciple 'from that hour' takes Jesus' mother into the family of believers to be their mother too" (Byrne, Life Abounding, 319).

31. "The scattering of 16:32 has been reversed through the 'gathering' which takes place around the crucified, symbolized by the union of the Mother and the Disciple in 19:27. The mother of Jesus, 'the woman' who now becomes a 'mother' in this new situation, will lead the way in that process. She is the woman whose pain of 'the hour' of giving birth now brings joy (see 16:21)" (Moloney, "Mary," 439).

worship she originated in anticipation of the "hour" (2:12) by now embracing the beloved disciple as her own son (19:26). By taking her as his mother to his own (19:27), the beloved disciple established the familial community of those who are to believe with the faith of the mother of Jesus, who said, "Do whatever he tells you" (2:5). Jesus told his disciples to love one another in the self-sacrificial way that he, the good shepherd and unique high priest, loved them (10:11, 15; 13:34; 15:12-13). They are to become a familial household of believers who worship by practicing the self-sacrificial worship that consists of obeying his commandment to love one another as he loved them to have divine life eternal (10:27-28; 12:25, 50; 17:2-3). The mutual acceptance of the mother of Jesus and the beloved disciple to form a new family thus serves as a model for the audience as believers to become a familial household of worship by loving one another for divine life eternal.[32]

Jesus, "knowing" that "everything" had already been accomplished (cf. 13:1, 3; 18:4), in order that the Scripture might be completed, said, "I thirst [διψῶ]" (19:28). He thus began to complete the Scripture from Ps 69 (LXX 68):22: " . . . for my thirst [δίψαν] they gave me sour wine [ὄξος] to drink." This is confirmed with the notice that a vessel full of "sour wine" (ὄξους) was standing there, that they put a sponge full of "sour wine" (ὄξους) to his mouth (19:29), and that he then took the "sour wine [ὄξος]" (19:30). By taking the sour wine and dying, in correspondence to the bitter cup of death the Father has given him to drink (18:11), Jesus did not just "fulfill" a single scriptural quotation (cf. 13:18; 17:12; 19:24), but "completed" one quotation of Scripture with another from the same Psalm. By dying in accord with Ps 69 (LXX 68):22, Jesus complemented Ps 69 (LXX 68):10, "zeal for your house will consume me" (2:17), which predicted his self-sacrificial death preliminary to his body being raised as the new personified temple or house for the true worship of the Father (2:16, 19, 21).

Before Jesus transformed the Jewish water for cleansing (2:6) into an abundance of good "wine" (2:7-10), he told his mother that his hour has not yet come (2:4). Jesus thus anticipated the hour of his death on the cross. Now that that hour has arrived (12:23; 13:31-32), Jesus drank the "sour wine" (19:30) corresponding to the bitter self-sacrificial death (18:11) that makes possible the abundant good "wine" symbolic of divine life eternal.

---

32. "As in the farewell discourse, Jesus is making preparation for his departure from the world. Implicit in the words, 'Look, your son!' and 'Look, your mother!' is a command, and the command is simply a particular instance of the 'new command I give you, that you love each other, just as I loved you, that you too love each other' (13:34), a command that came right on the heels of the announcement that 'Where I am going, you cannot come' (13:33)" (Michaels, *John*, 959).

Putting a sponge full of sour wine on a branch of hyssop, they "offered" (προσήνεγκαν) it to the mouth of Jesus (19:29) in an ironic act of worship, recalling Jesus' prediction to his disciples that "everyone who kills you will think he is offering worship [λατρείαν προσφέρειν] to God" (16:2).[33] This gesture evokes the Passover ritual. The Israelites used hyssop to sprinkle the blood of the Passover lambs on their doorposts to save them from the destruction God was bringing upon their Egyptian oppressors. This ritual was to be commemorated in future Passover celebrations (Exod 12:21–27). In addition, this happened on the day of preparation for the Passover, when the lambs were slaughtered in the temple (19:14). When Jesus took the sour wine offered to him on the hyssop and died (19:30), he accepted the ironic act of worship that enabled him to complete his own self-sacrificial act of worship, establishing him as the true Passover Lamb of God who takes away the sin of the world (1:29, 36). He thereby enables believers to worship by loving one another in the self-sacrificial way that he did (13:34; 15:12–13).

Jesus' powerful pronouncement when he took the sour wine, "It is accomplished [τετέλεσται]!" (19:30), climactically confirms not only the accomplishment of the Scripture to be "completed [τελειωθῇ]" (19:28), but that everything the Father had given him to "complete" (cf. 4:34; 5:36; 17:4, 23) has been "accomplished [τετέλεσται]" (19:28) by his self-sacrificial death.[34] Whereas Jesus was a passive recipient of a crown of thorns placed upon his "head" in mockery of his kingship (19:2), he now actively bowed his "head" as he sacrificed himself in death (19:30). Because one of his disciples "will give me over [παραδώσει με]," Jesus was troubled in "the spirit [τῷ πνεύματι]" (13:21; cf. 11:33). In ironic contrast, Jesus now majestically "gave over the spirit [παρέδωκεν τὸ πνεῦμα]" (19:30), his previously troubled human spirit, in death. He thereby ultimately laid down his own life, as an act of self-sacrificial worship, in accord with the command he received from his Father (10:18).

After Jesus announced, "I thirst" (19:28), and drank the bitter sour wine of death, he gave over not only his human spirit but the holy Spirit of God (19:30). Jesus had previously expressed his thirst to the Samaritan woman by saying, "Give me a drink" (4:7). He then disclosed his ability to give her the "living water" (4:10) that quenches one's thirst for divine life

---

33. The branches at the end of the stalk of hyssop "would have formed a little nest into which the soggy sponge would have been placed. Since crucified people were not raised very high off the ground, the soldiers would have had to lift the stalk barely above their own heads" (Köstenberger, *John*, 550).

34. Note the subtle progression from the work(s) (4:34; 5:36; 17:4), believers (17:23), and Scripture (19:28) that are "completed" (from τελειόω) to everything that is fully and finally "accomplished [from τελέω]" (19:28, 30).

eternal (4:14). On the last and great day of the feast of Tabernacles Jesus stood up in the temple and cried out, "If anyone thirsts, let him come to me and drink; the one who believes in me, as the Scripture said, 'From the belly of him will flow rivers of living water'" (7:37-38). Jesus said this about the Spirit, whom those believing in him were going to receive, for the Spirit had not yet been given, because Jesus had not yet been glorified (7:39). But now that the hour when Jesus was glorified by the Father by being lifted up/ exalted in crucifixion has arrived (12:23; 13:31-32), he gave over the Spirit, thus providing the "living water" for believers in him to drink and quench their thirst of divine life eternal.[35]

The beloved disciple "took" (ἔλαβεν) the mother of Jesus to his own to form a new family of believing disciples (19:27). Jesus complemented this when he "took" (ἔλαβεν) the sour wine, declared, "It is accomplished," bowed his head, and gave over the Spirit as he died (19:30), thus accomplishing the establishment of this new familial community. Now that Jesus has "given over" or "handed down" (παρέδωκεν) the Spirit by his self-sacrificial death, he can fulfill his promise to give his community of disciples another Paraclete, the Spirit of truth, to guide them in all truth (14:16-17, 26; 15:26; 16:13). This will enable his familial community of believing disciples, including all in the audience of believers, to become true worshipers who worship the Father, the God who is Spirit, in Spirit and truth (4:23-24) and thus, with the "living water" of the Spirit quench their thirst for divine life eternal (4:14; 7:37-39).[36]

It was the "preparation" day not only for the Passover (cf. 19:14) but also for the Sabbath, which made that Sabbath a "great day [μεγάλη ἡ ἡμέρα]" (19:31). This recalls that on the last "great day" (ἡμέρᾳ τῇ μεγάλῃ) of the feast of Tabernacles (7:37) Jesus transcended the water involved in the celebration of this feast with his promise of living water symbolic of the Spirit believers are to receive once Jesus has been glorified (7:38-39).[37] Now that Jesus has been glorified by being lifted up/exalted in crucifixion, he has fulfilled his promise as he gave over the Spirit (19:30). On the deeper, ironic level, that Sabbath was a "great day" because on its preparation day

35. Tabb, "Jesus' Thirst," 338-51.

36. "This final παραδίδωμι is the conclusion of a number of 'handing overs' within the Passion (18:2, 5, 35, 36; 19:11, 16). From the cross Jesus gives down to the seminal Christian community the eschatological gift of the Spirit, constituting the believers into a new household of God" (Coloe, *God Dwells*, 189). While in 19:30 the giving over of the Spirit is a general statement, implying that the recipients are the community of disciples, this becomes specific and explicit when the risen Jesus breathes on his disciples and tells them, "Receive the Holy Spirit" in 20:22. On the complementarity of these two bestowals of the Spirit, see Swetnam, "Bestowal," 556-76.

37. Carnazzo, *Seeing Blood and Water*, 63.

Jesus transcended the Jewish Passover feast by his act of self-sacrificial worship as the true Passover Lamb. This is confirmed by the notice that Jesus was already dead and thus did not need to have his legs broken (19:33) to hasten his death, like those crucified with him (19:32), so that the bodies did not remain on the cross on the Sabbath (19:31; cf. Deut 21:22-23), which underlines that his death was an act of self-sacrificial worship (cf. 10:18).

After Judas took the morsel of bread from Jesus, he "went out immediately" (ἐξῆλθεν εὐθύς) at night (13:30) to "give over" Jesus (cf. 6:64, 71; 12:4; 13:2, 11, 21; 18:2, 5) to a sacrificial death. This prompted Jesus to announce that now is the Son of Man glorified and God is glorified in him (13:31). In ironic contrast, blood and water "went out immediately" (ἐξῆλθεν εὐθύς) from the side of Jesus that one of the soldiers pricked with a spear to confirm his death during his glorification by crucifixion (19:34). The sacrificial death that Judas "went out immediately" to perpetrate ironically resulted in the life-giving blood and water that "went out immediately" from the side of the dead Jesus in fulfillment of the scriptural promise that rivers of living water will flow from the belly of him (7:38).[38] The life-giving blood and water, which is symbolic of the Spirit (7:39), that went out from the dead Jesus, as the true Passover Lamb of God (1:29, 36), thus correspond to and complement the Spirit Jesus "gave over" when he died as an act of self-sacrificial worship (19:30).

The blood essential for life and symbolic of his life-giving death went out immediately from the side of the dead Jesus followed by the water essential for life and symbolic of the Spirit (19:34). By following and flowing together with the blood, the water lends to the blood its natural cleansing as well as quenching qualities. On the symbolic level this means that the Spirit symbolized by the water enables the life-giving blood to cleanse or wash away the sin that leads to eternal death as well as to quench the thirst for divine life eternal. The blood and water that together went out of the Jesus lifted up and exalted in crucifixion as the true Passover Lamb of God brings to a climax all of the Gospel's previous indications of both the salvific cleansing and quenching effects of the death of Jesus as an act of self-sacrificial worship.

The Jesus whom God revealed to John as the one who baptizes with the Holy Spirit (1:33), John himself had just previously pointed out as the Lamb of God who takes away the sin of the world (1:29). That Jesus is "the one who baptizes" (ὁ βαπτίζων) with the Holy Spirit thus parallels and complements that he is "the one who takes away" (ὁ αἴρων) the sin of the world.

---

38. According to LXX Zech 14:8, "On that day living water will go out [ἐξελεύσεται] from Jerusalem."

John then repeated simply that Jesus is "the Lamb of God" (1:36) without further description. But his two previous descriptions of Jesus implicitly indicate that it is by baptizing or cleansing with the Holy Spirit that Jesus takes away or washes away the sin of the world as the Lamb of God. The cleansing water of the Holy Spirit that followed and flowed together with the blood from the side of the crucified Jesus (19:34) empowered that blood to wash or take away the sin of the world as the blood produced by the death of Jesus in an act of self-sacrificial worship as the true Passover Lamb of God.

The slaughter of the Passover lambs was considered an act of sacrificial worship and hyssop was used to apply the sacrificial blood that flowed from the slaughtered Passover lambs to the doors of the Israelites to save them from death (Exod 12:22).[39] The soldiers used hyssop, however, not to apply the blood of the Passover lambs but to give Jesus the sour wine that enabled him to accomplish his death (19:29-30) in an act of self-sacrificial worship as the true Passover Lamb of God. The sacrificial blood that flows from Jesus thus transcends that of the exodus event commemorated and celebrated at the Jewish feast of Passover. The self-sacrificial blood of Jesus saves not merely the Jewish people from death but takes away the sin of the whole world (1:29), saving the world from "the sin" of unbelief that brings eternal death (8:24) in order that believers may have divine life eternal (3:15-16).

Nicodemus was puzzled as to how one could be born again from above by water and the Spirit in order to see and enter the kingdom of God (3:3-5, 9). The water symbolic of the Spirit that went out from the side of Jesus gives the answer. The self-sacrificial blood of the Lamb of God makes the water and the Spirit available for regeneration. Jesus told Nicodemus that for this rebirth it was necessary for the Son of Man to be lifted up, so that all who believe in him might have divine life eternal (3:14-15). Now that Jesus has been lifted up in crucifixion, his self-sacrificial death as the Passover Lamb of God provides the life-giving blood that takes or washes away the sin of unbelief for those reborn of the cleansing water and Spirit that follow and flow together with the blood (19:34), so that they may believe and have divine life eternal. By the blood and water of the Spirit flowing from his death, Jesus "baptizes" with the Holy Spirit (1:33), transforming and transcending John's baptism with mere water (1:31), so that believers may be baptized and reborn from above in water and the Spirit in the sacrament of baptism.

During the wedding feast at Cana, Jesus, prior to his "hour" (2:4) of glorification by his self-sacrificial death, transformed the water used for Jewish ritual cleansing (2:6) into something eminently drinkable—choice

39. Moses told the Israelites to "sacrifice" (θύσατε) the Passover (lambs) (LXX Exod 12:21). And the Israelites are to tell their sons that this Passover (lamb) is a "sacrifice" (θυσία) to the Lord (LXX Exod 12:27).

wine in abundance (2:10). And now, during the hour of his self-sacrificial death, the water of the Spirit similarly transforms the cleansing blood of Jesus into something eminently drinkable. That the water of the Spirit follows and flows together with the blood from the side of Jesus (19:34) answers the Jews' objection which questioned how Jesus can give them his flesh to eat and his blood to drink. By his self-sacrificial death that produces life-giving blood together with the living water of the Spirit, Jesus provides the true life-giving food that is his flesh and the true life-giving drink that is his blood. By eating and feeding on his flesh and drinking his blood in the sacrament of the Eucharist, those baptized and reborn of water and the Sprit have divine life eternal within themselves (6:51–58).

The life-giving blood resulting from the self-sacrificial death of Jesus animates the water that follows and flows with it into the "living water" of the Spirit. This "living water" confirms Jesus' promise to the Samaritan woman that he can give the "living water" that definitively quenches one's deepest thirst for divine life eternal. Indeed, the water Jesus gives will become within the person of the one who drinks it an abundance of water gushing up to divine life eternal (4:10, 13–14; 7:37–39). The living water of the Spirit that follows and flows together with the life-giving blood of the self-sacrificial death of Jesus as the true Passover Lamb of God enables Samaritans as well as Jews to transcend their worship on Mount Gerizim and in the temple in Jerusalem. They and all believers may now become true worshipers who worship the Father, the God who is Spirit, in Spirit and truth (4:23–24)—the Spirit provided by the self-sacrificial death of Jesus (19:34) and the truth that he embodies (14:6), the truth that divine life eternal comes through self-sacrificial love.

Jesus laid down his clothes and washed his disciples' feet with water as a humble act of love (13:11) that symbolically anticipated the greater act of humble love he would demonstrate for them by laying down his life as an act of self-sacrificial worship (15:13). This washing was a "cleansing" (13:10–11) that gave the disciples a "share" with Jesus (13:8). He thus urged them to follow his example of love by washing one another's feet (13:14–15), thereby obeying his commandment to love one another in the self-sacrificial way that he loves them (13:34–35; 15:12–13). The blood and water that went out from the side of Jesus (19:34) fortifies the community of believers, by washing away their sin of unbelief in baptism and quenching their thirst for divine life eternal in the Eucharist, to love one another as Jesus loved them. From the abundant water of the Spirit that flows from within them (7:37–39), believers, by loving one another as Jesus loved them, can be a source for others of the divine life eternal they have within themselves (4:14; 6:53–54) resulting from the death of Jesus as an act of self-sacrificial worship.

The one who has seen the accomplishment of Jesus' self-sacrificial death that produced the life-giving blood and water of the Spirit (19:26-34) has testified and is still testifying (μεμαρτύρηκεν, perfect tense) with true testimony. Indeed "that one" (ἐκεῖνος), the one who has seen, the beloved disciple as the only male believer standing at the cross (19:26), knows that he speaks what is true (19:35a).[40] He invites the audience to join him in believing—that you "also" may believe (19:35b). By testifying, he anticipates and models for the audience the testifying they, as believing disciples, are to do—"You also will testify" (15:27), when the Paraclete, the Spirit of truth, comes and testifies about Jesus (15:26), enabling believers to worship in Spirit and truth (4:23-24). The believing audience can testify to the truth, and thus bring others to believe, based on what the narrator, an ideal, beloved disciple, has seen and testified about the death of Jesus as an act of self-sacrificial worship that provides the sacramental worship of baptism (water) and Eucharist (blood) for believers to have divine life eternal (3:14-16).[41]

The soldiers humiliated the crucified Jesus by taking his clothing so that the Scripture might be fulfilled, in which Jesus is the speaker of a prayer of lament uttered by the suffering just one in Ps 22 (LXX 21):19: "They divided my clothes among themselves, and for my clothing they cast lots" (John 19:24). They then gave him sour wine to drink (19:29-30), which alludes to another prayer of lament uttered by Jesus as the suffering just one in Ps 69 (LXX 68):22: "They gave gall for my food, and for my thirst they gave me sour wine to drink." In response to Jesus' scriptural prayers of lament "the things that happened" (cf. John 19:33-34) fulfill the Scripture, "Not a bone of him will be broken" (19:36), which alludes to a prayer of thanksgiving for divine rescue of the suffering just ones in Ps 34 (LXX 33):21: "The Lord watches over all their bones, not one of them will be broken."[42] A scriptural hymn of thanksgiving to God for protecting his suffering just ones thus answers Jesus' prayers of lament, distinguishing him as God's specially chosen, suffering just one, who offered his life to God in an act of self-sacrificial worship.[43]

---

40. On "that one" (ἐκεῖνος) as referring to the one who has seen (19:35), that is, the beloved disciple (19:26), see Mardaga, "Jn 19,35," 67-80. On the anonymity and identity of the beloved disciple, see Beck, "Whom Jesus Loved," 221-39.

41. "The Beloved Disciple is therefore portrayed as an eyewitness of the blood and water, yet clearly his witness is not simply to enable readers to believe that blood and water flowed from Jesus' side but to believe in the significance of this phenomenon, namely, that Jesus' death was a sacrifice that brought life" (Lincoln, *John*, 481).

42. For a discussion of the provenance and use of the scriptural quotation in John 19:36, see Schuchard, *Scripture*, 133-40.

43. As one of the thanksgiving psalms, Psalm 34 (LXX 33) "is an extension or complement of the lament. Recalling a past crisis of petition, thanksgiving psalms

That "not a bone of him will be broken" (John 19:36) in fulfillment of Scripture also reaffirms Jesus as the sacrificial Passover Lamb of God (1:29, 36). When the Israelites ate the slaughtered Passover lamb that was roasted intact (Exod 12:9), they were not to let any of it remain until morning, and "you shall not break a bone of it" (LXX Exod 12:10; see also 12:46; Num 9:12). In response to offering his life in an act of self-sacrificial worship as the Passover Lamb of God and the suffering just one, God allowed not a bone of Jesus to be broken. And this resulted in the flowing of the life-giving blood and water of the Spirit from the side of the dead Jesus (19:34). That not a bone of Jesus was broken, then, enabled him to provide the baptismal water that generates, and the eucharistic blood that sustains, the familial community of believers established by the beloved disciple and the mother of Jesus (19:26–27).[44]

And again another Scripture from Zech 12:10 says, "They will look upon the one they have pierced" (19:37).[45] This quote corresponds to the narrator's invitation to believe based on what the beloved disciple "has seen" (19:35). That they "will look" upon the one they have pierced means they will see what he "has seen"—the life-giving blood and water flowing from the pierced side of the crucified Jesus (19:34). This Scripture thus implicitly invites not only the Jews who asked Pilate that the legs of those crucified be broken and they be taken away (19:31), but also the soldiers who "saw" that Jesus was already dead so that one of them pricked his side (19:33–34), to "look upon" the life-giving blood and water flowing from the pierced Jesus in order to believe. But the audience, those who already believe, will continuously "look upon the one they have pierced" as an object of worship, contemplating the abundant, inexhaustible rivers of life-giving blood and water flowing from the dead Jesus, in order to sustain and renew the divine life eternal they have by believing (4:14; 6:53; 7:37–39).

The one who "has seen [ἑωρακώς]" (19:35) the cleansing and quenching blood and water that went out from the side of the crucified Jesus (19:34) has testified, so that "you also may believe" (19:35). This recalls and resonates with the healing of the man born blind, who was sent by Jesus to cleanse his eyes in the waters of Siloam (9:7). After Jesus told him, "You have seen [ἑώρακας] him" (9:37), he believed and worshiped Jesus as the Son

---

provide concrete testimony to answered prayer and display unwavering confidence in God's care and power to deliver" (Brown, "Psalms," 666).

44. "The combination of Passover and righteous sufferer traditions is also found in *Jub.* 49.13, where not breaking the bones of the lamb is linked with no bone of the children of Israel being broken" (Lincoln, *John*, 481).

45. For a discussion of the provenance and use of the scriptural quotation in John 19:37, see Schuchard, *Scripture*, 141–49; Cavicchia, "Guarderanno," 205–57, 423–74.

of Man (9:38). Now those who "will look upon" the one they have pierced (19:37) will see the cleansing and quenching blood and water, the symbols of the sacraments of baptism and the Eucharist, by which they may believe and worship Jesus. Now that Jesus has been lifted up/exalted/glorified in crucifixion as the final accomplishment of his self-sacrificial death, he magnetically draws all to himself (12:32), so that they will look upon the one they have pierced and see the life-giving blood and water that enable them to worship in order to have divine life eternal (3:14-16).

Jesus was speaking about the temple of his "body" (2:21) when he told the Jews, "Destroy this temple and in three days I will raise it" (2:19), so that it will replace the Jerusalem temple. After Joseph of Arimathea asked Pilate if he could take away the "body" of Jesus and then came and took away his "body" (19:38), both Joseph and Nicodemus (19:39; cf. 3:1-9; 7:50) took the "body" of Jesus (19:40). They "bound" his dead body with cloths (19:40), recalling that Jesus had raised the "bound" body of the dead Lazarus (11:44). They thus prepared it not only for burial but, ironically and unwittingly, to be raised by Jesus (10:18). Jesus' tomb was in a garden in the "place where" he was crucified (19:41) as an act of self-sacrificial worship that enabled his body, as the new temple, to be the "place where" it is necessary to worship (4:20). They "laid down" Jesus there because of the preparation day of the Jews (19:42). This complemented his "laying down" of his life to take it up again (10:18), and thus ironically prepared for the risen body of Jesus to replace the Jewish temple as the place for true worship.[46]

As an act of devotional worship, Mary anointed the feet of Jesus with a "pound" of very precious ointment (12:3) for the day of his "burial preparation" (12:7). Joseph and Nicodemus complemented this with an act of reverential worship of the dead Jesus, indicative that he is the true King of the Jews, when they bound his body in cloths along with a hundred "pounds" (19:39) of "spices" (ἀρωμάτων) in accord with the custom among Jews "to prepare for burial" (19:40).[47] They laid him in a new tomb, whose uniqueness is underlined by describing it with a double negative expression as a new tomb in which "no one had never" (οὐδέπω οὐδείς) been laid. Jesus' new and unique tomb, appropriate for his new and unique resurrection as the new temple (2:19, 21), was in a "garden" in the "place" where he was crucified (19:41). This recalls the "garden" as the "place" where Jesus gathered

---

46. On the link between the garden and temple symbolism, see Zimmermann, *Christologie der Bilder*, 166.

47. "Two men who had never dared to profess public allegiance to Jesus while he lived now seek to honor him in his death" (Duke, *Irony*, 110). According to LXX 2 Chr 16:14, when they buried King Asa, they laid him on a bier filled with "spices" (ἀρωμάτων) and various kinds of aromatics mixed into an ointment.

with his disciples in anticipation of his establishing a new "place" for true worship (4:20; 14:2). It is also a setting appropriate for a royal burial (19:41), as some of the kings of Judah were buried in gardens (2 Kgs 21:18, 26).[48]

To the dismay of the chief priests of the Jews (19:21), who denied the kingship of Jesus as well as their divine King in declaring that only Caesar is their king (19:15), many Jews read the title proclaiming Jesus as the King of the Jews, for the place "where he was crucified was near" the city of Jerusalem (19:20). In ironic contrast, there was no Jewish objection when the Jews Joseph and Nicodemus laid Jesus in the tomb in the garden "where he was crucified" (19:41), for his new and unique tomb "was near" (19:42). This implies a recognition by these Jews that Jesus indeed is not only the true King of the Jews but the divine King not of this world (18:36). They laid him there because of the preparation day of the "Jews" (19:42), ironically in preparation for his resurrection as the new temple for true worship (2:19, 21). This confirms for the audience that Jesus is worthy to be worshiped not only as the King of Israel/the Jews (1:49; 12:13; 19:3, 14, 19) but as the King of all peoples, indeed the divine King not of this world.[49]

Summary on 18:1–19:42

Jesus continued to allow himself to be the sacrificial victim as the band of soldiers, the tribune, and the Jewish officers arrested, bound, and led him before Annas first, for he was the father-in-law of Caiaphas, the high priest of that year (18:12–13). Caiaphas had advised the Jews that it was better for "one man" to die for the people (18:14; cf. 11:49–50). Despite Peter's violent assault of the high priest's servant (18:10), neither he nor any of the other disciples were arrested along with Jesus. This underlines the uniqueness of Jesus as the one high priest who sacrifices himself as the unique victim in contrast to a confusing plurality evident in the Jewish high priesthood. That both Annas and Caiaphas are referred to as high priest (18:19, 24) creates confusion for the audience about who is truly the high priest. This confusion reinforces the singularity of Jesus as the "one man" to die for the people, the one who offers his own life in an act of self-sacrificial worship as the one and only true high priest, the "one" shepherd (10:16) who gathers into "one" God's dispersed children (11:52) to share in divine life eternal (1:12).

Peter was very eager to fulfill the role of both the good shepherd and the disciple who lays down his life when he promised Jesus, "I will lay down my life for you" (13:37). Instead he fulfilled Jesus' prediction that he would

---

48. Brown, *Death*, 2.1268–70.
49. On John 19:12–42, see Heil, *Blood and Water*, 77–119.

deny him thrice (13:38; 18:17-18, 25-27). But, nevertheless, Peter entered the courtyard/sheepfold as one of the sheep for whom the good shepherd/high priest lays down his life. Before Peter, and any member of the audience, can be a disciple/shepherd who lays down his life for his friends (13:14-16, 37; 15:12-13), he must realize the need to be a disciple/sheep for whom the good shepherd and unique high priest Jesus first lays down his own life in an act of self-sacrificial worship for divine life eternal.

The Jews told Pilate that if "this one" were not doing evil, "we would not have given him over to you" (18:30). This associates them with Judas, repeatedly identified as the one who "betrayed" or "gave over" Jesus (18:2, 5; cf. 6:64, 71; 12:4; 13:2, 11, 21). But on the deeper level of the divine plan God "gave" his unique Son over to a self-sacrificial death, so that everyone who believes in him might not perish but might have divine life eternal (3:16). Accordingly, it is not "lawful" or "permitted" for the Jews to kill anyone (18:31; cf. 5:10), since Jesus will lay down his life on his own in accord with the command he received from his Father (10:18). This is confirmed by the notice that they said this "in order that the word of Jesus might be fulfilled that he said indicating the kind of death he was to die" (18:32; cf. 12:33)—a self-sacrificial death of being "lifted up/exalted" by God (divine passive) in crucifixion so that he might draw all "to myself" as both the personified place and object of true worship (12:32; 14:3).

As King, Jesus was born and came into the world, sent by the Father (5:43; 7:28; 8:42; 16:28) to lay down his life in love for others as an act of self-sacrificial worship for divine life eternal (3:16-17; 10:10-18; 12:50; 15:12-13), so that he might testify to the truth. Everyone who is of the truth "hears" his "voice" (18:37), that is, "hears" the "voice" of Jesus as the good shepherd/king and follows him (10:3-5, 16, 27) to have divine life eternal through self-sacrificial love for one another. Pilate, apparently exasperated, muttered to Jesus, "What is truth?" (18:38), an ironic question the audience can answer for themselves. As those who have heard the voice of Jesus as the good shepherd/king so that they are of the truth, believers are to appreciate that the truth to which Jesus testified consists of having divine life eternal through self-sacrificial love of one another. This is the truth by which true worshipers will worship the Father in "Spirit and truth" (4:23-24), in Jesus who is the personification of truth (14:6) as the good shepherd/king who lays down his life in self-sacrificial worship for divine life eternal.

Jesus' declaration that those who "gave him over" to Pilate to be crucified as a sacrificial victim have a greater "sin" (19:11) brings the audience to a climactic moment. The revelation Jesus gave Pilate inside the praetorium (18:33-38a; 19:1-3, 8-11) invites each member of the audience to make a personal decision to avoid not only Pilate's sin of unbelief but the "greater sin," the greater unbelief, of the individuals who rejected Jesus outside the praetorium (18:28–32, 38b–40; 19:4–7). All members of the audience, then, are called to believe in and worship the Jesus who has given believers the authority to become children of God (1:12) as the self-sacrificial Lamb of God who takes away the "sin" of the world (1:29, 36).

As the unique high priest who surpasses the Jewish high priest, Jesus will die not just for the unity of the nation but to gather into one the dispersed children of God (11:52), all believers (cf. 1:12) dispersed throughout the world. By not dividing his unified tunic (19:23), the soldiers advanced the goal of Jesus as the good shepherd/high priest to unify all into a believing, worshiping community (10:15–16; 17:11, 20–23). What the Gentile soldiers did with the clothing of the crucified Jesus ironically advanced the divine plan recorded in Jewish Scripture with Jesus as the speaker: "They distributed my clothes among themselves, and for my clothing they cast lots [Ps 22 (LXX Ps 21):19]" (19:24). The soldiers shared the clothes of Jesus among themselves (19:23), which points to individual Gentiles appropriating the divine life eternal Jesus' death will effect. And they cast lots for his seamless tunic, which demonstrates how Gentiles will preserve and participate in the unity and universality of the believing, worshiping community established by Jesus' death, his act of self-sacrificial worship, as the unique high priest.

With the arrival of the "hour" of his death Jesus invited the woman who is his mother to complete the initial family of faith and household of worship she originated in anticipation of the "hour" (2:12) by now embracing the beloved disciple as her own son (19:26). By taking her as his mother to his own (19:27), the beloved disciple established the familial community of those who are to believe with the faith of the mother of Jesus, who said, "Do whatever he tells you" (2:5). Jesus told his disciples to love one another in the self-sacrificial way that he, the good shepherd and unique high priest, loved them (10:11, 15; 13:34; 15:12–13). They are to become a familial household of believers who worship by practicing the self-sacrificial worship that consists of obeying his commandment to love one another as he loved them to have divine life eternal (10:27–28; 12:25, 50; 17:2–3). The mutual acceptance of the mother of Jesus and the beloved disciple to form a new family thus serves as a model for the audience as believers to become a familial household of worship by loving one another for divine life eternal.

Putting a sponge full of sour wine on a branch of hyssop, they "offered" it to the mouth of Jesus (19:29) in an ironic act of worship, recalling Jesus' prediction to his disciples that "everyone who kills you will think he is offering worship to God" (16:2). This gesture evokes the Passover ritual. The Israelites used hyssop to sprinkle the blood of the Passover lambs on their doorposts to save them from the destruction God was bringing upon their Egyptian oppressors. This ritual was to be commemorated in future Passover celebrations (Exod 12:21–27). In addition, this happened on the day of preparation for the Passover, when the lambs were slaughtered in the temple (19:14). When Jesus took the sour wine offered to him on the hyssop and died (19:30), he accepted the ironic act of worship that enabled him to complete his own self-sacrificial act of worship, establishing him as the true Passover Lamb of God who takes away the sin of the world (1:29, 36). He thereby enables believers to worship by loving one another in the self-sacrificial way that he did (13:34; 15:12–13).

The beloved disciple "took" the mother of Jesus to his own to form a new family of believing disciples (19:27). Jesus complemented this when he "took" the sour wine, declared, "It is accomplished," bowed his head, and gave over the Spirit as he died (19:30), thus accomplishing the establishment of this new familial community. Now that Jesus has "given over" or "handed down" the Spirit by his self-sacrificial death, he can fulfill his promise to give his community of disciples another Paraclete, the Spirit of truth, to guide them in all truth (14:16–17, 26; 15:26; 16:13). This will enable his familial community of believing disciples, including all in the audience of believers, to become true worshipers who worship the Father, the God who is Spirit, in Spirit and truth (4:23–24) and thus, with the "living water" of the Spirit quench their thirst for divine life eternal (4:14; 7:37–39).

Nicodemus was puzzled as to how one could be born again from above by water and the Spirit in order to see and enter the kingdom of God (3:3–5, 9). The water symbolic of the Spirit that went out from the side of Jesus gives the answer. The self-sacrificial blood of the Lamb of God makes the water and the Spirit available for regeneration. Jesus told Nicodemus that for this rebirth it was necessary for the Son of Man to be lifted up, so that all who believe in him might have divine life eternal (3:14–15). Now that Jesus has been lifted up in crucifixion, his self-sacrificial death as the Passover Lamb of God provides the life-giving blood that takes or washes away the sin of unbelief for those reborn of the cleansing water and Spirit that follow and flow together with the blood (19:34), so that they may believe and have divine life eternal. By the blood and water of the Spirit flowing from his death, Jesus "baptizes" with the Holy Spirit (1:33), transforming and transcending John's baptism with mere water (1:31), so that believers may be baptized and reborn from above in water and the Spirit in the sacrament of baptism.

During the wedding feast at Cana Jesus, prior to his "hour" (2:4) of glorification by his self-sacrificial death, transformed the water used for Jewish ritual cleansing (2:6) into something eminently drinkable—choice wine in abundance (2:10). And now, during the hour of his self-sacrificial death, the water of the Spirit similarly transforms the cleansing blood of Jesus into something eminently drinkable. That the water of the Spirit follows and flows together with the blood from the side of Jesus (19:34) answers the Jews' objection which questioned how Jesus can give them his flesh to eat and his blood to drink. By his self-sacrificial death that produces life-giving blood together with the living water of the Spirit, Jesus provides the true life-giving food that is his flesh and the true life-giving drink that is his blood. By eating and feeding on his flesh and drinking his blood in the sacrament of the Eucharist, those baptized and reborn of water and the Sprit have divine life eternal within themselves (6:51–58).

Jesus laid down his clothes and washed his disciples' feet with water as a humble act of love (13:11) that symbolically anticipated the greater act of humble love he would demonstrate for them by laying down his life as an act of self-sacrificial worship (15:13). This washing was a "cleansing" (13:10–11) that gave the disciples a "share" with Jesus (13:8). He thus urged them to follow his example of love by washing one another's feet (13:14–15), thereby obeying his commandment to love one another in the self-sacrificial way that he loves them (13:34–35; 15:12–13). The blood and water that went out from the side of Jesus (19:34) fortifies the community of believers, by washing away their sin of unbelief in baptism and quenching their thirst for divine life eternal in the Eucharist, to love one another as Jesus loved them. From the abundant water of the Spirit that flows from within them (7:37–39), believers, by loving one another as Jesus loved them, can be a source for others of the divine life eternal they have within themselves (4:14; 6:53–54) resulting from the death of Jesus as an act of self-sacrificial worship.

The soldiers humiliated the crucified Jesus by taking his clothing so that the Scripture might be fulfilled, in which Jesus is the speaker of a prayer of lament uttered by the suffering just one in Ps 22 (LXX 21):19: "They divided my clothes among themselves, and for my clothing they cast lots" (John 19:24). They then gave him sour wine to drink (19:29–30), which alludes to another prayer of lament uttered by Jesus as the suffering just one in Ps 69 (LXX 68):22: "They gave gall for my food, and for my thirst they gave me sour wine to drink." In response to Jesus' scriptural prayers of lament "the things that happened" (cf. John 19:33–34) fulfill the Scripture, "Not a bone of him will be broken" (19:36), which alludes to a prayer of thanksgiving for divine rescue of the suffering just ones in Ps 34 (LXX 33):21: "The Lord watches over all their bones, not one of them will be broken." A hymn of thanksgiving to God for protecting his suffering just ones thus answers Jesus' prayers of lament, distinguishing him as God's specially chosen, suffering just one, who offered his life to God in an act of self-sacrificial worship.

That "not a bone of him will be broken" (John 19:36) in fulfillment of Scripture also reaffirms Jesus as the sacrificial Passover Lamb of God (1:29, 36). When the Israelites ate the slaughtered Passover lamb that was roasted intact (Exod 12:9), they were not to let any of it remain until morning, and "you shall not break a bone of it" (LXX Exod 12:10; see also 12:46; Num 9:12). In response to offering his life in an act of self-sacrificial worship as the Passover Lamb of God and the suffering just one, God allowed not a bone of Jesus to be broken. And this resulted in the flowing of the life-giving blood and water of the Spirit from the side of the dead Jesus (19:34). That not a bone of Jesus was broken, then, enabled him to provide the baptismal water that generates and the eucharistic blood that sustains the familial community of believers established by the beloved disciple and the mother of Jesus (19:26–27).

The one who "has seen" (19:35) the cleansing and quenching blood and water that went out from the side of the crucified Jesus (19:34) has testified, so that "you also may believe" (19:35). This recalls and resonates with the healing of the man born blind, who was sent by Jesus to cleanse his eyes in the waters of Siloam (9:7). After Jesus told him, "You have seen him" (9:37), he believed and worshiped Jesus as the Son of Man (9:38). Now those who "will look upon" the one they have pierced (19:37) will see the cleansing and quenching blood and water, the symbols of the sacraments of baptism and the Eucharist, by which they may believe and worship Jesus. Now that Jesus has been lifted up/exalted/glorified in crucifixion as the final accomplishment of his self-sacrificial death, he magnetically draws all to himself (12:32), so that they will look upon the one they have pierced and see the life-giving blood and water that enables them to worship in order to have divine life eternal (3:14–16).

To the dismay of the chief priests of the Jews (19:21), who denied the kingship of Jesus as well as their divine King in declaring that only Caesar is their king (19:15), many Jews read the title proclaiming Jesus as the King of the Jews, for the place "where he was crucified was near" the city of Jerusalem (19:20). In ironic contrast, there was no Jewish objection when the Jews Joseph and Nicodemus laid Jesus in the tomb in the garden "where he was crucified" (19:41), for his new and unique tomb "was near" (19:42). This implies a recognition by these Jews that Jesus indeed is not only the true King of the Jews but the divine King not of this world (18:36). They laid him there because of the preparation day of the "Jews" (19:42), ironically in preparation for his resurrection as the new temple for true worship (2:19, 21). This confirms for the audience that Jesus is worthy to be worshiped not only as the King of Israel/the Jews (1:49; 12:13; 19:3, 14, 19) but as the King of all peoples, indeed the divine King not of this world.

9

The Risen Jesus Establishes the Worship for Divine Life Eternal (20:1—21:25)

The Risen Lord Ascends to the Father for Communal Worship (20:1-18)

Before Jesus raised Lazarus, he said, "Take away the stone" (11:39), which lay across the cave of his tomb (11:38), and then they "took away the stone" (11:41). When Lazarus came out, his face was wrapped in a "face cloth" (σουδαρίῳ) so that he had to be unwrapped by others (11:44). In contrast, when Mary Magdalene came to the tomb of Jesus, she saw that the "stone had been taken away" (20:1), the passive verb suggesting a divine rather than human agency. Inside the tomb Peter observed that the "face cloth" (σουδάριον) which had been on the head of Jesus "had been rolled up" (divine passive) apart "into one [εἰς ἕνα] place" (20:7). This symbolically corresponds to the purpose of Jesus' death, as an act of self-sacrificial worship, to gather all of the dispersed children of God "into one [εἰς ἕν]" (11:52). Then there will be "one" sheep herd, "one" shepherd (10:16), who has the divine authority to lay down his life on his own and to take it up again (10:18). The self-sacrificial death and resurrection of Jesus thus establishes the unity and universality of his believing and worshiping community.[1]

The one who "saw" the life-giving blood and water coming out of the dead Jesus (19:34) testified for the benefit of the audience, so that they may "believe" (19:35) to have divine life eternal (3:15-16). Complementing

---

1. "What the neatly folded and separately placed σουδάριον in Jesus' tomb indicates is that, whereas Lazarus was completely passive in his return to life, totally reliant upon the command of Jesus and needing others to remove the veil over his face, Jesus actively raised himself. The neatly folded, separately placed veil is the culminating indication of a majestic reassumption of life" (Byrne, *Life Abounding*, 330).

this, when the other disciple whom Jesus loved (20:2) entered the tomb and "saw" (20:8) how Jesus' burial cloths were left behind (20:7), he "believed" (20:8) in the resurrection of Jesus. This is confirmed by the notice that "they," that is, the other disciples, did not yet understand the Scripture—both the OT Scripture and the Scripture which is the Gospel (2:22; 20:30-31; 21:24-25)—that it was necessary for him to rise from the dead (20:9).[2] This invites the audience to join the beloved disciple in believing and Martha in believing and worshiping Jesus as "the resurrection and the life" (11:25-27). That Jesus himself has arisen from the dead reaffirms his promises to likewise raise on the last day to divine life eternal the believer and the one who feeds on his flesh and drinks his blood in the sacrament of the Eucharist (6:39-40, 44, 54).

When Mary Magdalene bent down into the tomb of Jesus (20:11), she observed two angels in white sitting there, one at the head and one at the feet, where the "body" of Jesus had been lying (20:12). This confirms Jesus' promise that in three days he would raise the destroyed temple (2:19) of his "body" (2:21). The risen Jesus then told her not to hold on to his body, for he had not yet ascended to the Father. Rather, she is to go to his brothers and tell them, "I am ascending to my Father and your Father, my God and your God" (20:17). This recalls that Jesus had told his disciples that he is going to his Father's house to prepare a "place" for them to worship (14:2). He will then come back and take them to himself so that where he is they also may be (14:3). He will thus introduce his brothers (cf. 19:26-27) into the "place," the familial, interpersonal relationship, he shares with his Father, so that his Father and God will be their Father and God. This relationship will enable his believing brothers and the audience to become true worshipers who worship the Father in Spirit and truth (4:23-24) for divine life eternal.[3]

Mary Magdalene spoke as a representative of the broader community when she declared that they have taken "the Lord" from the tomb, and "we" do not know where they laid him (20:2). But to the angels in the tomb she spoke for herself when she declared that they have taken away "my Lord,"

---

2. On Zech 6:12-13 as the referent for both 2:22 and 20:9 to highlight Jesus' resurrection as the rebuilding of the temple, see Kubiś, "Zechariah 6:12-13," 153-94. See also Moloney, "Know the Scripture," 97-111.

3. "As explained at length at the Supper, when Jesus has returned to the Father, a new mode of presence, transcending the limits of space and time, will be established (14:1-4)" (Byrne, *Life Abounding*, 333). "The intimacy of Jesus' relationship to God is now made available to believers" (Lincoln, *John*, 494). "Jesus' disciples are his 'brothers' in that they have the same 'Father' in heaven, the God of Israel whom they worship. ... This is a milestone in the Gospel, for it is the first and only instance (out of 120 in all!) in which God is explicitly identified as 'Father' of anyone except Jesus himself" (Michaels, *John*, 1002).

and "I" do not know where they have laid him (20:13). She continued to relate as an individual to the risen Jesus when she thought he was the gardener and ironically addressed him as "Lord," asking him to tell "me" where you have laid him, and "I myself" will take him away (20:15). After she recognized the risen Jesus (20:16), he told her not to hold on to him individualistically but to report to his brothers that he is ascending to his Father and God who is also their Father and God (20:17). She then announced to the disciples that she has seen "the Lord" (20:18), who is not only "my Lord" but "the" risen Lord to be worshiped together with his Father and God. She thus demonstrates the integration and interrelationship of personal and communal worship of both the risen Lord Jesus and God his Father for divine life eternal.[4]

The Climactic Worship of the Risen Jesus as My Lord and My God (20:19-31)

On the evening of that day, the first day of the week, the doors were locked where the disciples were for fear of the Jews (20:19a). Such fear prevented them from publicly confessing Jesus as the Christ (cf. 7:13; 19:38), in order not to be expelled from Jewish synagogue worship (9:22; 12:42), or be killed as an act of worship (16:2). But the risen Jesus then came and stood in their midst and said, "Peace be with you!" (20:19b). He thereby reaffirmed the giving of his own unique peace in his farewell address to them: "Peace I leave to you, my peace I give to you. Not as the world gives do I give to you. Do not let your hearts be troubled or afraid" (14:27; cf. 16:33). This repeated his previous exhortation, "Do not let your hearts be troubled" (14:1), because he is going to prepare a "place" for them to worship in the household of his Father (14:2). He will then come again and take them to himself, so that where he is—with his Father—they also may be. Their union with him and his Father is thus the "place" (14:3) where they may worship the Father in Spirit and truth (4:23-24).

After Jesus pronounced the word that brought them his peace and showed his hands and side to them, the disciples then "rejoiced," "seeing" the Lord (20:20). This fulfills Jesus' previous promise, "I will see you again, and your hearts will rejoice, and no one will take your joy away from you"

---

4. "Notice the steps she has traced. First, seeing the empty tomb, she is concerned to find '*her* Lord' (20:13); she then sees Jesus himself and takes him for the gardener (20:14-15); then she recognizes him, but only as *her* Teacher (20:16); now, after our Lord's revealing words, she finally knows that he is *the* Lord" (de la Potterie, *Hour*, 174; emphases original).

(16:22). To the Jews' request, "What sign do you show [δεικνύεις] us that you do these things" (2:18), Jesus replied by pointing to his resurrection, "Destroy this temple and in three days I will raise it" (2:19), a reference to the new temple of his risen body (2:21). The audience can appreciate that Jesus ironically answered the request of the Jews as he "showed" (ἔδειξεν) his disciples not merely a sign but the very hands and side of his risen body, the new temple itself. In being shown the "side" (πλευράν) of the risen Lord, the disciples see the pierced "side" (πλευράν) out of which flowed from the self-sacrificial death of Jesus the life-giving blood and the water symbolic of the Spirit (19:34) that enables them to become true worshipers in the new temple who worship the Father in Spirit and truth (4:23-24).[5]

Solemnly repeating, "Peace be with you" (20:21a), the risen Jesus reaffirmed the gift of his peace aimed at freeing his disciples from the fear of the Jews that finds them behind locked doors (20:19). He then commissioned them to move out from these doors, telling them, "As the Father has sent me, so I send you" (20:21b). In the prayer concluding his farewell address Jesus previously prayed to his Father for the mission he now imparts to his disciples, "As you have sent me into the world, so I have sent them into the world" (17:18; cf. 4:38). He prayed not only for his disciples but for those who will believe in him through their word (17:20). This accords with the fact that God sent his Son into the world so that the world might be saved through him (3:17), and that everyone who believes in him might have life eternal (3:16). The risen Jesus is thus sending his disciples out into the world to bring others to believe through their word, so that they may possess divine life eternal.

At the same time that Jesus sent his disciples on their mission (20:21), he "breathed on" (ἐνεφύσησεν) them and said to them, "Receive the Holy Spirit [πνεῦμα]" (20:22). God "breathed" (ἐνεφύσησεν) into the face of the first human being the breath of life, and the person became a living being (LXX Gen 2:7). An idolater does not recognize the Creator "breathing" (ἐμφυσήσαντα) into him a "living spirit [πνεῦμα ζωτικόν]" (Wis 15:11). Elijah "breathed" (ἐνεφύσησεν) on the dead son of a widow and he returned to life (3 Kgdms 17:21). God told Ezekiel to prophesy to the "Spirit" (πνεῦμα) to come from the four winds and "breathe" (ἐμφύσησον) into those slain that they may come to life. The "Spirit" (πνεῦμα) then entered into them and they came to life (LXX Ezek 37:9-10). Similarly, the risen Jesus "breathed"

---

5. "The future 'sign' of the crucified-risen Jesus as the New Temple promised indirectly by way of response to the demand of the Jews in Jn 2,18 is now fulfilled. . . . The risen Jesus is the 'sign' of the New Temple, and is himself in his intimate union with his Father the reality signified" (McCaffrey, *House*, 243).

upon his disciples the Holy Spirit that empowers them for their mission (20:21) to bring others to believe in order to have divine life eternal.[6]

The Jesus who "gave over" (παρέδωκεν) the Spirit when he died (19:30) invited his disciples to "receive" (λάβετε) the Holy Spirit (20:22), the Spirit of truth, which the world is not able to "receive [λαβεῖν]" (14:17a). It "remains" (μένει) with the disciples and will be in them (14:17b), as it "remains" (μένον) upon Jesus, the one who baptizes with the Holy Spirit (1:33), as the Lamb of God who takes away the sin of the world (1:29) through his self-sacrificial death. Similarly, the disciples have now been empowered to baptize with the Holy Spirit they have received from the risen Jesus and take away sins as they pronounce the word (cf. 17:20) of divine forgiveness, implicitly as they administer the sacrament of baptism to those who believe and refuse it to those who do not believe: "Whose sins you forgive are forgiven them, whose sins you retain are retained" (20:23). They may thereby fulfill their mission (20:21) of bringing others to believe, so that they do not die eternally in their sins (8:21, 24), but rather possess divine life eternal (3:15–16).

In receiving the "Holy Spirit" from the risen Jesus (20:22), the disciples received the "Holy Spirit" who will teach them everything and remind them of all that Jesus "told" them (14:26). Preeminent of all that Jesus "told" them is the commandment which is life eternal, the commandment the Father gave him to "tell" (12:49–50), the new commandment that they love one another in the self-sacrificial way that he loves them (13:34; 15:12). Failures to love one another in a selfless way are failures to love Jesus himself (14:15, 21; 15:10) and amount to sins against the new commandment Jesus gave for believers to have divine life eternal. The Holy Spirit that will remind believers of the new commandment to love one another in a self-sacrificial way in order to have life eternal is also the Holy Spirit that empowers believers to forgive (or retain) sins (20:23) against this commandment, so that believers also may not die eternally in their sins (cf. 8:21, 24).[7]

It was eight days later when the disciples were again inside the room, but now Thomas, absent previously (20:24), was with them (20:26a). Although they were still behind locked doors for fear of the Jews (20:19), the

---

6. On ancient embryology as the hermeneutical key for understanding "breath upon" in John 20:22, see Weissenrieder, "Spirit and Rebirth," 58–85.

7. "In its ongoing life the community will need both to celebrate and to draw upon the reconciliation won by the death of the Lamb (cf. 1 John 1:6–10). In this sense the sacrament of reconciliation that has evolved in the Catholic tradition has a genuine scriptural foundation here" (Byrne, *Life Abounding*, 336–37). On John 20:19–23 as providing insights into early Christian worship, see Nielsen, "Der erste Gottesdienst," 65–81. See also Coloe, *Household of God*, 167–91; Schneiders, "Raising of the New Temple," 337–55.

risen Jesus again came and stood in their midst and for a third, emphatic, and definitive time announced, "Peace be with you!" (20:19, 21, 26), aimed at alleviating their fear of publicly confessing and thus worshiping him (cf. 7:13; 19:38). Jesus then accommodated Thomas's demand for a personal, tangible encounter with his risen body (20:25), as he invited him to "bring your finger here and see my hands, and bring your hand and put it into my side, and do not become unbelieving but believing" (20:27). Thomas thus became "the Twin" (20:24) figuratively to those who saw the evidence that Jesus was risen from the dead (20:6, 8, 18, 20, 25). As their representative "Twin," Thomas complemented their seeing and believing with his climactic act of worshiping Jesus, whose risen body represents the new temple for worship (2:19-21), as he exclaimed, "My Lord and my God!" (20:28).[8]

The risen Jesus had commissioned Mary Magdalene to tell his disciples, "I am ascending to my Father and your Father, my God and your God" (20:17). Now that Jesus has ascended to the Father, Thomas's climactic act of confessional worship not only confirms but surpasses Jesus' announcement to Mary Magdalene.[9] Thomas demonstrates that believers can worship not only the Father but also the risen and ascended Son, the unique Son who has revealed and made the unseen God and Father visible to believers (1:18; 14:7-9), as "my Lord and my God" (20:28).[10] Thomas begins to fulfill Jesus' prediction that all may honor and thus worship the Son as they honor and thus worship the Father (5:23). His climactic act of worship confirms that Jesus has not made himself God or Son of God (5:18; 10:33), but has always been the divine Word and Son of God: "In the beginning was the Word, and the Word was with God, and the word was God" (1:1). That Word became human (1:14) in the person of Jesus Christ, the unique Son who revealed the God whom no one has ever seen (1:18).[11]

Nathanael worshiped Jesus, confessing, "Rabbi, you are the Son of God, you are the King of Israel!" (1:49). As spokesman for the Twelve, Peter worshiped Jesus, announcing, "We have believed and have come to know that you are the Holy One of God!" (6:69). The man born blind saw, believed

---

8. "In naming Jesus 'my God,' Thomas has moved away from strict Jewish monotheism, in which YHWH alone is God, into a new faith community of the brothers and sisters of Jesus (20:17)" (Coloe, *Household of God*, 189).

9. On the parallel roles of Mary Magdalene and Thomas, see Lee, "Partnership," 37-49.

10. "Earlier Jesus had said to that same disciple (Thomas), 'If you know me, you will know my Father also. From now on you do know him and have seen him' (14:7; cf. 5:23; 8:28). Thomas now knows that to have seen Jesus is indeed to have seen the Father (cf. 14:9)" (Byrne, *Life Abounding*, 338).

11. "The reader will know that, in fact, Jesus is not a human making himself God, but God already made human" (Duke, *Irony*, 77).

in Jesus as the Son of Man, and worshiped him (9:35–38). After affirming her belief in Jesus as "the resurrection and the life," Martha worshiped him, declaring, "You are the Christ, the Son of God, the one coming into the world!" (11:25–27). The crowds worshiped Jesus as he came into Jerusalem for the feast of Passover, proclaiming, "Hosanna! Blessed is he who comes in the name of the Lord, the King of Israel!" (12:13). And now Thomas's supreme christological confession of the lordship and divinity of the risen and ascended Jesus, worshiping him as "my Lord and my God!" (20:28), climactically confirms yet notably exceeds all of the narrative's previous acts of worshiping Jesus.

The risen Jesus' concluding words to Thomas, "Blessed are those who have not seen yet have believed" (20:29), refer to the audience. Even though the members of the audience have not seen the risen Lord himself like Mary Magdalene (20:18), the disciples (20:20, 25), and Thomas (20:27), nor even the burial cloths like Peter and the beloved disciple (20:6–8), they will still be blessed with divine life eternal for believing (3:15–16) without directly seeing the risen Lord. That the beloved disciple believed (20:8) before seeing the risen Lord himself testifies to the audience that they too can believe without seeing. By identifying with the characters in the narrative who have seen, they may likewise "see" based on their seeing. They have heard the testimony of those who have seen not only the burial cloths in the empty tomb but the risen Lord himself, so that they, along with Thomas as their figurative "Twin" (20:24), may worship the risen Jesus as "my Lord and my God!" (20:28).[12]

Although other revelatory signs Jesus did could be narrated (20:30), those written in this book are sufficient to generate and maintain the faith of the audience (20:31).[13] When life-giving blood and water flowed from the pierced side of Jesus as a result of his self-sacrificial death, the narrator spoke for the beloved disciple, who testified that he has personally seen this revelatory sign. With a direct appeal to the audience, he offered his true testimony, "so that you also may believe" (19:34–35). Reinforcing and advancing this previous appeal, the narrator states that all of the signs have been written "so that you may believe" (20:31). With this declaration of the

---

12. "Thomas thus functions as a representative character who brings into the text the experience of future believers. They, too, are absent from the experience of the historical Jesus and his resurrection appearances. They, too, know the apparent absence of Jesus. By narrating this scene, drawing on features of early Christian Eucharist, the evangelist makes available to later believers the Easter experience of the disciples" (Coloe, *Household of God*, 189).

13. On John 20:30–31 as indicative that the entire Fourth Gospel is understood to be "Scripture," see Moloney, "End of Scripture," 356–66.

purpose of the book the narrator climaxes all of the previous appeals for the audience to believe in and worship Jesus as the Christ (1:17, 41; 4:25-26, 29; 7:26-31, 41-42; 9:22; 10:24; 11:27), the Son of God (1:18, 49; 10:36; 11:27). They may thereby know and experience divine life eternal (3:14-18, 36; 5:24-26, 40; 6:40, 47, 53-58; 10:10, 28; 12:25, 49-50; 14:6; 17:2-3) in and through loving one another in the self-sacrificial way that Jesus loves (12:50; 13:34; 15:9-12).[14]

To Martha, the sister of Lazarus, whom he raised from the dead, Jesus proclaimed, "I am the resurrection and the life; whoever believes in me, even though he dies, will live, and all who live and believe in me will never die for eternity" (11:25-26). When he asked if she believed this, Martha affirmed her faith with an act of confessional worship, "Yes Lord, I have believed that you are the Christ, the Son of God, the one coming into the world!" (11:26-27). Now that Jesus has risen and ascended to the Father, the audience may similarly believe in and worship Jesus as the Christ, the Son of God, and thereby have divine life eternal now (20:31), as they look forward to living eternally even after dying (11:25-26). As Jesus affirmed in his final prayer to the Father who gave him, as the Son of God, authority over all people, so that he might give them life eternal: "This is eternal life, that they may know you, the only true God, and the one whom you sent, Jesus Christ" (17:1-3).[15]

A Eucharistic Meal with the Risen Lord (21:1-14)

The notice that "after these things Jesus again manifested himself to the disciples at the Sea of Tiberias" (21:1) invites the audience to link this scene to John 6 and its allusions to eucharistic worship. It recalls that "Jesus went across the Sea of Tiberias" (6:1) and that "boats came from Tiberias near the place where they ate the bread when the Lord gave thanks" (6:23), prefiguring the Eucharist.[16] Indicative of his leadership role, Simon Peter heads the list of seven disciples representative of the community of believers (21:2). This accords with his role as the spokesman for the disciples when he worshiped Jesus, proclaiming, "We ourselves have come to believe and have

---

14. "The whole purpose of the gospel has been to bring the reader to see in the humanity of Jesus, and above all in his death in sacrificial love on the cross, the only begotten Son who is always in the bosom of the unseen God (1:18), the 'I AM' (8:24) who reveals the essence of God to be love" (Byrne, *Life Abounding*, 341).

15. On John 20:1-31, see Heil, *Blood and Water*, 120-50.

16. These are the only occurrences of "Tiberias" in John, and the term "sea" occurs only in 6:1, 16, 17, 18, 19, 22, 25; and 21:1, 7.

come to know that you are the Holy One of God!" (6:69). Peter's leadership role is confirmed as he said to the other disciples, "I am going to fish," and they replied, "We are going with you," and then "they went out and embarked in the boat" (21:3). This recalls that the disciples similarly "embarked in a boat" (6:17) before Jesus manifested himself to them by performing the uniquely divine action of walking on the sea (6:19).[17]

Peter's declaration, "I am going to fish [ἁλιεύειν]" (21:3), carries both a literal and a symbolic meaning. In addition to catching fish for food, it symbolizes catching fish representative of people as future believers. In LXX Jer 16:16 God proclaims that he is sending for many fishermen and "they will fish" (ἁλιεύσουσιν) for "them," referring to the people of Israel (16:14–15).[18] But, as fishermen, the disciples "on that night caught nothing [οὐδέν]" (John 21:3). On the symbolic level of catching people to be believers, this resonates with Jesus' pronouncement in his farewell address to his disciples that "without me you can do nothing [οὐδέν]" (15:5). In the context this refers to their not being able to "bear fruit" (15:4), which, like catching fish, symbolically refers to bringing people to believe. That on that "night" the disciples caught nothing also recalls Jesus' statement to the disciples that "night is coming when no one can work" (9:4), that is, when he, as the "light" of the world (9:5), is absent.

Recalling that the disciples (20:10) did not yet "know" (ᾔδεισαν) the Scripture that it was necessary for Jesus to rise from the dead (20:9), the disciples did not "know" (ᾔδεισαν) that it was the risen Jesus when he stood on the shore in the early morning (21:4). The Jesus who promised his disciples that he would not leave them "orphans," but would come to them (14:18), now addressed them affectionately as "children" and established that they do not have any "fish to eat" (21:5).[19] Jesus then directed them to throw the net to the right side of the boat and "you will find [εὑρήσετε]" (21:6). The unexpressed object of what they will find allows for the disciples to find more than they expected—not only a great number of fish both for food and representative of people, but the unrecognized risen Jesus himself. This stands in notable contrast to what Jesus previously told the Jews, namely, "You will seek me and you will not find [εὑρήσετέ] me" (7:34, 36).[20]

17. Heil, *Jesus Walking*, 37–56. The verb "embark" (ἐμβαίνω) occurs in John only in 6:17, 24 and 21:3. The noun "boat" (πλοῖον) occurs only in 6:17, 19, 21, 22 and 21:3, 6, and its synonymous diminutive (πλοιάριον) only in 6:22, 23, 24 and 21:8.

18. In the synoptic gospel tradition Jesus promised to transform the fishermen he called to be his first disciples into "fishers of people" (Matt 4:18–22; Mark 1:16–20; see also Luke 5:1–11).

19. The word translated "fish to eat" (προσφάγιον) refers to a fish relish eaten with bread; see BDAG, 886.

20. That these are the only occurrences in John of "you will find" (εὑρήσετε)

After the disciples threw the net to the right side in accord with Jesus' instructions, "they were not able to draw it in because of the great number of fish" (21:6). This resolves the tension regarding their inability to catch anything. Now not only do they have fish to eat (21:5), but they have caught fish symbolically representative of great numbers of people. In LXX Hab 1:14-15 the fisherman "draws" (εἵλκυσεν) in the people, who are like "fish" (ἰχθύας), with his net. But the disciples are unable to "draw" (ἑλκύσαι) in the net because of the great number of "fish" (ἰχθύων), representative of people. In LXX Ezek 47:10 it is promised that when the life-giving waters flow from the eschatological temple of Jerusalem, the "fish" (ἰχθύες) will be like the "fish" (ἰχθύες) of the Great Sea—an "exceedingly great number" (πλῆθος πολὺ σφόδρα). And now that the disciples have followed the direction of the risen Jesus, the new "temple" for true worship (2:19-21), they are unable to draw in the net because of the "great number" (πλήθους) of "fish" (ἰχθύων).

Peter was the disciple who wanted to follow Jesus to the point of laying down his life for him (13:37). Instead, he denied Jesus thrice (18:17, 25-27), as Jesus predicted (13:38). But Jesus did tell Peter that he would follow him later (13:36). When the beloved disciple informed Peter that the one standing on the shore was the Lord, the naked Peter "girded" (διεζώσατο) his outer garment around him and threw "himself" (ἑαυτόν) into the sea (21:7). Peter thus began to follow Jesus, who "girded" (διέζωσεν) a towel around "himself [ἑαυτόν]" (13:4) and then washed the feet of the disciples and dried them with the towel with which he was "girded [διεζωσμένος]" (13:5), a ritualistic act symbolic of laying down his life for them.[21] When the other disciples reached the shore in the boat (21:8), they saw a "charcoal fire" there (21:9), recalling the "charcoal fire" around which Peter warmed himself (18:18) after his first denial of Jesus (18:17). Now, ironically, a charcoal fire warmed the meal with which the risen Jesus will nourish and reunite Peter and the disciples to himself.[22]

The disciples saw lying upon the charcoal fire fish and bread (21:9). The "fish" (ὀψάριον) recalls the two "fish [ὀψάρια]" (6:9) with which Jesus fed the great multitude with as much "fish" (ὀψαρίων) as they wanted (6:11).[23] And the "bread" (ἄρτον) they saw together with the fish on the charcoal fire recalls the "bread" (ἄρτον) the multitude ate when the Lord

---

strengthens this connection.

21. That these are the only occurrences in John of the verb "gird" (διαζώννυμι) strengthens this connection.

22. That these are the only occurrences in John of "charcoal fire" (ἀνθρακιά) strengthens this connection.

23. This term for "fish" (ὀψάριον) occurs in John only in 6:9, 11 and 21:9, 10, 13.

gave thanks (6:23).²⁴ Jesus' overabundant feeding of the great multitude with fish and bread thus indicated how he overabundantly feeds believers in the eucharistic meal. Indeed, in the Eucharist he nourishes them for a life they may have abundantly (10:10)— divine life eternal (6:27, 51, 54, 58; cf. 6:33, 35, 48, 53).

Jesus invited the disciples to bring some of the fish he had just directed them to catch (21:10), presumably to be added to the meal he is preparing (21:5). This indicates that Jesus not only feeds the disciples himself, but also has enabled them to provide an abundant supply of food, implicitly in the Eucharist, to nourish and sustain themselves for their mission of catching people to be believers. The word used to refer to the fish lying on the charcoal fire as well as to the fish Jesus now invited the disciples to bring to the meal is ὀψάριον (21:9–10), in contrast to ἰχθύς, the word employed for fish when the disciples caught the great number of fish in their net (21:6, 8). In accord with the double meaning of catching fish in this story, ὀψάριον refers to fish to be eaten, whereas ἰχθύς refers to fish that represent the people the disciples are to catch and bring into the worshiping community of believers for divine life eternal.²⁵

Whereas Jesus directed the disciples to bring some of the "fish" (ὀψαρίων) to be eaten (21:10), Peter drew in the net full of large "fish" (ἰχθύων) representative of the large number of people Jesus will enable the disciples to catch (21:11). The disciples were not able to "draw" (ἑλκύσαι) in the net because of the great number of fish/people (21:6). But the Peter whom Jesus rebuked for trying to prevent his self-sacrificial death (18:11) when he "drew" (εἵλκυσεν) his sword and cut off the right ear of the slave of the high priest (18:10), now empowered by the command of the risen Lord, "drew" (εἵλκυσεν) in the net full of fish/people to land.²⁶ This continues the unifying and universalizing purpose of the self-sacrificial death of Jesus, who declared, "When I am lifted up from the earth, I will draw [ἑλκύσω] all to myself" (12:32), indicating the kind of death he would die (12:33).

The soldiers' decision, "Let us not tear [σχίσωμεν]" the seamless tunic of the crucified Jesus, in accord with God's scriptural plan symbolically pointed to the unity his self-sacrificial death effects (19:24). Similarly, the net of so many fish that Peter drew in was not "torn" (ἐσχίσθη) but kept intact by God (divine passive), unifying the great quantity of distinctly

---

24. Except for John 13:18, the word "bread" (ἄρτος) occurs only in John 6 (twenty-one times) and 21:9, 13.

25. Pitta, "*Ichthys* ed *opsarion*, 348–64.

26. That these are the only occurrences in John of "he drew" (εἵλκυσεν) strengthens this connection.

numbered—one hundred fifty-three—fish/people in it (21:11).[27] The mention of the precise number of so many fish/people presupposes that each one was very carefully counted. This indicates that every individual person symbolized by the fish is important within the worshiping community of believers. Each and every believing person counts. As a result of the self-sacrificial death of Jesus that unifies all, none will be "lost" (3:16; 6:39; 10:28; 17:12; 18:9), so that all may be preserved and protected for divine life eternal.[28]

Jesus invited the disciples to the meal of fish and bread which he had provided for them, as he said to them, "Come, have breakfast" (21:12). This then completely resolved the tension regarding the disciples' recognition of Jesus (21:4). Not only have the beloved disciple and Peter recognized the Lord (21:7), but now the entire group recognized him, as none of the disciples dared to ask who he was, knowing that it was the Lord (21:12). Earlier at the Sea of Tiberias the disciples had gathered up the abundant leftovers after Jesus gave thanks and miraculously fed the large crowd with only five loaves of bread and two fish (6:1–13). Then boats came from Tiberias near the place where they ate bread, after "the Lord" gave thanks (6:23). Now the disciples knew that it is "the Lord," who is similarly feeding them with a meal of bread and fish symbolic of the Eucharist (21:9, 12–13). This provides a model for the audience of believers to recognize that Jesus, the risen Lord, is present as the ultimate host of every eucharistic meal they celebrate as a worshiping community.

When Jesus fed the large crowd, he "took" (ἔλαβεν) the "loaves of bread" (ἄρτους) and "gave" (διέδωκεν) them to those reclining and "likewise" (ὁμοίως) from the "fish" (ὀψαρίων), as much as they wanted (6:11). Similarly, he now "takes" (λαμβάνει) the "bread" (ἄρτον) and "gives" (δίδωσιν) it to the disciples, and the "fish" (ὀψάριον) "likewise [ὁμοίως]" (21:13). After Jesus fed the large crowd with fish and bread (6:1–13), he revealed himself as the "Bread of Life" that he gives as his flesh for the life of the world (6:51), a reference to the Eucharist (6:52–58). Jesus likewise fed the disciples with fish and bread (21:9–13), similarly suggesting the

---

27. That these are the only occurrences in John of the verb "tear" (σχίζω) strengthens this connection. On the relation of the 153 fish to Ezek 47:1–12, see Rastoin, "153 poissons," 84–92.

28. "Here the conservation of fish . . . hints at Jesus' repeated promise that he will keep his disciples safe, and that none of those whom the Father has given him will ever be lost" (Michaels, *John*, 1039). "In some respect that the author has not made explicit, though presumably intending his original readers to understand, it [the number 153] probably signifies perfection and completion: at the end of the age the church will have brought to Jesus all those that the Father has drawn to him for salvation (6:44)" (Byrne, *Life Abounding*, 347).

Eucharist. That Jesus fed the crowd with fish and an overabundance of bread and the disciples with bread and overabundance of fish reaffirms how he overabundantly feeds believers in the Eucharist with divine life eternal (6:54; 10:10). From this overabundance provided them in the Eucharist the audience as a worshiping community may nourish and sustain in and through the eucharistic meal the great number of people they will lead to become believers for divine life eternal.

The notice that this was now the third time that Jesus was "manifested" (ἐφανερώθη) to his disciples after being raised from the dead (21:14) forms a literary inclusion with this scene's introductory notice that Jesus again "manifested" (ἐφανέρωσεν) himself to the disciples and he "manifested" (ἐφανέρωσεν) in this way (21:1). The way in which the risen Jesus manifested himself was by providing the disciples with a eucharistic meal of bread and overabundant fish at the Sea of Tiberias (21:1–13), complementing his previous eucharistic meal of fish and overabundant bread for the great multitude at the Sea of Tiberias (6:1–13). This in turn recalls and resonates with how Jesus "manifested" (ἐφανέρωσεν) his glory (2:11), when at the wedding celebration in Cana he provided an overabundance of extraordinary wine (2:1–10) symbolic of the divine life eternal which is to be joyfully celebrated by the audience in their eucharistic meal of sacramental bread and wine.[29]

The Worship To Be Offered by Peter and by the Beloved Disciple (21:15–25)

Peter had distinguished himself from the other disciples when he promised to follow Jesus to the point of laying down his life for him (13:37). But instead he denied Jesus thrice (13:38; 18:17, 25–27). He continued to distinguish himself from the other disciples when he threw himself into the sea and swam toward Jesus while the others came in the boat (21:7–8), and again when he boarded the boat to draw in the net full of the great number of fish (21:11). Accordingly, Jesus inquired whether Peter will continue to distinguish himself from the others, when he asked Peter whether he loves Jesus more than the other disciples love him (21:15). Without daring to distinguish himself from the others, Peter simply affirmed, "Yes, Lord, you know that I love you," and then Jesus commanded him, "Feed my lambs" (21:15). Having fed the disciples with a meal of bread and fish symbolic of

---

29. "Both episodes [2:1–10 and 21:1–13] feature a revelation of the divine that for believers of subsequent generations continues sacramentally under the form of bread and wine" (Byrne, *Life Abounding*, 348). On the relation of John 21:1–14 to John 1–20 and to Luke 5:1–11, see Labahn, "Fischen nach Bedeutung," 115–40.

the Eucharist, the risen Jesus commissioned Peter likewise to feed, implicitly with the eucharistic meal, "my lambs," the followers who believe and belong to Jesus, the good shepherd (10:1-18, 26-29).

After Peter affirmed his love for Jesus a second time, Jesus commanded him, "Shepherd my sheep" (21:16). To "shepherd" (ποίμαινε) refers to caring for, protecting, guiding, or leading sheep.[30] This second command of Jesus to Peter could be paraphrased, "Be a shepherd [ποιμήν] to my sheep." Jesus demonstrated what it means to shepherd his sheep, as he, the good "shepherd," laid down his own life for the sheep as an act of self-sacrificial worship so that they may have divine life eternal (10:10-11, 28). Jesus first had to lay down his own life and take it up again in resurrection (10:17-18) before Peter can fulfill his promise to lay down his life (13:37). In other words, Peter had to be a sheep who followed Jesus before he can follow him as a shepherd. But now the risen Lord and good shepherd challenged and empowered Peter to demonstrate his love for Jesus by "shepherding my sheep," that is, by laying down his life as an act of self-sacrificial worship in love for them as Jesus loved them (13:34-35; 15:12-17).[31]

Saddened that Jesus would question his love for a third time, precisely in correspondence to his threefold denial of Jesus, Peter, for a third, emphatic, and definitive time, affirmed, "Lord, you know everything, you know that I love you" (21:17; cf. 16:30).[32] Jesus' third command to Peter, "Feed my sheep" (21:17), serves as a climactic combination of his first two commands. Whereas Jesus first commissioned Peter to "feed my lambs" (21:15) and then to "shepherd my sheep" (21:16), he now directed him to "feed my sheep." Having commanded Peter to "shepherd my sheep," Jesus thus empowered him to "feed my sheep" from the overabundance of bread (6:1-13) and fish (21:9-13) he supplied, which symbolically point to the overabundant, divine life eternal provided by the eucharistic meal. But the risen Jesus also empowered Peter to "feed," in the sense of nourish and sustain spiritually, "my sheep" by "shepherding" them, that is, by laying down his life for them in love, like the good shepherd, as an act of self-sacrificial worship for their divine life eternal.

Peter dressed himself when he girded his outer garment around himself, and went wherever he wished when he threw himself into the sea (21:7), and when he again boarded the boat to draw in the net full of fish

---

30. BDAG, 842.

31. On Peter being questioned by Jesus as to whether he has the love to lay down his life, see Shepherd, "Do You Love Me?," 777-92.

32. "An intensification in the exchange does, however, set in when Peter responds with deep emotion to a third round of questioning (v. 17)—doubtless because allusion to his triple denial is now clear" (Byrne, *Life Abounding*, 350).

(21:11). But, as Jesus assured him, when Peter grows old, he will stretch out his hands for someone else to dress him and take him where he does not wish to go (21:18), a reference to his eventual death. Indeed, Jesus said this to signify by what kind of death Peter would glorify, and thus offer worship to, God (21:19), a death similar to that of Jesus himself (12:33; 18:32). This reaffirms that Jesus' commissioning of Peter to shepherd and feed the sheep (21:15-17) means ultimately his laying down his own life for them in love. Jesus had declared that "I glorified" (ἐδόξασα) God by completing the work God gave him to do (17:4; cf. 13:31; 14:13; 17:1) with his self-sacrificial death as the good shepherd who laid down his life for the sheep. So also Peter, who had promised to lay down his life for Jesus (13:37), "will glorify" (δοξάσει) God by his death as an act of self-sacrificial worship.[33]

Jesus then said to Peter, "Follow me" (21:19b). After Peter turned and saw the beloved disciple following (21:20), he asked Jesus, "Lord, what about this one?" (21:21). Jesus replied to Peter, "If I want him to remain until I come, what is that to you?" And then Jesus emphatically reinforced his previous command to Peter by insisting, "As for you, follow me!" (21:22). At his final supper with his disciples Jesus had told Peter that where he is going Peter could not follow him now, but he would follow him later (13:36). But Peter protested, "Lord, why can I not follow you now? I will lay down my life for you" (13:37). Now, however, it is time for Peter to follow Jesus by finally laying down his life for the sheep like Jesus as an act of self-sacrificial worship that will glorify God (21:19a). Peter may thereby serve as an outstanding model for the audience of believers to love one another in a self-sacrificial way (13:34; 15:12, 17) that will glorify, and thus offer ethical worship to, God.

The word that the beloved disciple would not die went out to the "brothers" (21:23), not only the other disciples (20:17-18) but also the believers who became "brothers" and "sisters" of the beloved disciple, when he took the mother of Jesus to his own to form the familial worshiping community of believers (19:27). But Jesus only told Peter, reported twice, "If I want him to remain until I come, what is that to you?" (21:22, 23). Although the original beloved disciple may die before Jesus comes again, since the beloved disciple also represents the ideal and future believer (17:20), that Jesus wants the beloved disciple to remain challenges each member of the audience to be a beloved disciple, a believer who remains until Jesus comes again. "Remaining" until Jesus comes again includes "remaining" in the love of Jesus (15:9). And one "will remain" in the love of Jesus by keeping his

---

33. On the role of Peter in John 21:15-19, see Culpepper, "Peter as Exemplary Disciple," 165-78.

commandments (15:10), preeminently his new commandment to love one another in the self-sacrificial way that he loves (13:34; 15:12, 17) for divine life eternal (10:10–11; 12:50).

The narrator's affirmation that "this [οὗτος] is the disciple who testifies about these things" (21:24) serves as a further answer to Peter's previous question to Jesus about the beloved disciple following them, "Lord what about this one [οὗτος]?" (21:21). The narrator then characterized the beloved disciple as the implied author, the one who testifies about "these things," the events recorded in the book, and has written them as a foundation for the audience. The declaration that "we know [οἴδαμεν] that his testimony is true" (21:24) not only complements that the beloved disciple "knows [οἶδεν] that he speaks the truth" (19:35), but reaffirms the basis for the communal act of doxological worship introduced in the prologue, "We observed his glory, glory as of the unique one from the Father, full of a gift of truth" (1:14). The beloved disciple saw and testified to the life-giving blood and water flowing from the side of the dead Jesus (19:34), and "his testimony is true," so that the audience may believe (19:35) and express their belief in their communal worship of the Father and his unique Son.

That the beloved disciple has not only testified about these things but "written" them as true testimony (21:24) serves as another way for him to "remain" (21:22–23).[34] The book that he has written stands in continuity with the OT "scriptures," and just as they testify about Jesus (5:39; cf. 5:46), so this book offers true testimony to its future audiences. The narrator previously informed the audience that Jesus performed many other signs not written in this book, but that the ones that have been written are sufficient to provoke and strengthen their faith (20:30-31). To the communal confession, "We know that his testimony is true" (21:24), the narrator adds his own personal conclusion, "I do not think the world itself could contain the books that would be written," if all the things Jesus did were to be written (21:25). This rhetorical exaggeration assures the audience of even more reliable testimony than they have heard in this book to believe that Jesus is the Christ, the Son of God, and to express that faith by worshiping in Spirit and truth (4:23-24) to have divine life eternal in his name (20:31).[35]

---

34. "There is a sense, however, in which the Beloved Disciple, despite his death, does 'remain' (v. 24). He 'remains' and makes an irreplaceable contribution to the entire believing community through the testimony to the saving events and the written record of that testimony that he has 'authored' in the shape of the gospel" (Byrne, *Life Abounding*, 353).

35. "Flamboyant hyperbole of this nature was conventional at the end of literary works in the ancient world" (Byrne, *Life Abounding*, 353). On John 21:1-25, see Heil, *Blood and Water*, 151-67.

Summary on 20:1—21:25

Before Jesus raised Lazarus, the stone which lay across the cave of his tomb (11:38) had to be taken away (11:38-41). When Lazarus came out, his face was wrapped in a "face cloth" so that he had to be unwrapped by others (11:44). In contrast, when Mary Magdalene came to the tomb of Jesus, she saw that the "stone had been taken away" (20:1), the passive verb suggesting a divine rather than human agency. Inside the tomb Peter observed that the "face cloth" which had been on the head of Jesus "had been rolled up" (divine passive) apart "into one place" (20:7). This symbolically corresponds to the purpose of Jesus' death, as an act of self-sacrificial worship, to gather all of the dispersed children of God "into one" (11:52). Then there will be "one" sheep herd, "one" shepherd (10:16), who has the divine authority to lay down his life on his own and to take it up again (10:18). The self-sacrificial death and resurrection of Jesus thus establishes the unity and universality of his believing and worshiping community.

When Mary Magdalene bent down into the tomb of Jesus (20:11), she observed two angels in white sitting where the "body" of Jesus had been lying (20:12). This confirms Jesus' promise that in three days he would raise the destroyed temple (2:19) of his "body" (2:21). The risen Jesus then told her not to hold on to his body, for he had not yet ascended to the Father. Rather, she is to go to his brothers and tell them, "I am ascending to my Father and your Father, my God and your God" (20:17). This recalls that Jesus had told his disciples that he is going to his Father's house to prepare a "place" for them to worship (14:2). He will then come back and take them to himself so that where he is they also may be (14:3). He will thus introduce his brothers (cf. 19:26-27) into the "place," the familial, interpersonal relationship, he shares with his Father, so that his Father and God will be their Father and God. This relationship will enable his believing brothers and the audience to become true worshipers who worship the Father in Spirit and truth (4:23-24) for divine life eternal.

The Jesus who "gave over" the Spirit when he died (19:30) invited his disciples to "receive" the Holy Spirit (20:22), the Spirit of truth, which the world is not able to "receive" (14:17a). It "remains" with the disciples and will be in them (14:17b), as it "remains" upon Jesus, the one who baptizes with the Holy Spirit (1:33), as the Lamb of God who takes away the sin of the world (1:29) through his self-sacrificial death. Similarly, the disciples have now been empowered to baptize with the Holy Spirit they have received from the risen Jesus and take away sins as they pronounce the word (cf. 17:20) of divine forgiveness, implicitly as they administer the sacrament of baptism to those who believe and refuse it to those who do not believe:

"Whose sins you forgive are forgiven them, whose sins you retain are retained" (20:23). They may thereby fulfill their mission (20:21) of bringing others to believe, so that they do not die eternally in their sins (8:21, 24), but rather possess divine life eternal (3:15-16).

The risen Jesus had commissioned Mary Magdalene to tell his disciples, "I am ascending to my Father and your Father, my God and your God" (20:17). Now that Jesus has ascended to the Father, Thomas's climactic act of confessional worship not only confirms but surpasses Jesus' announcement to Mary Magdalene. Thomas demonstrates that believers can worship not only the Father but also the risen and ascended Son, the unique Son who has revealed and made the unseen God and Father visible to believers (1:18; 14:7-9), as "my Lord and my God" (20:28). Thomas begins to fulfill Jesus' prediction that all may honor and thus worship the Son as they honor and thus worship the Father (5:23).

The risen Jesus' concluding words to Thomas, "Blessed are those who have not seen yet have believed" (20:29), refer to the audience. Even though the members of the audience have not seen the risen Lord himself like Mary Magdalene (20:18), the disciples (20:20, 25), and Thomas (20:27), nor even the burial cloths like Peter and the beloved disciple (20:6-8), they will still be blessed with divine life eternal for believing (3:15-16) without directly seeing the risen Lord. That the beloved disciple believed (20:8) before seeing the risen Lord himself testifies to the audience that they too can believe without seeing. By identifying with the characters in the narrative who have seen, they may likewise "see" based on their seeing. They have heard the testimony of those who have seen not only the burial cloths in the empty tomb but the risen Lord himself, so that they, along with Thomas as their figurative "Twin" (20:24), may worship the risen Jesus as "my Lord and my God!" (20:28).

To Martha, the sister of Lazarus, whom he raised from the dead, Jesus proclaimed, "I am the resurrection and the life; whoever believes in me, even though he dies, will live, and all who live and believe in me will never die for eternity" (11:25-26). When he asked if she believed this, Martha affirmed her faith with an act of confessional worship, "Yes Lord, I have believed that you are the Christ, the Son of God, the one coming into the world!" (11:26-27). Now that Jesus has risen and ascended to the Father, the audience may similarly believe in and worship Jesus as the Christ, the Son of God, and thereby have divine life eternal now (20:31), as they look forward to living eternally even after dying (11:25-26). As Jesus affirmed in his final prayer to the Father who gave him, as the Son of God, authority over all people, so that he might give them life eternal: "This is eternal life, that they may know you, the only true God, and the one whom you sent, Jesus Christ" (17:1–3).

The soldiers' decision, "Let us not tear" the seamless tunic of the crucified Jesus, in accord with God's scriptural plan symbolically pointed to the unity his self-sacrificial death effects (19:24). Similarly, the net of so many fish that Peter drew in was not "torn" but kept intact by God (divine passive), unifying the great quantity of distinctly numbered—one hundred fifty-three—fish/people in it (21:11). The mention of the precise number of so many fish/people presupposes that each one was very carefully counted. This indicates that every individual person symbolized by the fish is important within the worshiping community of believers. Each and every believing person counts. As a result of the self-sacrificial death of Jesus that unifies all, none will be "lost" (3:16; 6:39; 10:28; 17:12; 18:9), so that all may be preserved and protected for divine life eternal.

Jesus invited the disciples to the meal of fish and bread which he had provided for them, as he said to them, "Come, have breakfast" (21:12). This then completely resolved the tension regarding the disciples' recognition of Jesus (21:4). Not only have the beloved disciple and Peter recognized the Lord (21:7), but now the entire group recognized him, as none of the disciples dared to ask who he was, knowing that it was the Lord (21:12). Earlier at the Sea of Tiberias the disciples had gathered up the abundant leftovers after Jesus gave thanks and miraculously fed the large crowd with only five loaves of bread and two fish (6:1–13). Then boats came from Tiberias near the place where they ate bread, after "the Lord" gave thanks (6:23). Now the disciples knew that it is "the Lord," who is similarly feeding them with a meal of bread and fish symbolic of the Eucharist (21:9, 12–13). This provides a model for the audience of believers to recognize that Jesus, the risen Lord, is present as the ultimate host of every eucharistic meal they celebrate as a worshiping community.

The notice that this was now the third time that Jesus was "manifested" to his disciples after being raised from the dead (21:14) forms a literary inclusion with this scene's introductory notice that Jesus again "manifested" himself to the disciples and he "manifested" in this way (21:1). The way in which the risen Jesus manifested himself was by providing the disciples with a eucharistic meal of bread and overabundant fish at the Sea of Tiberias (21:1–13), complementing his previous eucharistic meal of fish and overabundant bread for the great multitude at the Sea of Tiberias (6:1–13). This in turn recalls and resonates with how Jesus "manifested" his glory (2:11), when at the wedding celebration in Cana he provided an overabundance of extraordinary wine (2:1–10) symbolic of the divine life eternal which is to be joyfully celebrated by the audience in their eucharistic meal of sacramental bread and wine.

Saddened that Jesus would question his love for a third time, precisely in correspondence to his threefold denial of Jesus, Peter, for a third, emphatic, and definitive time, affirmed, "Lord, you know everything, you know that I love you" (21:17; cf. 16:30). Jesus' third command to Peter, "Feed my sheep" (21:17), serves as a climactic combination of his first two commands. Whereas Jesus first commissioned Peter to "feed my lambs" (21:15) and then to "shepherd my sheep" (21:16), he now directed him to "feed my sheep." Having commanded Peter to "shepherd my sheep," Jesus thus empowered him to "feed my sheep" from the overabundance of bread (6:1–13) and fish (21:9–13) he supplied, which symbolically point to the overabundant, divine life eternal provided by the eucharistic meal. But the risen Jesus also empowered Peter to "feed," in the sense of nourish and sustain spiritually, "my sheep" by "shepherding" them, that is, by laying down his life for them in love, like the good shepherd, as an act of self-sacrificial worship for their divine life eternal.

After Jesus directed Peter to follow him (21:19b), Peter turned and saw the beloved disciple following (21:20). He then asked Jesus, "Lord, what about this one?" (21:21). Jesus replied to Peter, "If I want him to remain until I come, what is that to you?" And then Jesus emphatically reinforced his previous command to Peter by insisting, "As for you, follow me!" (21:22). At his final supper with his disciples Jesus had told Peter that where he is going Peter could not follow him now, but he would follow him later (13:36). But Peter protested, "Lord, why can I not follow you now? I will lay down my life for you" (13:37). Now, however, it is time for Peter to follow Jesus by finally laying down his life for the sheep like Jesus as an act of self-sacrificial worship that will glorify God (21:19a). Peter may thereby serve as an outstanding model for the audience of believers to love one another in a self-sacrificial way (13:34; 15:12, 17) that will glorify, and thus offer ethical worship to, God.

Although the original beloved disciple may die before Jesus comes again, since the beloved disciple also represents the ideal and future believer (17:20), that Jesus wants the beloved disciple to remain (21:22, 23) challenges each member of the audience to be a beloved disciple, a believer who remains until Jesus comes again. "Remaining" until Jesus comes again includes "remaining" in the love of Jesus (15:9). And one "will remain" in the love of Jesus by keeping his commandments (15:10), preeminently his new commandment to love one another in the self-sacrificial way that he loves (13:34; 15:12, 17) for divine life eternal (10:10–11; 12:50).

The narrator characterized the beloved disciple as the implied author, the one who testifies about "these things" (21:24), the events recorded in the book, and has written them as a foundation for the audience. The declaration that "we know that his testimony is true" (21:24) not only complements that the beloved disciple "knows that he speaks the truth" (19:35), but reaffirms the basis for the communal act of doxological worship introduced in the prologue, "We observed his glory, glory as of the unique one from the Father, full of a gift of truth" (1:14). The beloved disciple saw and testified to the life-giving blood and water flowing from the side of the dead Jesus (19:34), and "his testimony is true," so that the audience may believe (19:35) and express their belief in their communal worship of the Father and his unique Son.

That the beloved disciple has not only testified about these things but "written" them as true testimony (21:24) serves as another way for him to "remain" (21:22–23). The book that he has written stands in continuity with the OT "scriptures," and just as they testify about Jesus (5:39; cf. 5:46), so this book offers true testimony to its future audiences. The narrator previously informed the audience that Jesus performed many other signs not written in this book, but that the ones that have been written are sufficient to provoke and strengthen their faith (20:30–31). To the communal confession, "We know that his testimony is true" (21:24), the narrator adds his own personal conclusion, "I do not think the world itself could contain the books that would be written," if all the things Jesus did were to be written (21:25). This rhetorical exaggeration assures the audience of even more reliable testimony than they have heard in this book to believe that Jesus is the Christ, the Son of God, and to express that faith by worshiping in Spirit and truth (4:23–24) to have divine life eternal in his name (20:31; 3:15–16).

10

Conclusion

Since there are detailed summaries at the conclusion of each of the preceding chapters, this final chapter will provide a brief synthetic overview of the various dimensions of the theme of worship that pervades the Gospel of John.

Worshiping Jesus

The prologue establishes Jesus, the Word that was with God and was God (1:1-2), as worthy of being worshiped. Its declaration of communal doxological worship sets a tone for worshiping Jesus: "The Word became flesh and dwelt among us, and we observed his glory, glory as of the unique one from the Father, full of a gift of truth" (1:14). Nathanael worshiped Jesus: "Rabbi, you are the Son of God, you are the King of Israel!" (1:49). As spokesman for the Twelve, Peter worshiped Jesus: "We have believed and have come to know that you are the Holy One of God!" (6:69). The man born blind saw, believed in Jesus as the Son of Man, and "worshiped" him (9:35-38). After affirming her belief in Jesus as "the resurrection and the life," Martha worshiped him: "You are the Christ, the Son of God, the one coming into the world!" (11:25-27). The crowds worshiped Jesus as he came into Jerusalem for the feast of Passover: "Hosanna! Blessed is he who comes in the name of the Lord, the King of Israel!" (12:13). And Thomas climactically worshiped the risen and ascended Jesus, as he declared, "My Lord and my God!" (20:28).

Mary not only fell at the feet of Jesus (11:32) in a gesture of worship, but also anointed his feet with perfumed oil and dried them with her hair (11:2; 12:3) as an act of devotional worship of Jesus. Overawed by Jesus' pronouncement of his divine identity as "I am," those arresting him "withdrew backwards and fell to the ground" (18:6), ironically placing them in a position of worshiping Jesus. Putting a sponge full of sour wine on a branch of hyssop, those crucifying Jesus "offered" it to his mouth (19:29) in an ironic act of worship, recalling Jesus' prediction to his disciples that everyone who kills them will think he is "offering" worship to God (16:2). Mary anointed the feet of Jesus with a pound of very precious ointment (12:3) as an act of devotional worship for the day of his "burial preparation" (12:7). Joseph and Nicodemus complemented this with an act of reverential worship of the dead Jesus, indicative that he is the true King of the Jews, when they bound his body in cloths along with a hundred pounds (19:39) of spices in accord with the custom among Jews "to prepare for burial" (19:40).

Worship by Jesus

John pointed to Jesus as the sacrificial Passover Lamb of God who takes away the sin of the world (1:29; cf. 1:36). In the context of the feast of Passover (6:4) Jesus indicated that he would sacrifice himself implicitly as the Passover Lamb, when he declared that "the bread that I will give is my flesh for the life of the world" (6:51). Jesus performs his act of sacrificial worship as the good shepherd who lays down his life for the sheep (10:11, 15), his beloved friends (15:13). No one takes his life from him, but he lays it down on his own (10:18). As the new and unique high priest, Jesus is the one man who will die for the people in an act of self-sacrificial worship (11:50). On the day of preparation for the Passover (19:14), when the lambs were slaughtered in the temple, Jesus was offered sour wine on hyssop (19:29), which was used to sprinkle the blood of the Passover lambs during the Exodus event (Exod 12:22). His self-sacrifice as the Passover Lamb of God was confirmed as his legs were not broken (19:33) in fulfillment of the Scripture that not a bone of the Passover lamb will be broken (19:36; cf. Exod 12:10, 46; Num 9:12).

The man born blind indicated that Jesus is a "worshiper of God" who does God's will, so that God listens to him (9:31). Martha acknowledged that whatever Jesus asks God, God will give him (11:22). Before he raised Lazarus from the dead (11:43), Jesus offered a prayer of thanksgiving to the Father for listening to him (11:41). As he approached the hour of his self-sacrificial death (12:27), Jesus prayed, "Father, glorify your name." In answer a voice came from heaven, "I have glorified and I will again glorify" (12:28). Jesus began the solemn prayer that followed his farewell address to his disciples, as "he raised his eyes to heaven" and said, "Father, the hour has come. Glorify your Son, so the Son may glorify you" (17:1). He went on to pray that the Father glorify him with the glory he had with him before the world existed (17:5). He then prayed that the Father keep his disciples "in your name that you have given me, so that they may be one as we are one" (17:11). Finally, he prayed for the unity of all future believers with the Father and the Son (17:21–24).

Worship through Jesus

Jesus' act of self-sacrificial worship enables the sacramental worship of baptism and the Eucharist, as indicated symbolically by the life-giving blood and water that went out from the side of the dead Jesus (19:34). By the blood and the water symbolic of the Spirit that flowed from his self-sacrificial death, Jesus "baptizes" with the Holy Spirit (1:33), transcending John's baptism with mere water (1:31). One may now see and enter the kingdom of God by being baptized and reborn from above in water and the Spirit (3:3–5) in the sacrament of baptism. When the risen Jesus breathed the Holy Spirit upon the disciples, he empowered them to baptize with the Holy Spirit and take away sins as they pronounce the word (cf. 17:20) of divine forgiveness, implicitly as they administer the sacrament of baptism (20:23). The water of the Spirit that flows together with the blood makes it drinkable, explaining how Jesus can give his flesh to eat and his blood to drink. He provides the true life-giving food that is his flesh and the true life-giving drink that is his blood in the sacrament of the Eucharist (6:51–58).

In his farewell address Jesus assured his disciples that their prayers would be answered if they pray through him: "Whatever you ask in my name, I will do it" (14:13), and, "If you ask me anything in my name, I will do it" (14:14). If the words of Jesus, particularly his word or commandment that they love one another in the self-sacrificial way that he loves them (13:34; 15:12, 17), remain in them, they may ask for whatever they want and it will be done for them (15:7). In their mission to "bear fruit" by bringing others to believe, whatever they ask the Father in the name of Jesus, he will give them (15:16; 16:23–27). If they love Jesus and keep his commandment to love one another (14:15), Jesus will ask the Father and he will give them another Paraclete to be with them always (14:16), the Spirit of truth (14:17, 26; 15:26; 16:13). This will enable them to become true worshipers who worship the Father in Spirit and truth (4:23), the Spirit that comes through the self-sacrificial death of Jesus (7:38–39; 19:34), and the truth that Jesus embodies (14:6)—that divine life eternal comes through self-sacrificial love.

Worship with Jesus

Near the feast of Passover (2:13) Jesus indicated that his risen body would replace the Jerusalem temple as the "place" of true worship (2:19-21; cf. 4:20-21). Jesus will transcend the feast of Tabernacles celebrated in the temple by providing living water symbolic of the Spirit (7:37-39; cf. 19:34). As the one whom the Father has "consecrated" (10:36), Jesus transcends the feast of Dedication celebrating the reconsecration of the temple (10:22). The "place" the risen and ascended Jesus will provide for true worship is not physical or geographical but his intimate union with his Father. In his Father's "household" of worship are many "dwellings," that is, divine interpersonal relationships, and Jesus' return to his Father prepares a "place" (14:2), his union with his Father, for believers to worship in union with him and his Father (14:3). Jesus ascended to his Father, who is also the Father of his believing brothers, to his God and their God (20:17), to form the "place" for worshiping both the Son and his Father (5:23). This is confirmed as Thomas climactically worshiped the risen Jesus: "My Lord and my God!" (20:28).

Jesus told Peter that unless he washes Peter's feet, he will have no "share with me" (13:8). He will thus not be able to participate in the worship for divine life eternal in the new communal household or temple into which Jesus' ritual washing of feet welcomes the disciples. Jesus then told him that the one who has "bathed," that is, has been "baptized," has no need except to have his feet washed, and then he is completely "clean" (13:10), ritually purified to share in worship with Jesus. By washing his disciples' feet, Jesus gave them a share with him in his self-sacrificial death symbolized by his washing of their feet. They are to metaphorically wash one another's feet (13:14-15) by loving one another in the self-sacrificial way that Jesus loves them (13:34; 15:12, 17). They are thus to love one another as an act of self-sacrificial worship in imitation of and in union with Jesus. Once Jesus has laid down his life for them, then they will be able to lay down their lives (13:37) in self-sacrificial love for one another in union with Jesus and thereby share with him in divine life eternal (10:28; 12:25, 50; 13:34; 17:2-3).

The Goal of Worship: Unity of All for Divine Life Eternal

Jesus lays down his life for his own sheep in an act of self-sacrificial worship (10:11, 15) to unite other sheep, future believers, so that "there will be one sheep herd, one shepherd" (10:16). As the good shepherd-high priest, Jesus will sacrifice himself so that he might gather into one the dispersed children of God (11:52). When Jesus is lifted up/exalted in his self-sacrificial death, he will draw all "to myself" (12:32); he will prepare a "place" for all believers to worship, as he takes them "to myself," so that where he is they also may be—united with him and his Father (14:3). Jesus prayed that future believers may all be one in union with him and his Father (17:20–21). The soldiers' decision, "Let us not tear" the seamless tunic of the crucified Jesus, symbolically pointed to the unity his self-sacrificial death effects (19:24). That the face cloth which had been on the head of Jesus had been rolled up apart "into one place" (20:7) symbolically corresponds to the purpose of Jesus' death, as an act of self-sacrificial worship, to establish the unity and universality of his believing and worshiping community.

The ultimate goal of Jesus laying down his life as an act of self-sacrificial worship is to unite all people as believers into a worshiping community for divine life eternal (10:10–11, 15, 28). The life-giving blood and water that flowed from the side of the self-sacrificed Jesus (19:34) provides the basis for baptismal and eucharistic worship. Believers reborn from water and the Spirit in the sacrament of baptism (3:3–5) may have divine life eternal (3:15–16). A believer who eats the flesh of Jesus and drinks his blood in the Eucharist has divine life eternal, and Jesus will raise him on the last day (6:54). Believers are to pray through Jesus for whatever they need to keep Jesus' commandment to love one another in the self-sacrificial way that he loves (13:34; 15:12) for divine life eternal (12:50). The Gospel of John was written so that its audiences may believe that Jesus is the Christ, the Son of God (20:31a), and thereby have eternal life (17:3). By believing, and expressing that belief in and through all of the dimensions of their liturgical and ethical worship, they may have divine life eternal in his name (20:31b).

Bibliography

Ashton, John. *The Gospel of John and Christian Origins*. Minneapolis: Fortress, 2014.
Atkinson, Kenneth. "Synagogue." In *Eerdmans Dictionary of the Bible*, edited by David Noel Freedman, 1260–62. Grand Rapids: Eerdmans, 2000.
Barker, Margaret. *King of the Jews: Temple Theology in John's Gospel*. London: SPCK, 2014.
Beasley-Murray, George R. *John*. WBC 36. 2nd ed. Nashville: Nelson, 2000.
Beck, David R. "'Whom Jesus Loved': Anonymity and Identity. Belief and Witness in the Fourth Gospel." In *Characters and Characterization in the Gospel of John*, edited by Christopher W. Skinner, 221–39. LNTS 461. London: Bloomsbury, 2012.
Bennema, Cornelis. *Encountering Jesus: Character Studies in the Gospel of John*. Milton Keynes, UK: Paternoster, 2009.
———. "Mimesis in John 13: Cloning or Creative Articulation?" *NovT* 56 (2014) 261–74.
———. *The Power of Saving Wisdom: An Investigation of Spirit and Wisdom in Relation to the Soteriology of the Fourth Gospel*. Eugene, OR: Wipf and Stock, 2007.
Bevere, Allan R. "Circumcision." In *Eerdmans Dictionary of the Bible*, edited by David Noel Freedman, 256. Grand Rapids: Eerdmans, 2000.
Blaine, Bradford B. *Peter in the Gospel of John: The Making of an Authentic Disciple*. Academia Biblica 27. Atlanta: Society of Biblical Literature, 2007.
Block, Daniel I. *For the Glory of God: Recovering a Biblical Theology of Worship*. Grand Rapids: Baker Academic, 2014.
Borchert, Gerald L. *Worship in the New Testament: Divine Mystery and Human Response*. St. Louis: Chalice, 2008.
Brodie, Thomas L. *The Gospel according to John: A Literary and Theological Commentary*. New York: Oxford University Press, 1993.
Brown, Raymond E. *The Death of the Messiah: From Gethsemane to the Grave: A Commentary on the Passion Narratives in the Four Gospels*. ABRL. 2 vols. New York: Doubleday, 1994.
———. *The Gospel according to John*. AB 29–29A. Garden City, NY: Doubleday, 1966–70.
———. *An Introduction to the Gospel of John*. Edited, updated, introduced, and concluded by Francis J. Moloney. AYBRL. New Haven, CT: Yale University Press, 2003.
Brown, Sherri. *Gift upon Gift: Covenant through Word in the Gospel of John*. Princeton Theological Monograph Series 144. Eugene, OR: Pickwick, 2010.

———. "John the Baptist: Witness and Embodiment of the Prologue in the Gospel of John." In *Characters and Characterization in the Gospel of John*, edited by Christopher W. Skinner, 147–64. LNTS 461. London: Bloomsbury, 2012.

———. "What Is Truth? Jesus, Pilate, and the Staging of the Dialogue of the Cross in John 18:28–19:16a." *CBQ* 77 (2015) 69–86.

Brown, William P. "Psalms, Book of." *NIDB* 4.661–80.

Bruner, Fredrick Dale. *The Gospel of John: A Commentary*. Grand Rapids: Eerdmans, 2012.

Burer, Michael H. *Divine Sabbath Work*. Bulletin for Biblical Research Supplements 5. Winona Lake, IN: Eisenbrauns, 2012.

Burnett, Joel. "Dedication, Feast Of." In *Eerdmans Dictionary of the Bible*, edited by David Noel Freedman, 335. Grand Rapids: Eerdmans, 2000.

Burridge, Richard A. *Imitating Jesus: An Inclusive Approach to New Testament Ethics*. Grand Rapids: Eerdmans, 2007.

Byrne, Brendan. *Life Abounding: A Reading of John's Gospel*. Collegeville, MN: Liturgical, 2014.

Campbell, Alistair. "Worship in the New Testament." In *In Praise of Worship: An Exploration of Text and Practice*, edited by David J. Cohen and Michael Parsons, 70–83. Eugene, OR: Pickwick, 2010.

Carnazzo, Sebastian A. *Seeing Blood and Water: A Narrative-Critical Study of John 19:34*. Eugene, OR: Pickwick, 2012.

Cassidy, Richard S. *Four Times Peter: Portrayals of Peter in the Four Gospels and at Philippi*. Collegeville, MN: Liturgical, 2006.

Cavicchia, A. "'Guarderanno a Colui che hanno trafitto': Studio di ermeneutica cristologica su Zac 12,10 in Gv 19,37." *Anton* 87 (2012) 205–57, 423–74.

Cho, Sukmin. *Jesus as Prophet in the Fourth Gospel*. New Testament Monographs 15. Sheffield, UK: Sheffield Phoenix, 2006.

Cohee, Peter. "John 1.3–4." *NTS* 41 (1995) 470–77.

Coloe, Mary L. "Anointing the Temple of God John 12:1–8." In *Transcending Boundaries: Contemporary Readings of the New Testament*, edited by Rekha M. Chennattu and Mary L. Coloe, 105–18. Biblioteca di Scienze Religiose 187. Rome: Libreria Ateneo Salesiano, 2005.

———. *Dwelling in the Household of God: Johannine Ecclesiology and Spirituality*. Collegeville, MN: Liturgical, 2007.

———. *God Dwells with Us: Temple Symbolism in the Fourth Gospel*. Collegeville, MN: Liturgical, 2001.

———. "Welcome into the Household of God: The Foot Washing in John 13." *CBQ* 66 (2004) 400–15.

———. "The Woman of Samaria: Her Characterization, Narrative, and Theological Significance." In *Characters and Characterization in the Gospel of John*, edited by Christopher W. Skinner, 182–96. LNTS 461. London: Bloomsbury, 2012.

Cullmann, Oscar. *Early Christian Worship*. Lima, OH: Wyndham Hall, 1953.

Culpepper, R. Alan. "The Johannine *hypodeigma*: A Reading of John 13:1–38." *Semeia* 53 (1991) 133–52.

———. "Peter as Exemplary Disciple in John 21:15–19." *PRSt* 37 (2010) 165–78.

Day, Peggy L. "Adulteress." In *Eerdmans Dictionary of the Bible*, edited by David Noel Freedman, 23. Grand Rapids: Eerdmans, 2000.

De la Potterie, Ignace. *The Hour of Jesus: The Passion and the Resurrection of Jesus According to John*. New York: Alba House, 1989.

Duke, Paul D. *Irony in the Fourth Gospel*. Atlanta: John Knox, 1985.

Giblin, Charles Homer. "Mary's Anointing for Jesus' Burial-Resurrection (John 12,1–8)." *Bib* 73 (1992) 560–64.

Gieschen, C. A. "Baptism and the Lord's Supper in the Gospel of John." *CTQ* 78 (2014) 23–45.

Gignac, Francis T. "The Use of Verbal Variety in the Fourth Gospel." In *Transcending Boundaries: Contemporary Readings of the New Testament*, edited by Rekha M. Chennattu and Mary L. Coloe, 191–200. Biblioteca di Scienze Religiose 187. Rome: Libreria Ateneo Salesiano, 2005.

Gordley, Matthew. "The Johannine Prologue and Jewish Didactic Hymn Traditions: A New Case for Reading the Prologue as a Hymn." *JBL* 128 (2009) 781–802.

Gorman, Frank H. "Passover, Feast Of." In *Eerdmans Dictionary of the Bible*, edited by David Noel Freedman, 1013–14. Grand Rapids: Eerdmans, 2000.

Grigsby, B. "Washing in the Pool of Siloam—A Thematic Anticipation of the Johannine Cross." *NovT* 27 (1985) 227–35.

Gunawan, H. P. "Jesus as the New Elijah: An Attempt to the Question of John 1:21." *Sino-Christian Studies* 9 (2010) 29–53.

Gundry, Robert H. "In My Father's House Are Many *Monai* (John 14:2)." *ZNW* 58 (1967) 68–72.

Heil, John Paul. *Blood and Water: The Death and Resurrection of Jesus in John 18–21*. CBQMS 27. Washington: Catholic Biblical Association, 1995.

———. *Hebrews: Chiastic Structures and Audience Response*. CBQMS 46. Washington, DC: Catholic Biblical Association of America, 2010.

———. "Jesus as the Unique High Priest in the Gospel of John." *CBQ* 57 (1995) 729–45.

———. *Jesus Walking on the Sea: Meaning and Gospel Functions of Matt 14:22–33, Mark 6:45–52 and John 6:15b–21*. AnBib 87. Rome: Biblical Institute, 1981.

———. *The Letters of Paul as Rituals of Worship*. Eugene, OR: Cascade, 2011.

———. "A Rejoinder to 'Reconsidering the Story of Jesus and the Adulteress (John 7:53—8:11).'" *Église et Théologie* 25 (1994) 361–66.

———. "The Story of Jesus and the Adulteress (John 7,53—8,11) Reconsidered." *Bib* 72 (1991) 182–91.

———. *Worship in the Letter to the Hebrews*. Eugene, OR: Cascade, 2011.

Holleran, J. Warren. "Seeing the Light: A Narrative Reading of John 9." *ETL* 69 (1993) 5–26, 354–82.

Hoskins, Paul M. *Jesus as the Fulfillment of the Temple in the Gospel of John*. Paternoster Biblical Monographs. Eugene, OR: Wipf and Stock, 2007.

Hurtado, Larry W. *At the Origins of Christian Worship: The Context and Character of Earliest Christian Devotion*. Grand Rapids: Eerdmans, 1999.

Hylen, Susan E. *Imperfect Believers: Ambiguous Characters in the Gospel of John*. Louisville: Westminster John Knox, 2009.

Jenney, Timothy P. "Tabernacles, Feast Of." In *Eerdmans Dictionary of the Bible*, edited by David Noel Freedman, 1270–71. Grand Rapids: Eerdmans, 2000.

Keener, Craig S. *The Gospel of John: A Commentary*. 2 vols. Peabody, MA: Hendrickson, 2003.

Kerr, Alan R. *The Temple of Jesus' Body: The Temple Theme in the Gospel of John*. JSNTSup 220. Sheffield, UK: Sheffield Academic, 2002.

Kim, Sang-Hoon. *Sourcebook of the Structures and Styles in John 1–10: The Johannine Parallelisms and Chiasms*. Eugene, OR: Wipf and Stock, 2014.

Koester, Craig R. "Messianic Exegesis and the Call of Nathanael (John 1.45–51)." *JSNT* 39 (1990) 23–34.

———. *The Word of Life: A Theology of John's Gospel*. Grand Rapids: Eerdmans, 2008.

Köstenberger, Andreas J. *John*. BECNT. Grand Rapids: Baker, 2004.

Kubis, A. "Zechariah 6:12–13 as the Referent of γραφή in John 2:22 and 20:9: A Contribution to Johannine Temple-Christology." *Biblical Annals* 2 (2012) 153–94.

Labahn, M. "Fischen nach Bedeutung—Sinnstifung im Wechsel literarischer Kontexte: Der wunderbare Fischfang in Johannes 21 zwischen Inter- und Intratextualität." *SNTSU* 32 (2007) 115–40.

Lee, Dorothy A. *Flesh and Glory: Symbolism, Gender and Theology in the Gospel of John*. New York: Crossroad, 2002.

———. "The Gospel of John and the Five Senses." *JBL* 129 (2010) 115–27.

———. *Hallowed in Truth and Love: Spirituality in the Johannine Literature*. Eugene, OR: Wipf and Stock, 2012.

———. "Martha and Mary: Levels of Characterization in Luke and John." In *Characters and Characterization in the Gospel of John*, edited by Christopher W. Skinner, 197–220. LNTS 461. London: Bloomsbury, 2012.

———. "Partnership in Easter Faith: The Role of Mary Magdalene and Thomas in John 20." *JSNT* 58 (1995) 37–49.

Léon-Dufour, Xavier. *To Act according to the Gospel*. Peabody, MA: Hendrickson, 2005.

Lincoln, Andrew T. *The Gospel According to Saint John*. BNTC. Peabody, MA: Hendrickson, 2005.

Mardaga, Hellen. "The Repetitive Use of ὑψόω in the Fourth Gospel." *CBQ* 74 (2012) 101–17.

———. "The Use and Meaning of ἐκεῖνος in Jn 19,35." *Filología Neotestamentaria* 20 (2007) 67–80.

McCaffrey, James. *The House with Many Rooms: The Temple Theme of Jn. 14,2–3*. AnBib 114. Rome: Biblical Institute, 1988.

McGowan, Andrew B. *Ancient Christian Worship: Early Church Practices in Social, Historical, and Theological Perspective*. Grand Rapids: Baker Academic, 2014.

Menken, Maarten J. J. "The Translation of Ps 41:10 in John 13:18." *JSNT* 40 (1990) 61–79.

Michaels, J. Ramsey. *The Gospel of John*. NICNT. Grand Rapids: Eerdmans, 2010.

Miller, E. L. "The Logic of the Logos Hymn: A New View." *NTS* 29 (1983) 552–61.

———. *Salvation-History in the Prologue of John: The Significance of John 1:3–4*. NovTSup 60. Leiden: Brill, 1989.

Moloney, Francis J. "Can Everybody be Wrong? A Reading of John 11.1–12.8." *NTS* 49 (2003) 505–27.

———. "'For As Yet They Did Not Know the Scripture' (John 20:9): A Study in Narrative Time." *ITQ* 79 (2014) 97–111.

———. "The Gospel of John: The 'End' of Scripture." *Int* 63 (2009) 356–66.

———. "The Gospel of John as Scripture." *CBQ* 67 (2005) 454–68.

———. *The Gospel of John*. SP 4. Collegeville, MN: Liturgical, 1998.

———. *Love in the Gospel of John: An Exegetical, Theological, and Literary Study*. Grand Rapids: Baker, 2013.

———. "Mary in the Fourth Gospel: Woman and Mother." *Salesianum* 51 (1989) 421–40.
Morgan-Wynne, John. *The Cross in the Johannine Writings*. Eugene, OR: Pickwick, 2011.
Neyrey, Jerome H. *Give God the Glory: Ancient Prayer and Worship in Cultural Perspective*. Grand Rapids: Eerdmans, 2007.
———. *The Gospel of John in Cultural and Rhetorical Perspective*. Grand Rapids: Eerdmans, 2009.
Nicklas, Tobias. "'Unter dem Feigenbaum'. Die Rolle des Lesers im Dialog zwischen Jesus und Natanael (Joh 1.45–50)." *NTS* 46 (2000) 193–203.
Nielsen, Helge Kjaer. "Der erste Gottesdienst: Eine Analyse von Joh 20, 19–23." *SNTSU* 28 (2003) 65–81.
Nielsen, Jesper Tang. "The Narrative Structures of Glory and Glorification in the Fourth Gospel." *NTS* 56 (2010) 343–66.
Perrin, Nicholas. *Jesus the Temple*. Grand Rapids: Baker Academic, 2010.
Phillips, Peter M. *The Prologue of the Fourth Gospel: A Sequential Reading*. LNTS 294. London: T. & T. Clark, 2006.
Pitta, A. "*Ichthys* ed *opsarion* in Gv 21,1–14: semplice variazione lessicale o differenza con valore simbolico?" *Bib* 71 (1990) 348–64.
Quek, Tze-Ming. "A Text-Critical Study of John 1.34." *NTS* 55 (2009) 22–34.
Rastoin, Marc. "Encore une fois les 153 poissons (Jn 21,11)." *Bib* 90 (2009) 84–92.
Schneiders, Sandra M. "The Raising of the New Temple: John 20.19–23 and Johannine Ecclesiology." *NTS* 52 (2006) 337–55.
Schuchard, Bruce G. *Scripture within Scripture: The Interrelationship of Form and Function in the Explicit Old Testament Citations in the Gospel of John*. SBLDS 133. Atlanta: Scholars, 1992.
Shepherd, David. "'Do You Love Me?': A Narrative-Critical Reappraisal of ἀγαπάω and φιλέω in John 21:15–17." *JBL* 129 (2010) 777–92.
Smith, Dwight Moody. "When Did the Gospels Become Scripture?" *JBL* 119 (2000) 3–20.
Swetnam, James. "Bestowal of the Spirit in the Fourth Gospel." *Bib* 74 (1993) 556–76.
Tabb, B. "Jesus' Thirst at the Cross: Irony and Intertextuality in John 19:28." *EvQ* 85 (2013) 338–51.
Thettayil, Benny. *In Spirit and Truth: An Exegetical Study of John 4:19–26 and a Theological Investigation of the Replacement Theme in the Fourth Gospel*. CBET 46. Leuven: Peeters, 2007.
Thomas, John Christopher. *Footwashing in John 13 and the Johannine Community*. JSNTSup 61. Sheffield, UK: Sheffield Academic, 1991.
Wanke, Joachim. "δεῖπνον." *EDNT* 1.281–82.
Weissenrieder, A. "Spirit and Rebirth in the Gospel of John." *Religion & Theology* 21 (2014) 58–85.
Yee, Gale A. *Jewish Feasts in John's Gospel*. Wilmington, DE: Michael Glazier, 1989.
Zimmermann, Ruben. *Christologie der Bilder im Johannesevangelium: Die Christopoetik des vierten Evangeliums unter besonderer Berücksichtigung von Joh 10*. WUNT 2/171. Tübingen: Mohr Siebeck, 2004.

Scripture Index

OLD TESTAMENT

Genesis
1:1	6
2:7	149
27:35	23
28:12	25, 28
28:17	25, 28

Exodus
12	18, 26
12:7–11	33n13
12:9	33, 138, 145
12:10	138, 145, 168
12:14	33
12:21–27	132, 143
12:21	135n39
12:22	135, 168
12:27	135n39
12:46	138, 168
14:13–31	53
16:4–36	53
16:4	54
16:15	54
17:3	54
19:8	30
19:11	29
19:16	29
20:8–11	49
24:3	30
24:7	30
24:16–17	32, 44
25:9	10
28:31	128n26
36:29	128n26
40:34	11
40:35	11

Leviticus
16:34	80
21:16–23	119
23:40	65, 73

Numbers
9:12	138, 145, 168
11:1	54
14:27	54
14:29	54
17:6	54
17:20	54
21:9	35, 45

Deuteronomy
16:14	65, 73
18:15	17n4, 53
18:18	17n4, 53
21:22–23	134

Judges
14:6	39n28
14:19	39n28
15:14	39n28

1 Kingdoms
10:10	39n28

3 Kingdoms

8:10	11
8:11	11
17:21	149

2 Kings

17:24–41	38
21:18	140
21:26	140

2 Chronicles

3:1	103n22
16:14	139n47

Nehemiah

9:15	54

1 Maccabees

4:48	71, 75

2 Maccabees

6:28	98n9
6:31	98n9

4 Maccabees

17:22–23	98n9

Psalms

22:19	129, 137, 142, 144
34	137n43
34:21	137, 144
41:10	99, 114
LXX 68:10	33, 33n11, 86, 93
69:10	131
69:22	131, 137, 144
LXX 77:16	60
LXX 77:20	60
LXX 77:24	54
LXX 81:6	71, 75
LXX 103:15	30
LXX 117:25	85

Wisdom

15:11	149

Sirach

31:27	30
31:28	30
44:16	98n9
50:25–26	38

Hosea

2:14–16	29n1

Amos

9:13–14	29

Micah

4:1	24
4:4	24

Habakkuk

1:14–15	155

Zephaniah

3:14–15	86

Zechariah

3:8	24
3:10	24
6:12–13	147n2
9:9	86
12:10	138
14:8	60, 134n38

Isaiah

2:2	89, 94
6:3	90
6:10	89
9:1	8n11
25:6–8	30
29:13	18n9, 51
40:3	17
42:1	20, 27
44:3	38n27

52:13—53:12	18–19, 26	1:1–2	6n4, 7, 9–10, 11, 13, 14, 19, 58, 64, 96, 99, 111, 112, 116, 167
53:1	89		
54:4–8	29n1		
56:7	33	1:1	5, 5n2, 6, 6n4, 8, 10, 12, 17, 26, 34, 36, 41, 43, 45, 46, 47, 50, 151
62:4–5	29n1		

Jeremiah

		1:2	5, 5n2, 6n4, 7, 8, 12
2:2	29n1	1:3–5	68, 90, 94
16:14–15	154	1:3–4	7, 8, 9, 10, 12, 13, 15, 16, 18, 26, 31, 36, 46, 56, 59, 64, 72, 77, 89
16:16	154		

Ezekiel

		1:3	5, 7, 7n8, 8, 9, 10, 12, 13, 14
16:8	29n1		
23:4	29n1	1:4–5	14
37:9–10	149	1:4	5, 5n2, 7, 7n8, 8–9, 10, 12, 34, 64
47:1–12	157n27		
47:1	60	1:5	5, 5n2, 7–8, 9, 63
47:10	155	1:6–13	5–6, 6n3, 8–10
		1:6–8	14
		1:6	5, 6n3, 8, 9, 10, 11, 16, 20, 22, 26

Daniel

		1:7–8	20
7:13–14	25, 28	1:7	5, 8, 9, 12, 15, 16, 18, 24, 26
		1:8	5, 8, 13, 15, 16
		1:9–11	21
		1:9–10	14

NEW TESTAMENT

		1:9	5, 8, 9, 10, 12, 17, 18, 31, 34, 44, 53, 77, 90, 94

Matthew

4:16	8n11	1:10	5–6, 9, 10, 18, 19, 26, 87
4:18–22	154n18	1:11	6, 9, 14, 18, 24, 42, 103, 127, 130

Mark

1:16–20	154n18	1:12–13	14, 49
7:4	18n9	1:12	2, 6, 6n3, 9, 12, 15, 16, 19, 24, 26, 32, 34, 35, 36, 38, 39, 44, 45, 46, 64, 66, 70, 74, 82, 89, 92, 100, 119, 121, 124, 127, 129, 140, 142
7:7	18n9		

Luke

5:1–11	154n18, 158n29		
		1:13	6, 6n3, 10, 35, 45, 66

John

		1:14–18	6, 10–14, 19, 26
1–20	158n29	1:14	2, 6, 6n4, 10–11, 12, 13, 14, 15, 16, 17, 18, 19, 20, 21, 25, 26, 27,
1:1–18	4, 5–15, 95		
1:1–5	5, 5n2, 6–8		

John (continued)

1:14 (continued)	28, 32, 33, 34, 36, 40, 41, 43, 44, 45, 46, 47, 51, 55, 59, 61, 65, 67, 70, 71, 73, 74, 75, 77, 78, 80, 89, 91, 94, 102, 104, 111, 113, 115, 116, 151, 161, 166, 167
1:15	6, 12, 15, 17, 18, 19, 20, 22, 26
1:16–17	23
1:16	6, 12, 13, 15
1:17	6, 13, 15, 16, 17, 20, 29, 30, 40, 41, 47, 56, 64, 72, 77, 80, 102, 104, 111, 115, 153
1:18	6, 6n4, 13, 14, 15, 17, 21, 26, 27, 33, 36, 46, 50, 58, 64, 151, 153, 163
1:19–51	4, 16–28, 29
1:19–28	16–18, 26
1:19	16, 20, 22, 30
1:20	16, 17, 18, 26
1:21	17, 26
1:22	17
1:23	17, 18, 26
1:24	17
1:25	17
1:26	17, 18, 19, 21, 22, 26, 30, 35, 45
1:27	18, 19, 26
1:28	18, 22, 26, 29
1:29–34	18–21, 26
1:29	2, 18, 19, 20, 21, 22, 23, 25, 26, 27, 28, 32, 36, 38, 41, 45, 46, 47, 52, 53, 54, 55, 57, 58, 63, 64, 69, 70, 72, 80, 81, 83, 84, 93, 95, 121, 123, 124, 126, 127, 132, 134, 135, 138, 142, 143, 145, 150, 162, 168
1:30	19
1:31	19, 20, 22, 23, 24, 27, 30, 31, 35, 44, 45, 135, 143, 169
1:32–33	32, 41, 44, 47, 66, 80
1:32	20, 22, 25, 28, 35, 37, 40, 45, 47
1:33	20, 21, 21n14, 22, 25, 26, 27, 28, 30, 35, 37, 38, 39n29, 40, 45, 46, 47, 56, 102, 114, 115, 134, 135, 143, 150, 162, 169
1:34	20, 25, 27, 28
1:35–42	21–22, 27
1:35	21, 22
1:36	2, 21, 22, 23, 25, 27, 32, 38, 45, 46, 52, 54, 57, 58, 72, 81, 83, 84, 93, 95, 121, 123, 124, 126, 132, 134, 135, 138, 142, 143, 145, 168
1:37–38	23
1:37	21, 22
1:38	21, 21n14, 22, 27, 118
1:39	21, 22, 23, 25, 27, 32, 44
1:40	22, 23, 25
1:41	22, 23, 25, 118, 153
1:42	22
1:43–51	22–25, 27
1:43	22, 29
1:44	22
1:45	23, 24, 27, 52, 118, 127
1:46	23, 24, 27, 127
1:47	23, 24, 27
1:48	23, 31
1:49	1, 20n12, 24, 25, 27, 28, 31, 36, 38, 41, 44, 46, 47, 52, 53, 56, 67, 71, 74, 75, 86, 93, 118, 122, 125, 140, 145, 151, 153, 167
1:50	24, 31, 32, 44, 50, 52
1:51	25, 28, 33, 36, 45, 46, 50, 70, 89, 94

SCRIPTURE INDEX

2:1—4:54	4, 29–48	2:19–21	41, 43, 47, 48, 85, 90, 94, 96, 113, 151, 155, 170
2:1–12	29–32		
2:1–11	37, 38, 39, 42, 43, 44, 46, 48, 49, 63, 73	2:19	33, 49, 52, 58, 69, 74, 79, 83, 84, 85, 86, 89, 93, 94, 131, 139, 140, 145, 147, 149, 162
2:1–10	55, 71, 158, 164		
2:1–5	130		
2:1	29, 30		
2:2	30	2:20	33
2:3	30	2:21	33, 49, 62, 64, 65, 66, 67, 69, 73, 74, 79, 80, 83, 84, 85, 86, 89, 93, 94, 131, 139, 140, 145, 147, 149, 162
2:4	30, 58, 61, 73, 95, 130, 131, 135, 143		
2:5	30, 131, 142		
2:6–9	31, 44		
2:6–7	41	2:22	34, 35, 43, 45, 47, 147, 147n2
2:6	30, 32, 37, 38, 46, 131, 135, 143	2:23	34, 35, 42, 45, 52
2:7–10	32, 131	2:24	34
2:7	30	2:25—3:1	34
2:8	31	2:25	34
2:9–10	41	3:1–21	34–36
2:9	31, 37, 37n25, 39, 47, 63, 73	3:1–9	139
		3:2	34, 36, 46, 66
2:10	31, 37, 44, 50, 69, 70, 136, 143	3:3–5	2, 59, 67, 68, 72, 74, 96, 113, 135, 143, 169, 171
2:11	31, 32, 34, 36, 43, 44, 45, 46, 48, 52, 59, 158, 164	3:3	35, 66, 67, 102, 114, 122, 128
		3:4	35
2:12	32, 33, 43, 44, 48, 130, 131, 142	3:5	35, 37, 38, 39n29, 40, 45, 46, 47, 66, 102, 114, 122
2:13–25	32–34		
2:13–21	42, 45, 103	3:7	128
2:13	32, 49, 52, 57, 82, 83, 92, 170	3:9	135, 143
		3:13–15	50
2:14–23	49	3:13–14	36, 46
2:14–22	57, 83, 92	3:14–18	153
2:14–16	52, 86, 93	3:14–17	110
2:14–15	32, 33, 70	3:14–16	111, 137, 139, 145
2:14	50, 58	3:14–15	35, 38, 45, 76, 126, 135, 143
2:15–22	58		
2:15	50	3:14	54, 61, 64, 73, 86, 88, 89, 93, 94, 99, 100, 114, 124
2:16–21	50		
2:16–17	96, 113		
2:16	32, 61, 80, 102, 131	3:15–16	49, 53, 104, 106, 135, 146, 150, 152, 163, 166, 171
2:17	33, 33n11, 34, 43, 48, 52, 86, 93, 131		
2:18	33, 52, 54, 149	3:15	54, 68, 74, 99, 100, 114
2:19–22	43, 70		

John (*continued*)

3:16–17	111, 112, 116, 122, 141
3:16	36, 38, 41, 46, 47, 53, 57, 79, 91, 100, 104, 118, 121, 141, 149, 157, 164
3:17–18	126
3:17	41, 47, 79, 87, 90, 91, 100, 111, 149
3:19–21	36, 46
3:19	53
3:21	66
3:22–36	37–38, 108
3:22–24	97n8
3:22	37, 39n29
3:25	37, 97n8
3:26	37, 39n29
3:27	37
3:29	37, 37n25, 39, 47, 63, 65, 73, 108
3:31	128
3:34	38, 40, 46, 47, 52, 56
3:35	38, 46
3:36	38, 46, 49, 53, 153
4:1–42	38–41
4:1	39n29
4:2	39n29
4:6	38, 39, 126
4:7	38, 132
4:8	41
4:9	38, 41
4:10–14	39n29
4:10	38, 39, 40, 43, 46, 47, 48, 60, 132, 136
4:11	39
4:12	39
4:13–14	39, 46, 136
4:14	40, 43, 48, 49, 53, 54, 60, 61, 73, 97n6, 133, 136, 138, 143, 144
4:15	39, 46
4:16	39, 46
4:17	39, 46
4:18	39, 46, 62
4:19	40, 42, 47
4:20–24	50
4:20–21	61, 170
4:20	40, 47, 80, 103, 104, 117, 139, 140
4:21	40, 47, 80, 87, 94, 103
4:22	40, 41, 47, 62, 80
4:23–24	2, 4, 40, 41, 42, 43, 47, 48, 56, 59, 61, 62, 64, 66, 67, 68, 72, 73, 74, 80, 87, 94, 96, 102, 104, 105, 109, 111, 112, 113, 115, 116, 122, 133, 136, 137, 141, 143, 147, 148, 149, 161, 162, 166
4:23	51, 59, 169
4:25–26	40, 153
4:25	50, 109, 116
4:27	41
4:28	40, 50
4:29	41, 153
4:30	41
4:32	54
4:34	54, 58, 67, 70, 74, 77, 111, 132, 132n34
4:35	106
4:36	41, 49, 53, 88, 106
4:38	149
4:39–42	88, 106
4:39	41
4:40–41	41
4:40	42, 102, 114
4:41	65, 102, 114
4:42	41, 42, 47, 50, 53, 63, 67, 74, 80, 87, 102, 115, 126
4:43–54	42–43
4:43	42
4:44	42
4:45	42
4:46–54	70
4:46–53	49, 77
4:46	42, 43, 48
4:47	42, 90
4:48	42
4:49	42, 47
4:50	43, 47, 63, 65, 73

4:51	43, 48	6:4	52, 57, 82, 83, 92, 168
4:52	43, 48	6:5–13	53
4:53	43, 48	6:5	85
4:54	43, 48	6:9	155, 155n23
5:1—10:42	4, 49–75	6:10	53
5:1–47	49–52, 70	6:11	53, 79, 83, 91, 155, 155n23, 157
5:1–18	59, 72	6:12	54
5:1	49	6:14	53, 77n4
5:2–9	49	6:15	53, 85
5:8–13	50	6:16	53, 153n16
5:8–9	52, 71	6:17	53, 153n16, 154, 154n17
5:8	49, 51	6:18–21	53
5:9–18	67	6:18	153n16
5:9	49	6:19	153n16, 154, 154n17
5:10–13	50	6:20	56
5:10	121, 141	6:21	154n17
5:14	58, 59, 63, 72, 73	6:22	53, 153n16, 154n17
5:15	50	6:23	53, 79, 91, 153, 154n17, 156, 157, 164
5:16	50, 109	6:24–25	53
5:17	50	6:24	154n17
5:18	50, 51, 52, 58, 59, 71, 72, 80, 151	6:25	153n16
5:20	51, 67, 74	6:26–59	72
5:21	51, 56	6:26	53
5:22–26	125	6:27	54, 156
5:22	51	6:30	54
5:23	51, 52, 65, 71, 75, 151, 163, 170	6:31	54, 55
5:24–26	153	6:32	54
5:24	51, 52, 53, 65, 71	6:33	156
5:25	71, 75	6:35	54, 60, 118, 156
5:26	71, 75	6:36	54
5:27	125	6:37	68, 74, 110
5:30	58, 67, 70, 74, 77	6:38	58, 67, 70, 74, 77
5:36	132, 132n34	6:39–40	111, 118, 147
5:39	166	6:39	60, 110, 157, 164
5:40	153	6:40	54, 56, 60, 153
5:41	51	6:41	54
5:42	51	6:43	54
5:43	51, 88, 122, 141	6:44	60, 89, 94, 147
5:44	51, 59	6:46	64
5:46	52, 127, 166	6:47	153
5:47	52	6:48	118, 156
6:1–71	52–57	6:49	55
6:1–13	55, 71, 157, 158, 159, 164, 165	6:50–58	121
6:1	153, 153n16		
6:2	52, 85		

John (continued)

6:50	55
6:51–58	2, 136, 144, 169
6:51	55, 63, 69, 72, 83, 97n6, 99, 99n13, 114, 118, 156, 157, 168
6:52–58	157
6:53–58	153
6:53–54	136, 144
6:53	55, 56, 60, 72, 138, 156
6:54	55, 55n16, 56, 60, 72, 147, 156, 158, 171
6:55	56, 72
6:56	55n16, 60, 103, 107, 115
6:57	55n16
6:58	55, 55n16, 72, 97n6, 99, 99n13, 114, 156
6:59	58
6:62	58
6:63	56, 72
6:64	56, 57, 58, 84, 95, 121, 134, 141
6:66	87, 118
6:67	56
6:68	56, 82, 92
6:69	56, 67, 71, 72, 74, 75, 82, 92, 151, 154, 167
6:70	99, 114
6:71	57, 58, 84, 95, 121, 134
7:1—10:21	57–70
7:1–52	57–61
7:1	58, 80, 141
7:2	57
7:4	58
7:5	58
7:6	61, 63, 64, 73
7:7	87
7:8	58, 61, 73
7:10	58
7:13	148, 151
7:14	58, 59, 62
7:16–17	58
7:16	63, 64
7:17	58
7:18	58
7:19	80
7:21	67, 74
7:23	59, 67, 72
7:25	80
7:26–31	153
7:28	59, 62, 111, 122, 141
7:30	61, 73, 95
7:31	63, 64, 80
7:32	62, 80
7:34	154
7:35	87, 93
7:36	154
7:37–39	39n29, 62, 133, 136, 138, 143, 144, 170
7:37–38	125, 133
7:37	60, 60n26, 62, 133
7:38–39	133, 169
7:38	60, 60n26, 61, 73, 134
7:39	2, 61, 73, 133, 134
7:41–42	153
7:43	128
7:45	62, 80
7:48	62
7:50	139
7:53—8:11	3, 61–63
7:53	61
8:1	61
8:2	62
8:3–10	73
8:3	62
8:4–6	62
8:7	62, 65, 73
8:8	62
8:9	62
8:10	62
8:11	62, 73
8:12–59	63–65
8:12	63, 64, 66, 68, 118
8:20	64, 95
8:21	64, 150, 163
8:24	64, 99, 118, 125, 150, 163
8:28	64, 86, 88, 89, 93, 94, 99, 124, 126
8:30–31	64

SCRIPTURE INDEX

8:30	80	9:38	1, 68, 74, 87, 89, 93, 139, 145
8:32	64	9:39	90
8:34	64	10:1–21	68–70
8:35	108, 115	10:1–18	159
8:37	80	10:1	120, 123
8:39–41	64	10:2–5	68
8:40	64, 80	10:2–3	120
8:42	122, 141	10:3–5	122, 141
8:44	64	10:3–4	95
8:45–46	64	10:3	123
8:49	65	10:4–5	119
8:50	65	10:7	68, 120
8:51	65, 97n6	10:8	123
8:52	65, 97n6	10:9	68, 104, 117
8:54	65, 76	10:10–18	122, 141
8:56	65, 73	10:10–11	91, 94, 118, 159, 161, 165, 171
8:58	65, 73	10:10	69, 84, 88, 101, 104, 117, 153, 156, 158
8:59	65, 66, 73		
9:1–41	66–68, 70, 90	10:11–15	119
9:1	66	10:11–12	95
9:2	66	10:11	69, 70, 71, 74, 81, 82, 88, 92, 101, 104, 108, 112, 115, 117, 118, 120, 123, 124, 125, 128, 130, 131, 142, 168, 170
9:3–4	67, 74		
9:3	66		
9:4	66, 154		
9:5	66		
9:6	66		
9:7	66, 67, 96, 113, 138, 145		
9:8	86	10:12	117
9:11	67, 96, 113	10:13	84
9:14	67	10:14	120
9:15	67, 96, 113	10:15–18	123
9:16	128	10:15–16	129, 142
9:22	16n3, 68, 74, 82, 90, 92, 94, 109, 148, 153	10:15	69, 70, 71, 74, 82, 91, 92, 94, 95, 101, 108, 112, 115, 117, 118, 124, 125, 128, 130, 131, 142, 168, 170, 171
9:24	67, 74, 76		
9:30	67, 74		
9:31	67, 70, 74, 77, 79, 91, 105, 115, 168		
9:32–33	68, 74	10:16	81, 82, 92, 119, 120, 122, 123, 140, 141, 146, 162, 170
9:34	68, 74		
9:35–38	90, 94, 96, 100, 113, 152, 167		
		10:17–18	81, 96, 119, 123, 159
9:35–37	89	10:17	69, 74, 104, 124
9:35	68, 74, 87, 93	10:18	69, 70, 74, 83, 90, 92, 94, 101, 105, 114, 121, 124, 127, 132, 134, 139, 141, 146, 162, 168
9:36–37	68, 74		
9:37	87, 93, 138, 145		

John (*continued*)

10:19	128
10:22–42	70–71
10:22	70, 170
10:23	70
10:24	70, 153
10:25	88
10:26–29	159
10:26–27	81, 82, 92
10:27–30	123
10:27–28	128, 131, 142
10:27	119, 122, 123, 141
10:28	70, 71, 81, 97n6, 118, 125, 153, 157, 159, 164, 170, 171
10:30	71, 75
10:31	70
10:32	70, 71
10:33	71, 75, 151
10:34–35	71, 75
10:36	71, 75, 82, 92, 112, 125, 153, 170
10:38	71, 75
10:42	80
11:1—12:50	4, 76–94
11:1–46	76–80
11:1–3	76
11:2	78, 84, 93, 96, 167
11:4	76, 78, 79, 88, 90, 91, 94
11:5	108, 115
11:11	108, 115
11:14	77
11:17–18	77
11:21	77, 78
11:22	77, 78, 79, 91, 105, 115, 168
11:23–24	77
11:24–27	78, 91
11:25–27	147, 152
11:25–26	153, 163, 167
11:25	77, 79, 91, 104, 118
11:26–27	153, 163
11:26	77, 77n4, 97n6
11:27	1, 77, 77n4, 78, 91, 125, 153
11:30	78
11:32	1, 78, 84, 93, 118, 167
11:33	132
11:38–41	162
11:38	146, 162
11:39	78, 84, 91, 93, 96, 146
11:40	78, 79, 83, 85, 88, 90, 91, 94
11:41	1, 79, 91, 110, 146, 168
11:42	79, 85, 91
11:43	85, 168
11:44	79, 118, 139, 146, 162
11:45	79, 80
11:46	80
11:47–57	80–83
11:47–48	82, 92
11:47	80, 117, 121
11:48	80, 82, 92, 103, 117, 119, 140
11:49–50	119, 140
11:49	80, 81, 114, 118
11:50–52	96, 117, 119, 122
11:50	80, 81, 82, 92, 114, 118, 121, 124, 126, 129, 168
11:51–52	82, 92
11:51	81, 90, 94, 117, 118, 119
11:52	82, 90, 92, 94, 117, 118, 119, 121, 124, 129, 140, 142, 146, 162, 170
11:53	83, 85, 92, 117
11:55	82, 83, 92
11:56	83, 92
11:57	83, 92
12:1–11	83–85
12:1	83, 85, 95
12:2	83
12:3	78, 84, 93, 96, 139, 167, 168
12:4	84, 96, 121, 134, 141
12:5	84
12:6	84
12:7	84, 96, 139, 168
12:8	84

Reference	Pages
12:9	85
12:10	85
12:11	85
12:12–16	85–86
12:12	85, 95
12:13	85, 86, 87, 93, 122, 125, 126, 140, 145, 152, 167
12:14	86
12:15	86, 125
12:16	86, 93
12:17–36	87–89
12:17	87
12:18	87
12:19	87
12:20–21	122
12:20	87, 93
12:21	87, 93, 100
12:22	87, 94
12:23	87, 88, 89, 94, 95, 100, 124, 131, 133
12:24	88, 106
12:25	88, 98, 110, 116, 131, 142, 153, 170
12:26	88, 98, 103
12:27	1, 88, 95, 102, 110, 168
12:28	1, 88, 110, 168
12:29	88
12:30	88
12:31	110, 116
12:32–34	124
12:32	89, 94, 103, 106, 107, 121, 122, 123, 126, 139, 141, 145, 156, 171
12:33	89, 94, 103, 121, 141, 156, 160
12:34	89, 94
12:35	8
12:36	89
12:37–50	89–91
12:37	89
12:38	89
12:39	89
12:40	89
12:41	90
12:42	90, 94, 109, 148
12:43	90, 94
12:44–45	90, 94
12:46	90, 94, 118
12:47–50	107
12:47	90, 94
12:48–50	107n29
12:48	105
12:49–50	150, 153
12:49	90, 94, 101, 105, 111
12:50	2, 90, 94, 101, 105, 111, 120, 122, 131, 141, 142, 153, 161, 165, 170, 171
13:1—17:26	4, 95–116
13:1–38	95–101
13:1	95, 96, 97, 100, 101, 103, 114, 130, 131
13:2	95, 97, 100, 102, 121, 134, 141
13:3	96, 103, 131
13:4	96, 128, 155
13:5	96, 97, 113, 155
13:6–7	97
13:7	98, 113
13:8	97, 98, 113, 128, 136, 144, 170
13:9	97
13:10–11	136, 144
13:10	97, 107, 170
13:11	97, 99, 114, 121, 134, 136, 141, 144
13:12–15	109
13:12–13	97, 113
13:14–16	103, 120, 141
13:14–15	136, 144, 170
13:14	97, 100, 113, 114
13:15	98, 99, 104, 113
13:16	98, 99, 109
13:17	98, 103
13:18	55n16, 98, 99, 100, 114, 131, 156n24
13:19	99
13:20	99
13:21	100, 102, 121, 132, 134, 141
13:23	129
13:26–27	100
13:30	100, 134

John (*continued*)

13:31–32	131, 133
13:31	100, 110, 124, 134, 160
13:32	100
13:33	100, 102, 103, 114
13:34–35	136, 144, 159
13:34	2, 100, 101, 104, 105, 107, 108, 111, 114, 120, 131, 132, 142, 143, 150, 153, 160, 161, 165, 169, 170, 171
13:35	101, 108, 114
13:36	101, 103, 155, 160, 165
13:37	101, 120, 140, 141, 155, 158, 159, 160, 165, 170
13:38	101, 120, 141, 155, 158
14:1–31	102–6
14:1	102, 148
14:2	102, 103, 104, 105, 106, 107, 108, 115, 117, 140, 147, 148, 162, 170
14:3	103, 104, 117, 121, 141, 147, 148, 162, 170, 171
14:4	103
14:5	104
14:6	104, 111, 112, 118, 122, 136, 141, 153, 169
14:7–9	104, 115, 151, 163
14:10–11	105, 115
14:10	104, 108, 115
14:12	105, 115
14:13–14	107, 108, 109, 115, 116
14:13	105, 108, 115, 160, 169
14:14	105, 115, 169
14:15	105, 150, 169
14:16–17	133, 143
14:16	105, 109, 115, 169
14:17	2, 105, 108, 109, 115, 150, 162, 169
14:18	105, 154
14:19	105
14:21	150
14:23–24	107n29
14:23	105, 108, 115
14:25	108, 110, 115
14:26	2, 106, 109, 115, 133, 143, 150, 169
14:27	148
14:30–31	110, 116
15:1–17	106–8
15:1	106
15:2	106, 107
15:3	107
15:4	107, 108, 115, 154
15:5	107, 108, 115, 154
15:6	107, 108, 115
15:7	107, 108, 109, 115, 116, 169
15:8	108
15:9–12	153
15:9	108, 115, 160, 165
15:10	108, 109, 115, 116, 150, 161, 165
15:11	108, 110, 116
15:12–17	159
15:12–13	120, 122, 130, 131, 132, 136, 141, 142, 143, 144
15:12	2, 108, 109, 111, 116, 120, 150, 160, 161, 165, 169, 170, 171
15:13	108, 112, 115, 118, 120, 125, 136, 144, 168
15:14	108, 115
15:15	108, 115
15:16	108, 109, 115, 116, 169
15:17	108, 115, 120, 160, 161, 165, 169, 170
15:18—16:33	109–10
15:18	109, 110, 116
15:19	109
15:20	109

15:26	2, 109, 115, 133, 137, 143, 169	17:20	149, 150, 160, 162, 165, 169
15:27	137	17:21–24	169
16:1	110	17:21	1
16:2	109, 132, 142, 148, 168	17:22	112, 116
16:4	110	17:23	112, 116, 132, 132n34
16:6	110	17:24	1, 112, 116
16:11	110, 116	17:25	1
16:13	2, 109, 116, 133, 143, 169	17:26	113, 116
		18:1—19:42	4, 117–45
16:14	109, 116	18:1–27	117–20
16:15	109, 116	18:1	117
16:21	130	18:2	117, 118, 121, 134, 141
16:22	109, 116, 149		
16:23–27	169	18:3	117
16:23	109, 116	18:4	118, 131
16:24	109, 116	18:5	118, 121, 127, 134, 141
16:25	110		
16:26	110, 116	18:6	118, 127, 168
16:27	110, 116	18:7	118
16:28	110, 116, 122, 141	18:8	118, 127
16:30	159, 165	18:9	118, 119, 157, 164
16:32	130	18:10	119, 140, 156
16:33	110, 116, 148	18:11	119, 131, 156
17:1–26	110–13, 117	18:12–13	119, 140
17:1–3	153, 164	18:14	119, 121, 140
17:1–2	124	18:15	119, 120
17:1	1, 110, 111, 160, 169	18:16	120
17:2–3	131, 142, 153, 170	18:17–18	120, 140
17:2	110	18:17	155, 158
17:3	110, 111, 171	18:18	155
17:4	111, 132, 132n34, 160	18:19	119, 122n7, 140
		18:20	58
17:5	1, 111, 169	18:22	123n10
17:6	111	18:24	119, 140
17:7	111	18:25–27	120, 140, 155, 158
17:8	111	18:28—19:11	121–24
17:9	112	18:28–32	124, 142
17:10	112	18:28	121
17:11	1, 112, 129, 142, 169	18:29	121, 122, 123
17:12	118, 131, 157, 164	18:30	121, 127, 141
17:15	112	18:31	121, 141
17:17	112	18:32	121, 141, 160
17:18	112, 149	18:33–38	124, 141
17:19	112	18:33	122, 127
17:20–23	129, 142	18:35	122, 127
17:20–21	112, 116, 171		

John (*continued*)

18:36	122, 123, 125, 126, 127, 140, 145
18:37	122, 123, 127, 141
18:38–40	124, 142
18:38	122, 141
18:39	123, 127
18:40	123
19:1–3	124, 141
19:1	123
19:2	123, 132
19:3	123, 123n10, 140, 145
19:4–7	124, 142
19:4	123
19:5	123, 126, 127
19:6	126
19:7	125
19:8–11	124, 141
19:10	124, 126
19:11	124, 125, 128, 141
19:12–42	125–40
19:12	125
19:13–14	126
19:13	125
19:14	126, 127, 132, 133, 140, 143, 145, 168
19:15	126, 127, 140, 145
19:16	127
19:17	127
19:18	127
19:19	127, 140, 145
19:20	127, 140, 145
19:21	127, 140, 145
19:22	127
19:23	128, 129, 142
19:24	128, 129, 131, 137, 142, 144, 156, 164, 171
19:25–26	129
19:25	129, 130
19:26–34	137
19:26–27	138, 145, 147, 162
19:26	129, 130, 131, 137, 137n40, 142
19:27	130, 131, 133, 142, 143, 160
19:28	131, 132, 132n34
19:29–30	135, 137, 144
19:29	131, 132, 142, 168
19:30	131, 132, 132n34, 133, 133n36, 134, 143, 150, 162
19:31	133, 134, 138
19:32	134
19:33–34	137, 138, 144
19:33	134, 168
19:34–35	152
19:34	2, 134, 135, 136, 138, 143, 144, 145, 146, 149, 161, 166, 169, 170, 171
19:35	137, 137n40, 138, 145, 146, 161, 166
19:36	137, 137n42, 138, 144, 145, 168
19:37	138, 138n45, 139, 145
19:38	139, 148, 151
19:39	139, 168
19:40	139, 168
19:41	139, 140, 145
19:42	139, 140, 145
20:1—21:25	4, 146–66
20:1–18	146–48
20:1	146, 162
20:2	147
20:6–8	152, 163
20:6	151
20:7	146, 147, 162, 171
20:8	147, 151, 152, 163
20:9	147, 147n2, 154
20:10	154
20:11	147, 162
20:12	147, 162
20:13	148
20:15	148
20:16	148
20:17–18	160
20:17	147, 148, 151, 162, 163, 170
20:18	148, 151, 152, 163
20:19–31	148–53
20:19–23	150n7
20:19	148, 149, 150, 151

20:20	148, 151, 152, 163	21:12	157, 164
20:21	149, 150, 151, 163	21:13	155n23, 156n24, 157
20:22	133n36, 149, 150, 150n6, 162	21:14	158, 164
		21:15–25	158–61
20:23	150, 163, 169	21:15–19	160n33
20:24	150, 151, 152, 163	21:15–17	160
20:25	151, 152, 163	21:15	158, 165
20:26	150, 151	21:16	159, 165
20:27	151, 152, 163	21:17	159, 165
20:28	1–2, 151, 152, 163, 167, 170	21:18–19	101
		21:18	160
20:29	152, 163	21:19	160, 165
20:30–31	147, 152n13, 161, 166	21:20	160, 165
		21:21	160, 161, 165
20:30	152	21:22–23	161, 166
20:31	1, 152, 153, 161, 163, 166, 171	21:22	160, 165
		21:23	160, 165
21:1–25	161n35	21:24–25	147
21:1–14	153–58, 158n29	21:24	161, 166
21:1–13	158, 164	21:25	161, 166
21:1	153, 153n16, 158, 164		
21:2	153	**Acts of the Apostles**	
21:3	154, 154n17	3:22	17n4
21:4	154, 157, 164	7:37	17n4
21:5	154, 155, 156		
21:6	154, 154n17, 155, 156	**1 Corinthians**	
		6:11	97n8
21:7–8	158		
21:7	153n16, 155, 157, 159, 164	**Ephesians**	
		5:26	97n8
21:8	154n17, 155, 156		
21:9–13	157, 159, 165	**Titus**	
21:9–10	156	3:5	97n8
21:9	155, 155n23, 156n24, 157, 164		
		Hebrews	
21:10	155n23, 156	10:22	97n8
21:11	156, 157, 158, 160, 164		
21:12–13	157, 164		

Author Index

Ashton, John., 7n7, 7n8, 7n9
Atkinson, Kenneth., 58n22

Barker, Margaret., 78n5
Beasley-Murray, John R., 35n19, 36n21, 54n13, 55n15, 79n8
Beck, David R., 137n40
Bennema, Cornelis., 23n19, 40n32, 49n2, 50n3, 66n43, 68n48, 78n6, 98n9
Bevere, Allan, R., 59n23
Blaine, Bradford B., 22n15
Block, Daniel I., 2n3
Borchert, Gerald L., 1n1
Brodie, Thomas L., 119n1
Brown, Raymond E., 2n2, 81n14, 123n10, 140n48
Brown, Sherri., 3n5, 3n6, 3n7, 16n2, 30n4, 30n5, 37n23, 59n25, 62n32, 63n36, 122n8
Brown, William P., 137n43
Bruner, Frederick Dale., 8n10, 17n6, 19n10, 20n12
Burer, Michael H., 50n5
Burnett, Joel., 70n52
Burridge, Richard A., 98n9
Byrne, Brendan., 11n20, 31n8, 33n12, 35n16, 35n17, 35n18, 37n24, 40n31, 41n35, 42n36, 43n39, 50n4, 54n12, 55n16, 58n21, 59n24, 60n29, 61n30, 63n35, 64n37, 64n38, 65n42, 66n44, 67n46, 68n48, 69n49, 69n50, 70n53, 71n54, 76n1, 76n2, 77n3, 79n6, 79n9, 82n16, 83n21, 85n26, 86n29, 86n30, 87n31, 87n32, 88n35, 90n39, 95n1, 97n5, 99n12, 99n13, 100n14, 101n16, 103n21, 104n23, 105n25, 107n30, 108n32, 110n35, 111n37, 112n39, 121n4, 121n6, 122n9, 123n11, 125n15, 126n18, 126n21, 127n23, 128n24, 130n30, 146n1, 147n3, 150n7, 151n10, 153n14, 157n28, 158n29, 159n32, 161n34, 161n35

Campbell, Alistair., 2n2
Carnazzo, Sebastian A., 133n37
Cassidy, Richard S., 22n15
Cavicchia, A., 138n45
Cho, Sukmin., 40n31, 42n36
Cohee, Peter., 7n8
Coloe, Mary L., 11n20, 32n9, 32n10, 38n26, 39n28, 40n30, 41n35, 43n41, 57n20, 58n21, 60n26, 60n27, 63n36, 64n38, 65n39, 65n42, 71n54, 84n23, 89n36, 96n3, 96n4, 98n10, 98n11, 102n18, 103n20, 103n22, 106n26, 108n33, 126n21, 128n26, 130n28, 133n36, 150n7, 151n8, 152n12
Cullmann, Oscar., 1n1, 2n2, 35n18
Culpepper, R. Alan., 98n9, 160n33

Day, Peggy L., 62n33
De la Potterie, Ignace., 127n22, 148n4

Duke, Paul D., 9n14, 23n18, 31n8, 82n15, 122n7, 124n13, 139n47, 151n11

Giblin, Charles Homer., 84n22
Gieschen, C. A., 2n2
Gignac, Francis T., 55n16
Gordley, Matthew., 6n4
Gorman, Frank H., 53n9
Grigsby, B., 67n46
Gunawan, H. P., 17n4
Gundry, Robert H., 102n19

Heil, John Paul,, 3n4, 3n6, 53n10, 61n31, 82n15, 97n8, 119n1, 120n3, 124n14, 126n21, 128n26, 140n49, 153n15, 154n17, 161n35
Holleran, J. Warren., 68n48
Hoskins, Paul M., 11n20, 89n36, 121n6
Hurtado, Larry W., 2n2
Hylen, Susan E., 39n30, 78n5

Jenney, Timothy P., 57n20

Keener, Craig S., 9n16, 11n21, 14n27, 19n10, 36n20, 69n51, 126n20
Kerr, Alan R., 32n10
Kim, Sang-Hoon., 6n4
Koester, Craig R., 1n1, 12n22, 24n20
Köstenberger, Andreas J., 8n11, 8n12, 10n19, 11n21, 14n27, 17n5, 17n6, 20n11, 20n12, 22n17, 34n15, 36n21, 83n18, 97n5, 129n27, 132n33
Kubis, A., 147n2

Labahn, M., 158n29
Lee, Dorothy A., 1n1, 51n6, 77n4, 78n5, 84n22, 84n23, 85n25, 151n9
Léon-Dufour, Xavier., 98n9
Lincoln, Andrew T., 5n2, 6n5, 7n6, 9n13, 10n17, 11n22, 19n10, 21n13, 23n19, 25n25, 30n3, 31n7, 35n18, 36n21, 40n33, 41n35, 43n38, 52n8, 57n20, 60n28, 63n36, 76n2, 80n11, 85n25, 85n27, 86n29, 88n33, 90n38, 96n3, 97n5, 97n7, 99n12, 99n13, 100n15, 101n17, 105n25, 106n28, 107n29, 110n34, 112n38, 112n41, 123n12, 126n18, 137n41, 138n44, 147n3

Mardaga, Hellen., 36n19, 137n40
McCaffrey, James., 102n18, 149n5
McGowan, Andrew B., 3n6
Menken, Maarten J. J., 99n13
Michaels, J. Ramsey., 6n5, 9n15, 14n27, 16n1, 17n3, 17n5, 17n7, 19n10, 20n11, 22n16, 24n21, 24n22, 25n23, 25n24, 30n4, 31n6, 32n9, 34n14, 36n21, 40n33, 42n37, 43n39, 43n40, 51n6, 52n7, 53n11, 55n14, 55n17, 56n18, 57n19, 60n26, 61n30, 62n34, 65n40, 65n41, 67n46, 68n48, 69n50, 76n1, 76n2, 79n7, 79n8, 81n13, 82n16, 83n19, 84n22, 85n28, 88n34, 90n40, 91n41, 95n2, 96n3, 97n5, 99n12, 100n14, 100n15, 105n25, 106n27, 108n31, 108n32, 110n34, 110n36, 112n40, 113n42, 121n5, 122n8, 124n13, 125n16, 126n19, 126n20, 128n24, 131n32, 147n3, 157n28
Miller, E. L., 5n2, 7n7, 7n8
Moloney, Francis, J., 3n7, 10n18, 12n23, 13n24, 13n25, 13n26, 18n8, 29n2, 36n21, 55n15, 77n4, 80n12, 95n1, 96n3, 99n13, 130n31, 147n2, 152n13
Morgan-Wynne, John., 35n18, 89n37

Neyrey, Jerome H., 1n1, 2n2
Nicklas, Tobias., 24n21
Nielsen, Helge Kjaer., 150n7
Nielsen, Jesper Tang., 11n22

AUTHOR INDEX

Perrin, Nicholas., 26n25
Phillips, Peter M., 7n8, 10n18, 11n22
Pitta, A., 156n25

Quek, Tze-Ming., 20n12

Rastoin, Marc., 157n27

Schneiders, Sandra M., 150n7
Schuchard, Bruce G., 128n25, 137n42, 138n45
Shepherd, David., 159n31
Smith, Dwight Moody., 3n7

Swetnam, James., 133n36

Tabb, B., 133n35
Thettayil, Benny., 40n33
Thomas, John Christopher., 96n4

Wanke, Joachim., 83n20
Weissenrieder, A., 150n6

Yee, Gale A., 49n1

Zimmermann, Ruben., 139n46

www.ingramcontent.com/pod-product-compliance
Lightning Source LLC
Chambersburg PA
CBHW031428150426
43191CB00006B/440